Cisco IOS Access Lists

D1384618

Cisco IOS Access Lists

Jeff Sedayao

O'REILLY®

Beijing · Cambridge · Farnham · Köln · Paris · Sebastopol · Taipei · Tokyo

Cisco IOS Access Lists

by Jeff Sedayao

Copyright © 2001 O'Reilly & Associates, Inc. All rights reserved.
Printed in the United States of America.

Published by O'Reilly & Associates, Inc., 101 Morris Street, Sebastopol, CA 95472.

Editor: Jim Sumser

Production Editor: Emily Quill

Cover Designer: Ellie Volckhausen

Printing History:

June 2001: First Edition.

Nutshell Handbook, the Nutshell Handbook logo, and the O'Reilly logo are registered trademarks of O'Reilly & Associates, Inc. The association between the image of a burro and Cisco IOS access lists is a trademark of O'Reilly & Associates, Inc. Cisco IOS and and all Cisco-based trademarks are registered trademarks of Cisco Systems, Inc.

Many of the designations used by manufacturers and sellers to distinguish their products are claimed as trademarks. Where those designations appear in this book, and O'Reilly & Associates, Inc. was aware of a trademark claim, the designations have been printed in caps or initial caps.

While every precaution has been taken in the preparation of this book, the publisher assumes no responsibility for errors or omissions, or for damages resulting from the use of the information contained herein.

Library of Congress Cataloging-in-Publication Data

Sedayao, Jeff.
    Cisco IOS access lists/Jeff Sedayao.
        p. cm.
    ISBN 1-56592-385-5
    1. Computer networks--Security measures. 2. Cisco IOS. 3. Computer networks--Access
        control. I. Title.

TK5105.59 .S444 2001
005.8--dc21   2001033174

ISBN: 1-56592-385-5
[M]

Table of Contents

Preface

Building and maintaining a network involves more than just making sure that packets can flow between devices on the network. As a network administrator, you also want to ensure that only the right people can access resources on your network, and that your network will continue to run even if parts of that network fail or are configured incorrectly. Your organization may have directives that you need to implement, like using cheaper network paths whenever possible. In short, while maintaining connectivity is important, you also need to implement security, robustness, and business policies with your network.

This book is about network policies and how to implement those policies using Cisco IOS access lists. I present a way to think about access lists and network policy, describe how access lists are built, and give examples of how to apply those access lists in different situations. Along the way, there are a number of side-bars and notes about concepts and information important to using access lists, and at the end of the book, there are appendixes with useful reference material.

A brief note about what I cover: the access lists in this book deal only with the Internet Protocol (IP), though you could probably use many of the same techniques with other network protocols as well. While all the examples involve Cisco IOS access lists, many of the concepts are generic and can be applied to other router vendors' equipment. I've tried to make the examples in this book applicable to as many IOS versions as possible; most examples should work with Versions 10.* and above. If a feature is only available later or is known to fail with certain platforms and versions, I try to point that out. Please note, also, that the terms "access list" and "access control list" are used interchangeably throughout the book.

It is unfortunate that the general policy mechanism for Cisco routers is known as an access list. The term *access* connotes that access lists apply only to the area of security, while in fact access lists are used for a whole range of policies, not just for security concerns. I envision this book as a guide and reference for implementing network policies with access lists on Cisco routers.

Organization

Chapter 1, *An Introduction to Network Policies and Cisco Access Lists*, motivates our discussion of access lists by giving examples of why you need to implement network policies. It then describes a framework for thinking about access lists and provides an idea of how we use access lists and the tools for implementing policy.

Chapter 2, *Access List Basics*, describes access list fundamentals: the format of the basic types, masking, and ways to maintain access lists. It also discusses some tricks and traps of access lists (like the difference between network masks and access list masks), some common mistakes, and ways to reduce the number of access list entries and access list changes you may need to make.

Chapter 3, *Implementing Security Policies with Access Lists*, shows how to use access lists to implement security policies. It has examples of access lists that control access to router resources and to hosts, and discusses the tradeoffs of different kinds of access lists. The chapter includes explanations of how certain protocols work and ends with a discussion of access list alternatives.

Chapter 4, *Implementing Routing Policies with Access Lists*, describes using access lists to control routing. Network administrators typically use access lists for routing to make sure that their networks are robust and to implement business policy decisions; I include a number of examples demonstrating these tasks.

Chapter 5, *Debugging Access Lists*, is about (what else?) debugging access lists. It first goes over how to check that your access lists are correct, and then shows what to do if you discover that they are wrong.

Chapter 6, *Route Maps*, describes more advanced forms of access lists, including community lists, AS path access lists, and route maps. The chapter goes over policy routing and ends with a discussion of using access lists and routes with BGP, the Border Gateway Protocol.

Chapter 7, *Access List Case Studies*, concludes the book with some case studies of how different types and applications of access lists are used together in a variety of scenarios. There are three cases: an example of routers that connect sites within an organization, a firewall example, and a BGP routing example.

Appendix A, *Extended Access List Protocols and Qualifiers*, has a number of tables listing keywords and qualifiers for extended access lists.

Appendix B, *Binary and Mask Tables*, contains a decimal/binary conversion chart and a table of prefix lengths and their corresponding network masks, access list masks, and valid networks.

Appendix C, *Common Application Ports*, contains a table of commonly used application ports.

Audience

This book is designed for network administrators and others who use Cisco routers to implement policies, whether the policies are for security or to ensure that networks are robust. Basic knowledge of Cisco routers and TCP/IP is assumed. Those who are relatively new to using Cisco routers should start with Chapter 1 and work their way through Chapter 5. Network administrators who need to implement policy-based routing using route maps, whether with interior routing protocols or with BGP, should read Chapter 6. Chapter 7 contains case studies that readers may find useful.

Administrators who are experienced in using Cisco routers can use this book as a reference for policy implementation, debugging, and access lists in general. Chapter 2 describes masking techniques that may reduce access list sizes and reduce the number of necessary changes. Chapters 3, 4, 6, and 7 have many examples of implementing basic security, robustness, and business policies. Readers interested in debugging access list problems should find Chapter 5 useful. The three appendixes contain helpful reference tables of access list keywords, decimal to binary conversions, and masks and ports that common applications use. Network administrators may find the table showing network masks, access list masks, and valid networks for each possible prefix length particular useful.

Conventions used in this book

I have used the following formatting conventions in this book:

- *Italic* is used for router commands (commands that are typed at the router command prompt, whether in privileged mode or not), as well as for emphasis and the first use of technical terms.

- `Constant width` is used for router configurations (configuration commands that are either typed in while in configuration mode or read in from files loaded over the network). It is also used for strings and keywords that are part of configuration commands.

- `Constant width italic` is used for replaceable text.

- **`Constant width bold`** is used for user input.

We'd like to hear from you

While the editors, the technical reviewers, and I have done our best to make sure that all the examples are correct, we may have gotten something wrong. Certainly, with all the different versions of IOS out there, there will be cases in which these examples won't work. If you do find an error or come across an example where something doesn't work under a particular IOS version, we'd like to hear from you.

Please address comments and questions concerning this book to the publisher:

> O'Reilly & Associates, Inc.
> 101 Morris Street
> Sebastopol, CA 95472
> (800) 998-9938 (in the United States or Canada)
> (707) 829-0515 (international or local)
> (707) 829-0104 (fax)

There is a web page for this book, which lists errata, examples, or any additional information. You can access this page at:

> *http://www.oreilly.com/catalog/cisrtlist*

To comment or ask technical questions about this book, send email to:

> *bookquestions@oreilly.com*

For more information about books, conferences, software, Resource Centers, and the O'Reilly Network, see the O'Reilly web site at:

> *http://www.oreilly.com*

Acknowledgments

There are several people and organizations I want to acknowledge. Clinton Wong needs to be mentioned because he was the person who let me know that O'Reilly was looking for authors in this area. Several organizations deserve thanks, particularly O'Reilly & Associates for being interested in my book, Intel for giving me the chance to learn about Cisco routers, and Cisco for making the routers I am writing about. I'd like to thank my editors—Mike Loukides, Simon Hayes, and Jim Sumser—for putting up with me through all of these years. Andre Paree-Huff, Sally Hambridge, Lynne Marchi, and Mark Degner deserve acknowledgment for providing excellent technical reviews. Finally, I'd like to thank Susan, Stephanie, Kevin, and Chris for enduring me throughout the writing of this book, and to Mom and Dad for watching the kids numerous times while I went off writing.

In this chapter:
- *Policy sets*
- *The policy toolkit*

1

Network Policies and Cisco Access Lists

In the best of all possible worlds, network administrators would never need network policies. Crackers would never break into a router to invade a network, routers would never pass bad routing information, and packets would never take network paths that network administrators did not intend. Sadly, we live in a hostile, imperfect world. Consider the following scenarios:

- Crackers penetrate Company A's public web site. The intruders replace the company's web content with pornography. Company A's management and public relations are consumed with dealing with the resulting negative publicity, much to the detriment of the company's core business.

- A network administrator works at Site O, one of many sites within a large, geographically dispersed intranet. Instead of typing "19", he types "10" ("9" and "0" are next to each other on the keyboard) when configuring a local router. As a result, Site O begins to advertise a route to network 10.0.0.0/8 instead of network 19.0.0.0/8. Since network 10.0.0.0/8 belongs to Site P, users on network 10 are unable to access the rest of the intranet. Network 19.0.0.0/8 users are also isolated because their route in Site P is also not getting advertised. Users at Sites O and P can't do any work requiring access to network resources outside their respective sites.

- A company has two connections to the Internet through different Internet service providers (ISPs), both at the same bandwidth. This has been implemented to provide backup routing in case one connection goes down. One of the ISPs has traffic-based prices while the other has a fixed price. To reduce costs, the company wants to use the fixed-price ISP unless the line to it goes down, in which case it will use the traffic-based Internet connection. Because a routing policy has not been implemented to enforce this preference, all Internet IP traffic passes through the usage-based connection, forcing the company to incur higher than necessary costs.

What can we conclude by looking at these scenarios? We see that crackers may try to penetrate networks, router configuration mistakes can happen, and network traffic may not flow through the path that network administrators intend. We see that these problems can occur accidentally or intentionally, often despite good intentions. In all these cases, if certain network policies had been formulated and enforced, costly problems could have been avoided.

Let's look more closely at these scenarios. The first involves crackers breaking into a web site and modifying the contents. What kind of policy could prevent this situation? Allowing only HTTP (web) access to the web server from the Internet can greatly reduce the probability of a break-in, since such a policy makes it much more difficult for crackers to exploit operating system weaknesses or application software security holes. Even if someone gains access to the web server, preventing the use of services such as Telnet or FTP to or from the Internet would make it difficult to exploit the server as a platform for further attacks. It would also be difficult to upload pictures or other content to the server.

This first scenario deals with *security*. A network administrator must worry about the definitive network security concerns: unauthorized modification of information, denial-of-service attacks, unauthorized access, and eavesdropping. Throughout this book, you'll learn how to use Cisco access lists to enforce security policies.

The intranet scenario describes how a configuration mistake at one site in an enterprise network can create problems for another site far away. In this case, an intranet Site O advertised a route for a Site P, causing users in Site O and Site P to be cut off from the rest of the intranet. Again, why are both cut off? Typos happen. Errors in judgment happen. Even with injections of bad routing information and the best of intentions, a network should keep running. Network policies that help retain tight control over routes can minimize the impact of human error.

This scenario illustrates the *robustness* problem. This problem is conceptually different from the first scenario and, in many ways, more difficult to deal with. In the security-oriented scenario, we are trying protect against hostile attacks. In the intranet scenario, we are trying to protect against operator mistakes. The difference in intent makes it much harder to anticipate where a problem can occur. Despite the difficulty, it is important that this type of scenario be anticipated. As intranets and the Internet become mission critical, configuration errors should not shut down networks. Configuration errors become more and more common as intranets and the Internet get bigger—the larger a network is, the more components it has that can fail in strange ways. Also, as more people are involved with maintaining a network, the greater the chance that one of them will make a configuration mistake. Access policies can minimize these risks. Maintaining a healthy and robust network is a major motivation for network access policies, as we will see repeatedly in future chapters.

In the final scenario, traffic should go to the cheaper path, which is identical to the other path in every respect except for the way it is billed. In this scenario, security and robustness are not prime motivations. Instead, nontechnical business factors drive traffic policy. *Business drivers* are a third major motivation for network access policies.

So these are the three key concerns that motivate the need for access policies: security, robustness, and business drivers. It should be mentioned that they are not always easily separated and distinct. Security is often (and should be) a major business reason for access policies. Good security also helps with network robustness: preventing denial-of-service attacks keeps the network up and healthy. Conversely, policies intending to maintain network robustness—minimizing the impact of accidental misconfiguration and equipment failures—can also minimize the impact of deliberate sabotage. Having a highly available, robust network is often a business goal that is key to an organization's effectiveness. Despite some overlap, I mention our three motivations as separate goals because they are distinct and important enough to help us focus on why we implement access policies.

Policy sets

Now that you know why you should have policies, how do you implement them in Cisco router networks? How are Cisco access lists involved with policy at all? In this section, I describe a conceptual framework that can help with the design and implementation of policies. The key concept in this framework is the *policy set*.

If you think about policies in general (not just network access policy), every policy has two parts, *what* and *how*. "What" designates the objects included in a policy. "How" describes how those objects are affected by the policy. When a policy is enforced, some set of objects or is evaluated against whether it is affected by that policy. Let's look at policies in a department store. The store has a policy on business hours. Employees may come in during a specific range of hours, and customers are allowed in during another range. How is this policy divided into the two parts? The affected objects (the "what") are the store's employees and customers. The "how" is that employees are allowed in during certain hours, and customers are permitted to shop during certain hours. Of course, people other than employees, such as delivery workers, also go into stores. As each person goes in, the policy is enforced, and we check to see whether they are employees, deliverers, or customers. If they are customers, they may enter only during certain hours.

Let's look at other policies a store might have. Many stores do not permit customers to bring in knapsacks or large bags. The "what" in the policy are the knapsacks and large bags brought by people coming to a store. The "how" is a rule forbidding customers from bringing them into the store and forcing them to check those items into lockers or drop them off in some area. Also, stores typically have a policy that only employees may enter certain areas. The "what" in this policy is employees. The "how" is that only employees are permitted in some area.

When implementing traffic policies in Cisco router networks, we have to partition them in a similar way. The "what" of a policy, the set of objects affected, is what I will call the *policy set*. Let's look at the policy sets in the department store example. For the business-hours policy, the policy set consists of the store's customers. For the knapsack policy, the policy set consists of the knapsacks and large bags that customers bring into the store. For the restricted-area policy, the policy set is made up of the stores' employees.

Policy sets are defined using a series of *policy set entries*. These entries include or exclude objects of interest from a policy set. Let's go back to our department store policies to show how these policy set entries work. The store may have a policy that only employees who have undergone cashier training, supervisors, or managers may operate a cash register. In this case, the policy set is made of employees with the approved characteristics. We define the policy set with the following policy set entries:

```
Employees with cashier training
Supervisors
Managers
```

When an employee tries to operate a cash register, he enters an employee ID number, which is checked against a database to see whether the employee is in the policy set. Is he an employee with cashier training? Is he a supervisor? Is he a manager? If any of these conditions apply, that employee is permitted to operate the cash register. In our knapsack policy example, knapsacks and large bags are included in our policy set, which is defined with the following policy set entries:

```
Knapsacks
Large bags
```

To enforce this policy, each person coming into the store with a bag is checked. Is the bag a knapsack? Then it is not permitted. Is the bag very large? Again, it is not permitted. If it is not one of the choices in the policy set (a purse, say), the policy does not apply, and the customer may bring the bag into the store.

If the store changes its policy to allow large bags containing merchandise to be returned or exchanged, the policy set is then defined with the following policy set entries:

```
Knapsacks
Exclude large bags with merchandise for exchange or return
Large bags
```

When this bag policy is enforced, people coming into the store have their bags checked. Do they have a knapsack? The bag may not be brought in. Does the bag have merchandise to exchange or return? Then it may be brought in. Is the bag large? If so, it may not be brought in. Policy set entries, as mentioned earlier, can either include or exclude objects from the policy set.

Characteristics of policy sets

Notice that we add each entry to the policy set in the order specified. This is important because objects are compared sequentially against a policy set. As soon as an object matches a policy set entry, no more matching is done. If we had the policy set entries in the following order:

```
Knapsacks
Large bags
Exclude large bags with merchandise for exchange or return
```

then "Large bags" are matched before excluding large bags with merchandise to be exchanged, and no exception is made.

Enforcing policies takes up resources and has costs. The longer the policy set, the longer it takes to enforce the policy, and more resources are required. Using our department store example, if our policy set spelled out different colors of knapsacks and bags:

```
Green knapsacks
Purple knapsacks
Red knapsacks
Beige knapsacks
All other knapsacks
Aquamarine bags
Blue bags
Yellow bags
Exclude pink bags with merchandise for exchange or return
Exclude all large bags with merchandise for exchange or return
All other bags
```

it would obviously take longer for an employee to inspect incoming bags. The number of points where policies are enforced also has an effect on resources. A store with many entrances would need to have an employee at each entrance to enforce the bag policy. This is why many department stores have only one entrance: to minimize the number of employees needed to enforce such a policy.

Policy sets in networks

In network policies, policy sets are sets of the network objects that pass through or into a router. The three types of network objects that routers process are host IP addresses, packets, and routes. Network administrators implement policies by defining policy sets of these objects and applying rules to them. The policies are enforced as routers check the host IP addresses, packets, and network numbers going through them to see if they are members of a defined policy set. If so, rules are applied to those network objects.

Policy sets of host IP addresses

Let's give a few examples to show how network policies and policy sets work. I'll describe a network policy, then break down each policy into a policy set and its rules. Let's start with the following policy:

Only hosts in network 192.168.30.0/24 can log into Router A

This is the network analog of the department store policy of allowing only employees into certain areas. In this case, the policy set is composed of the IP addresses in the network 192.168.30.0/24, which we can define as follows:

Policy Set #1: Hosts with IP addresses in network 192.168.30.0/24

We implement this policy by allowing only hosts in the policy set to log into Router A. The rule that we apply is the following:

Router logins are permitted only from Policy Set #1

When someone tries to log into the router, the IP address of the host is checked. If the IP address is in Policy Set #1, the person is permitted to log on. This is one way of limiting who can make changes to a router.

For convenience, policy sets are labeled with numbers and, in some instances, names. This permits us to reuse policy sets. Let's add another policy as follows:

Only hosts in network 192.168.30.0/24 may use Router A as an NTP (time) server

We can then have the following policy setting without redefining a new policy set:

Only hosts in Policy Set #1 may use the NTP Service

Policy sets of packets

The previous example showed how sets of host addresses form a policy set. Another type of network object that can be used to form policy sets is a *packet*. A security-oriented policy might state:

Only web traffic is allowed to Host A

Such a policy is designed to prevent scenarios like the one mentioned previously, where a web server was penetrated and altered. The policy set in this example consists of IP packets carrying the HTTP protocol (the web protocol) going to Host A:

Policy Set #101: HTTP Packets to Host A

The policy set is applied against the router interface leading to Host A:

> Only packets in Policy Set #101 can pass through the router interface leading to Host A

Only packets in Policy Set #101 are allowed through the interface to the host. Since web packets are the only packets defined in Policy Set #101, traffic to Host A is effectively limited to web traffic.

In addition to host IP addresses and packets, policy sets can be comprised of routes. A policy might say the following:

> Accept only routes to network 192.168.65.0/24 from other routers

A policy like this could be used to send only traffic to network 192.168.65.0/24 through a given router. It might also be used if we know that only routes to 192.168.65.0/24 arrive at the router. Any other routes received would be there only because of configuration mistakes (robustness being the key concern) or intentional attacks (security the key concern). Whatever our motivation, the policy set would be the following:

> Policy Set #2: Network 192.168.65.0/24

How would the policy set be affected? It would be as follows:

> Routing protocol: Accept only Policy Set #2

The result would be that network 192.168.65.0/24 is the only route allowed into the router's routing table.

Complex policy sets

As policies get more complex, it can be difficult to separate out a policy set. Take the following policy:

> Network traffic should pass through Organization X only as a last resort

In other words, traffic should not go through Organization X unless no other route is available. This type of policy deals with scenarios like those discussed previously, where for business reasons like cost, certain network paths are preferred. How do we specify a policy set for this? Because traffic will not flow through a router to a given destination unless routing information exists for that destination, we can implement this policy by defining a policy set of all the routes going through Organization X:

> Policy Set #3: All routes going through Organization X

We can then weight the metrics of the routes from the policy set to make them less appealing to routing processes and usable only as a last resort:

> Routing protocol: Add extra routing metric values to routes in Policy Set #3

So far, I have focused only on policy sets, so you might be wondering how Cisco access lists come into the picture. The function of Cisco access lists is to hold the specification of a policy set. The term "access list" is somewhat deceptive in that it implies only a security function. Though access lists are indeed used for security functions, they are properly understood as a general mechanism used by Cisco routers to specify a set of network objects subject to policy. Access lists are built of access list entries, which directly correspond with policy set entries.

The framework described here is useful because it helps us think about network policies in ways that are almost directly translatable into Cisco access lists. In future chapters, I will almost always define network policies in terms of a policy set and a policy imposed upon it.

The policy toolkit

What do we do with our policy sets once we define them? How can we use those policy sets to prevent the described scenarios from happening? This section talks about the "policy toolkit," a set of four "tools" that are general techniques for manipulating policy sets.

As we know, policy sets can be described as the "what" of a policy. The policy tools fit into our conceptual framework as the "how." Once we define a policy set, we must do something with it to implement a policy. There are four kinds of tools we can use with policy sets to implement network policy. These tools control the following:

- Router resources
- Packets passing through the router
- Routes accepted and distributed
- Routes based on characteristics of those routes

It may not be obvious why a network administrator would use these tools. To understand this, think about the functions that a router performs in a network. First, in many ways, a router functions like a host in that there are certain services it provides—logins, network time, SNMP MIB data. These are *router resources* that a network administrator can control. Secondly, a router's key function is to forward packets from one network interface to another. Hence the network administrator can do *packet filtering*, i.e., can control the packets passing through the router. The last key function of a router is to accept and distribute routing information. Thus, there must be a way to control routes that are accepted and distributed. The most common way to do this is with the routes themselves: by filtering routes based on their network numbers. A second, more complex way to filter routes is to use another characteristic of the routes, like last hop or some other arbitrary route attribute. It can be argued that all route filtering is done based on some route characteristic, be it the network number or some other attribute, but we keep them in separate categories because route filtering based on route characteristics tends to be much more complex than filtering using network numbers. Controlling routes based on route properties also tends to use radically different access list constructs.

For each of the four policy tools, I describe the typical policy set and provide an example of how the tool is used. I'll come back to these examples in later chapters when I show how to build and use access lists.

Controlling router resources

In the original scenarios, we saw how letting unauthorized people log into a web server created problems. Similar problems can arise when unauthorized people are allowed to log into routers. Logins over the Internet can allow the theft of passwords and therefore the penetration of networks. Problems occur when unqualified people are allowed to make changes. For these reasons, as well as in a more general sense, network administrators need to have control over the resources on a router. The main concern here is, of course, security, but network robustness and business policy also play a large part.

Earlier in this chapter, I mentioned that policy sets are composed of one of three things: host IP addresses, packets, or network addresses. When we control router resources, the policy set we use consists of host IP addresses: the IP addresses of systems that can access the resource. Let's look at a policy that defines which machines can access a certain router, restricting router logins to the hosts at IP addresses 192.168.30.1 and 192.168.33.5. Figure 1-1 shows how the network is configured with the router, the two hosts allowed to access it, and other hosts and networks.

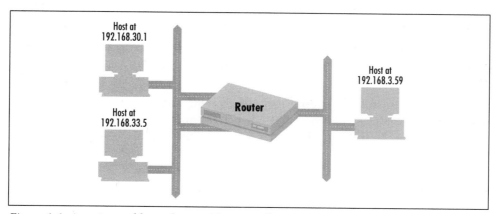

Figure 1-1. A router and hosts that could potentially access it

The first step in defining the access policy is to define the policy set of hosts that can access the router. We do that as follows:

> Policy Set #1: IP address 192.168.30.1
>
> Policy Set #1: IP address 192.168.33.5
>
> Policy Set #1: No other IP addresses

Each of the first two policy set entries adds a specific IP address to the policy set: Policy Set #1 contains the IP addresses 192.168.30.1 and 192.168.33.5. The third entry explicitly denies all other IP addresses.

Once the policy set is defined, we apply Policy Set #1 to router logins:

> Router logins: Use Policy Set #1

The policy we have just defined says that only hosts with IP addresses 192.168.30.1 and 192.168.33.5 may log into the router.

Controlling packets passing through a router

On the Internet, high-profile web servers are constantly probed for potential security vulnerabilities and opportunities for crackers to penetrate a web server and alter its contents. These web servers can be substantially protected from this and other kinds of attacks by limiting the type of packet a router passes on to the servers. With this policy tool, also known as *packet filtering*, we define in our policy sets the kinds of IP packets that can pass through router interfaces. Packet filtering with access lists is a very common use of Cisco routers, particularly as part of firewalls. Although the primary concern here is security, robustness and business policy are also considerations, since an organization may find that certain kinds of packets cause problems. It may decide that it doesn't want a certain type of network traffic passing through, thus conserving bandwidth or reducing costs.

Almost all organizations now have some kind of web presence, so let's use the web server example to show how to specify a packet-filtering policy.

The policy will limit access to a web server on an interface of a router to the web protocols HTTP and SSL. Figure 1-2 shows a typical network configuration that a company might use for this purpose.

This configuration shows a web server 192.168.35.1 on router interface Ethernet 0. The interface Ethernet 1 connects to other hosts and network segments with the company, while the serial line connects directly to the Internet.

First, let's specify the policy set:

> Policy Set #101: HTTP packets to the host at 192.168.35.1
>
> Policy Set #101: SSL packets to the host at 192.168.35.1
>
> Policy Set #101: No other packets

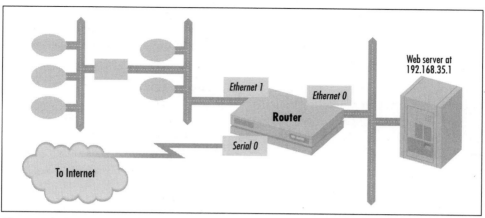

Figure 1-2. Restricting packets to a web server

The first two policy set entries permit HTTP and SSL. The last entry excludes all other packets.

Finally, the policy set is applied to the router interface:

> Ethernet interface 0: Apply Policy Set #101 to outgoing packets

The result is that the web server at 192.168.35.1 on interface Ethernet 0 can be accessed only with web protocols.

Controlling routes accepted and distributed

In a previous scenario, a typographic error by a network administrator at one site causes both the site's own users and those at a remote site to lose network connectivity. Networks would function perfectly if routers always distributed routes correctly and with the metrics and directionality that the network designers intended. But as I said, operator mistakes do happen. In another scenario, network traffic paths are not optimal to an organization in terms of cost. Often the desire for traffic between networks to flow in certain paths goes against what would naturally happen with no intervention. To prevent routing errors from causing problems and to implement traffic-flow preferences, network implementers use the policy tool called *route filtering*. Route-filtering policies specify what routes are accepted into a router and what routes and routing metric values are distributed from a router. The policy sets used are composed of network numbers and are applied to routing protocols to indicate what routes are accepted and distributed from a router or what route metric values those routes should contain.

The main motivations for using this policy tool are robustness and business policy. A network administrator wants to make sure that a network operates despite the presence of configuration mistakes, or a business may decide it wants traffic flowing over some paths instead of others to make a cost-effective use of bandwidth. Security can also be a motivation for implementing these policies since one way to attack a network is to inject bad routing information. Route filtering can effectively stop this attack.

Let's look at a simple but very common application of route filtering. To implement such a policy, we first need to define what networks we want to accept. We then declare that these routes are the only routes accepted by a given routing protocol. In this example, we accept only two routes, 192.168.30.0/24 and 192.168.33.0/24, into an EIGRP routing process 1000. Figure 1-3 shows this network configuration.

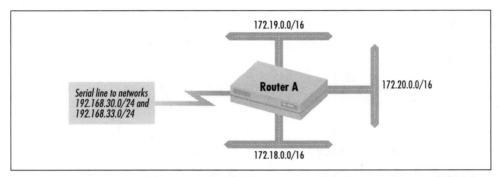

Figure 1-3. A configuration where route acceptance and distribution must be controlled

The policy set used with route filtering is composed of network numbers. For this example, we have the following policy set:

Policy Set #2: Network 192.168.30.0/24

Policy Set #2: Network 192.168.33.0/24

Policy Set #2: No other networks

It contains the two networks we specified and excludes all other networks. We then use this policy set to express the routes accepted for a given routing process:

Routing process EIGRP 1000 accepts only routes in Policy Set #2

Only routes for networks 192.168.30.0/24 and 192.168.33.0/24 are accepted by EIGRP routing process 1000. All other routes are excluded, so only traffic for the two networks included will be permitted through the router.

Controlling routes accepted and distributed based on route characteristics

Networks would be much easier to configure and manage if network numbers were the only criteria we had for route policies, but there are other criteria for making routing decisions, including route characteristics. For instance, in a previous scenario, a company connecting to the Internet wants to prefer all routes coming from a particular Internet service provider. An ISP may want to route traffic depending on preferences that its customers send along with their route advertisements. In these cases, policy decisions must be made on some route characteristic other than just the network number. Like the previous policy tool, the policy sets themselves are still made up of network numbers, but membership in this type of policy set is based on route characteristics. Although this kind of access policy is typically implemented when dealing with Internet connectivity using the BGP-4 routing protocol, it can be done with interior routing protocols as well. The main motivations for using this technique are business drivers and robustness, but security (e.g., preventing denial-of-service routing attacks) can also drive its use.

In the next example, we'll see how to control routing based on the properties of routes. In this case, we route based on the path that routing information has taken. Organization A has a policy to never route traffic through Organization B. Figure 1-4 shows how network connectivity might look in this situation.

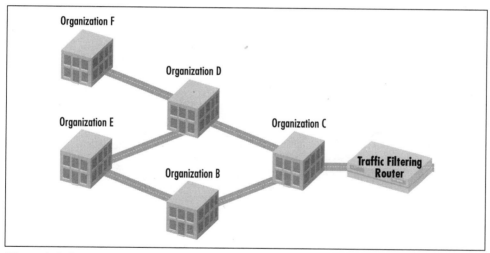

Figure 1-4. Organization A restricting traffic based on paths

Organization A connects to other organizations through a number of paths, some that go through Organization B and some that do not. The policy's goal is to prevent traffic leaving Organization A from going through Organization B. To do this, Organization A needs to reject all routes with a path through Organization B. We build a policy set containing only routes that do not pass through Organization B:

    Policy Set #100: Exclude all routes passing through Organization B

    Policy Set #100: Include all other routes

Then we apply the policy set to a route process:

BGP Routing process #65001: Accept only routes in Policy Set #100

on the router connecting Organization A to Organization C.

Putting it all together

These four policy tools are the fundamental techniques that network designers use to create and maintain secure and stable networks. Think of them as four different ways to keep networks running. When faced with an Internet or intranet network policy issue, you can deal with it by controlling router resources, packet filtering, or managing route distribution based on network numbers or route characteristics. We have seen how hosts, packets, and routes are controlled through access lists. Another way to think about these tools is to picture the router as a giant filter, taking in service requests from hosts, packets, or routes, and then either forwarding them, modifying them, or dropping them. When we want to implement a network policy, we use our four policy tools as different types of filters on the routers. The actual filters are defined in access lists.

In this book, we'll see how to use access lists to apply these four categories of policy controls, and will return to these examples in future chapters to demonstrate how access lists are used.

2

Access List Basics

In Chapter 1, I talked about the need for network policies. I also described how to build policy sets, how policy sets map to access lists, and how to manipulate policy sets. However, before actually implementing any policies, we must first understand how to create and manipulate access lists. This chapter covers the two basic access list types and how to build and maintain them. The first kind of access list is the *standard access list*, used to build policy sets of IP addresses or IP networks. In describing the standard access list, we will examine the basic syntax used in all Cisco access lists, including the basic permit/deny operation for including or excluding network objects from a policy set, address specification and masking, and the sequence used in processing access lists. The standard access list cannot cover all the policies we may wish to specify, particularly when we want to do packet filtering, which leads us to the second type of access list: the *extended access list*. This kind of list extends the format of the standard access list to specify packet filtering policies. Once we have learned to build the basic access list types, the chapter covers how to optimize, build, and maintain access lists.

Standard access lists

Also in Chapter 1, we discussed the motivations for implementing access policies. All three motivations—security, robustness, and business drivers—are reasons to use the standard access list. With these reasons in mind, a network administrator typically uses standard access lists to implement three types of policy controls:

- Access to router resources
- Route distribution
- Packets passing through a router

These policy controls require policy sets of IP addresses or network numbers, so the standard access list is used to build policy sets of either IP addresses or network numbers. Once policy sets are defined with standard access lists, the access list can restrict access to network resources, determine which routes are accepted and distributed, and change routing metrics to influence traffic behavior. To illustrate how the standard access list is used, let's look again at the first example from Chapter 1, which deals with controlling router resources. Recall that Figure 1-1 showed a router that we control and the hosts that are allowed to access its resources. We defined Policy Set #1, consisting of the hosts allowed to log into the router, as follows:

> Policy Set #1: IP address 192.168.30.1
>
> Policy Set #1: IP address 192.168.33.5
>
> Policy Set #1: No other IP addresses

How does this policy set map to actual access lists? Here is the mapping:

```
access-list 1 permit 192.168.30.1
access-list 1 permit 192.168.33.5
access-list 1 deny 0.0.0.0 255.255.255.255
```

The number after the **access-list** keyword is the access list number, so in this example, we define access list 1. The number also specifies what kind of access list it is. Different types of access lists for different network protocols use different ranges of access list numbers (e.g., IP uses 1–99 for standard access lists and 100–199 for extended access lists; IPX uses 800–899 for its standard access lists, while DECnet uses 300–399). The first two entries use the keyword **permit**, which includes the IP address listed in the entry into our policy set. In this example, we first include the IP address 192.168.30.1 into our policy set, followed by IP address 192.168.33.5. The third entry contains the keyword **deny**, which excludes the IP addresses following from the policy set. IP address and wildcard mask 0.0.0.0 255.255.255.255 means that we should match all packets. Combined with the **deny** keyword, this excludes all other packets (we'll discuss this mask format later in the chapter). It should be noted that access lists can be entered in the router's configuration only after you have obtained full privileges on the router and entered global configuration mode.

What do we do with the policy set we have just defined? In the example, we want to control router login access. The policy set application is summarized as:

> Router logins: Only from hosts with IP addresses defined in Policy Set #1

In Cisco router configuration language, this maps to be:

```
line vty 0 4
access-class 1 in
```

The first command line states that we are about to define some attributes about virtual terminal sessions (`line vty`), the Telnet sessions that allow people to log into the router. In this command we state that we will have five possible simultaneous sessions, labeled 0 to 4. The next command line states that the policy set defined by access list 1, our selected set of IP addresses, is the group of IP addresses that have access to the virtual terminal sessions. Only Telnet sessions initiated from hosts with those sets of IP addresses will be allowed to use one of the five available logins. In this way, we have just specified what IP addresses can telnet into our router. The *line* command makes all the following options we set apply to all possible Telnet sessions. We can also apply different access lists for each session.

The implicit deny

Notice that we have used **deny** to exclude all other IP addresses from our policy set. The keyword **deny** is used to specify what is not included in the policy set. For example:

```
access-list 2 deny 192.168.30.1
access-list 2 permit 192.168.33.5
```

Access list 2 does not include IP address 192.168.30.1 in the policy set but does include 192.168.33.5. These two access list entries are equivalent to the following single entry:

```
access-list 2 permit 192.168.33.5
```

This is because access lists have an *implicit deny* at the end of them. Everything not explicitly permitted in the standard access list is denied. Similarly, in access list 1 listed earlier, we could have used the following as our access list:

```
access-list 1 permit 192.168.30.1
access-list 1 permit 192.168.33.5
```

and omitted the final deny completely.

The implicit deny is a key feature of Cisco access lists. It is a behavior that effects the way access lists are written, generally making them easier to deal with. We will use this feature extensively.

Standard access lists and route filtering

Previously, I mentioned that the standard access list is also used in route filtering. This means that we can use standard access lists to build policy sets of routes. Let's go back to the example in Chapter 1 that illustrated how to filter routes. The network configuration is shown in Figure 2-1.

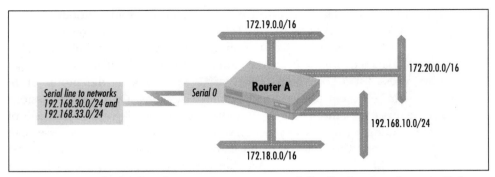

Figure 2-1. A configuration where route acceptance and distribution must be controlled

We want a policy that restricts Router A (in Figure 2-1) so it forwards only traffic destined for the two networks 192.168.30.0/24 and 192.168.33.0/24 through the line on serial interface 0. We can implement this by configuring Router A to accept only routing information for these two networks from over the serial line. Traffic between the networks connected to Router A, 172.18.0.0/16, 172.19.0.0/16, 172.20. 0.0/16, and 192.168.10.0/24, should be permitted, along with any traffic between those networks and the two networks on the other side of the serial line. All other traffic should be dropped. In addition to preventing the router from carrying unwanted traffic, this policy also prevents routing problems in case a configuration error (here or elsewhere) sends other routes to Router A over the serial line. To implement the policy, we need to configure the router to accept only the routes 192.168.30.0/24 and 192.168.33.0/24. Here is the policy set specification:

> Policy Set #2: Route 192.168.30.0/24
>
> Policy Set #2: Route 192.168.33.0/24
>
> Policy Set #2: No other routes

When translated into standard access list notation, this policy set specification yields:

```
access-list 2 permit 192.168.30.0
access-list 2 permit 192.168.33.0
```

This access list includes the two networks 192.168.30.0/24 and 192.168.33.0/24 in the policy set. We do not need an access list entry that excludes all other routes because the implicit deny at the end of access lists takes care of this. With the policy set established, we then apply it to a routing process. In our route distribution example, we specified this by saying:

> Routing process EIGRP #20: Accept only routes in Policy Set #2 inbound from interface serial 0

The analogous route configuration commands are:

```
router eigrp 20
distribute-list 2 in Serial0
```

The first line specifies the route protocol and EIGRP autonomous system (AS) number involved. The second line says that for this particular EIGRP routing process, only the routes in access list 2 from routing protocol updates over serial interface 0 will be accepted.

Access list wildcard masks

An optional *wildcard mask* can be used to include many addresses in a policy set. For example:

```
access-list 3 permit 192.168.30.0 0.0.0.255
access-list 3 permit 192.168.33.5
```

means that all the hosts on network 192.168.30.0/24 are included in our policy set, as well as the host with IP address 192.168.33.5. The wildcard mask is interpreted as a bit mask where 1 indicates "match anything" in the corresponding bit in the IP address, and 0 means match the IP address exactly in that bit position. Making the last octet of a mask all 1's (255) means match anything in the final octet. Thus every host in the network 192.168.30.0/24 is included in the policy set. If we apply the list to the virtual terminal lines:

```
line vty 0 5
 access-class 3 in
```

all the hosts in the 192.168.30.0/24 network and the host at 192.168.33.5 can log into the router. Another way to think about this is that a 1 is a wildcard for that particular bit position. Any value, 0 or 1, in the corresponding bit position is considered a match.

Specifying hosts in a subnet versus specifying a subnet

It is important to distinguish between specifying a network number for inclusion in a policy set and specifying all of the hosts in a network in a policy set. Using the previous example, the access list entry:

```
access-list 3 permit 192.168.30.0 0.0.0.255
```

includes all of the hosts in network 192.168.30.0/24 in a policy set. This is not the same as:

```
access-list 4 permit 192.168.30.0
```

This access list entry includes the single IP address 192.168.30.0 in a policy set. 192.168.30.0 could be one of two things: a host IP address (a strange one at that, since hosts typically do not have 0 in the last octet) or a network number. The entry does not include all of the hosts in network 192.168.30.0/24. If we use access list 4 in an **access-class** statement such as:

```
line vty 0 4
 access-class 4 in
```

only a host with the strange but potentially valid IP address of 192.168.30.0 would be permitted to have login access to the router. Access list 4 would more typically be used to build a policy set of a network addresses in a routing context:

```
router eigrp 100
 distribute-list 4 in Serial0
```

Here, only the route to network 192.168.30.0 would be permitted into the routing table via the EIGRP routing protocol.

If we were building a policy set of network addresses, the address/mask pair **192. 168.30.0 0.0.0.255** would include the network 192.168.30.0/24. But it would also include networks like 192.168.30.0/25, 192.168.30.128/25, and 192.168.30.192/ 26 that have different mask lengths. In general, it is best to be as specific as possible when defining policy sets. Including more than necessary can lead to unexpected behavior such as having unanticipated routes in a policy set.

Access list wildcard masks versus network masks

One of the most commonly used access list wildcard masks specifies all the hosts in a network or a network subnet, as we saw in the previous example. Let's define a router's interface Ethernet 0 on network 192.168.30.0/24 with the IP address 192. 168.30.1. We use the following statements in the router:

```
interface Ethernet 0
ip address 192.168.30.1 mask 255.255.255.0
```

The *network mask* (often called a *subnet mask*) is **255.255.255.0.** The leftmost 24 bits have a value of 1, corresponding to the first three octets of the Ethernet IP address, which define the network number. They also correspond to the "24" used when we describe the network as 192.168.30.0/24. The remaining eight bits in this network's IP addresses identify the host. To get all of the hosts in Network 192. 168.30.0/24 into a policy set, we use the following access list entry:

```
access-list 3 permit 192.168.30.0 0.0.0.255
```

The *access list wildcard mask* is 0.0.0.255 (the rightmost eight bits are set to 1). This is a wildcard mask that matches all the addresses in the network, and it has 0 in the bit positions where the network mask has 1 and 1 where the mask has 0.

Let's look at another example of network masks and access list wildcard masks that match all of the addresses in that network. For network 172.28.0.0/16, the network mask is **255.255.0.0.** Each of the leftmost 16 bits has the value of 1. These 16 bits correspond to the first two octets in the IP address, which define the network number. The remaining 16 bits in the network's IP addresses identify the host. If we need an access list address and wildcard mask combination that include all the addresses in 172.28.0.0/16 in a policy set, we would use `172.28.0.0 0.0.255.255`. The access list wildcard mask `0.0.255.255` has 1 in the 16 rightmost bits and 0 in the leftmost 16, while the network mask `255.255.0.0` has 0 in the 16 rightmost bits and 1 in the leftmost 16. Note again that the access list wildcard mask has 0 in the bit positions where the network mask has 1 and 1 where the network mask has 0. A fairly common mistake is to use a network's network mask when you want to match all of a network's hosts instead of an access list wildcard mask.

Generally, for a network specified as A.B.C.D/n, the access list wildcard mask that matches all addresses in a network will have 1's in the *32–n* rightmost bits and 0 in the leftmost *n* bits. For the network 192.168.32.0/26, the access list wildcard mask that matches all entries is `0.0.0.63` (six 1's in the rightmost column). The network mask on the interface is `255.255.255.192`. For a supernet such as 192.168.80.0/22, the access list wildcard mask that matched all the addresses in it would be `0.0.3.255` while the network mask on the interface would be `255.255.252.0`.

The implicit wildcard mask

Earlier, we saw an IP address and wildcard mask combination of:

```
0.0.0.0 255.255.255.255
```

Since each bit is a 1 in this mask, any IP address on any network will be matched. This construct is very useful, and we'll see this address/mask combination used repeatedly in both basic access lists and in extended access lists.

We've also seen access lists in which no mask is included. In the first example, we defined a policy set that included the addresses 192.168.30.1 and 192.168.33.5. The access list evolved to be the following:

```
access-list 1 permit 192.168.30.1
access-list 1 permit 192.168.33.5
```

As I mentioned previously, a 0 in a bit position indicates that there should be a match at exactly that bit position. Thus, the access list could have been written as:

```
access-list 1 permit 192.168.30.1 0.0.0.0
access-list 1 permit 192.168.33.5 0.0.0.0
```

The lack of an explicit wildcard mask implies a default mask of `0.0.0.0`.

The same applies to network numbers as well as hosts. The access list:

```
access-list 2 permit 192.168.30.0
access-list 2 permit 192.168.33.0
```

includes 192.168.30.0/24 and 192.168.33.0/24 (assuming a typical class C network mask). It can also be written as:

```
access-list 2 permit 192.168.30.0 0.0.0.0
access-list 2 permit 192.168.33.0 0.0.0.0
```

The implicit wildcard mask is a handy feature that saves typing. We'll be using this feature of standard access lists repeatedly.

Sequential processing in access lists

You will recall from Chapter 1 that access list entries are processed sequentially in the order in which they are entered. For each network object a router sees, it starts at the beginning of the access list with the first entry and checks for a match. If not, it continues down the list of entries until there is a match or no more entries. However, as soon as a match is found, no more matches are made, which makes the order of the entries in our list a very important consideration. Let's look at an example:

```
access-list 4 permit 192.168.30.0 0.0.0.255
access-list 4 deny 192.168.30.70
```

Access list 4 includes the IP address 192.168.30.70. This address is included even though there is an explicit deny of the IP address. If the router controls a resource such as login access with access list 4, and then a host with 192.168.30.70 requests use of that resource, the router would see that 192.168.30.70 was in the policy set specified by access list 4 and allow the request. No more matches are made, and the entry on the second line is never reached. Access list 4 effectively specifies a policy set composed of all the addresses in network 192.168.30.0/24, including 192.168.30.70.

On the other hand, IP address 192.168.30.70 is not in the policy set specified by access list 5:

```
access-list 5 deny 192.168.30.70
access-list 5 permit 192.168.30.0 0.0.0.255
```

When the router checks 192.168.30.70 against access list 5, it matches on the first line. The address is explicitly excluded. Although both access lists have the same entries, the entries are in a different order. Access list 5 specifies a policy set of all the IP addresses in network 192.168.30.0/24 except 192.168.30.70.

Standard access lists and packet filtering

At the beginning of this section, I mentioned that standard access lists are also used to control packets flowing through a router. Network administrators use standard access lists in this fashion when certain hosts need total access to hosts on a particular subnet. Figure 2-2 shows a network configuration used to protect a set of hosts that process payroll information.

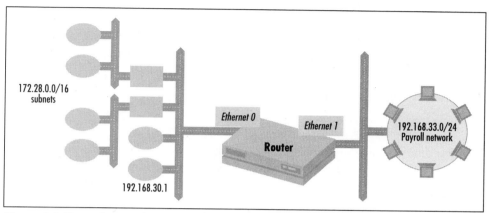

Figure 2-2. Using the standard access list for packet filtering

The router shown has two interfaces, Ethernet 0 and Ethernet 1. Network 192.168. 33.0/24, where the payroll hosts live, is on the Ethernet 1 interface while the rest of the network is reachable through the Ethernet 0 interface. We wish to limit access to the payroll systems on network 192.168.33.0/24 to the following hosts: 192.168.30.1, 172.28.38.1 (and no other host on network 172.28.38.0/24), and any remaining host in network 172.28.0.0/16. The hosts that can send traffic to the payroll hosts on network 192.168.33.0/24 should still be able to send any kind of IP traffic to that network. No other hosts have any business with the payroll systems and should have no access whatsoever.

To implement this policy, let's first define a policy set containing the hosts that can access the payroll machines:

Policy Set #6: host with IP address 192.168.30.1

Policy Set #6: host with IP address 172.28.38.1

Policy Set #6: no other host on subnet 172.28.38.0/24 of network 172.28.0.0/16

Policy Set #6: any remaining hosts in network 172.28.0.0/16 not previously excluded

This policy set needs to be applied to any packet going out to interface Ethernet 1 where network 192.168.33.0/24 is attached:

Ethernet interface 1: Apply Policy Set #6 to outgoing packets

Policy Set #6 translates into the following standard access list:

```
access-list 6 permit 192.168.30.1
access-list 6 permit 172.28.38.1
access-list 6 deny 172.28.38.0 0.0.0.255
access-list 6 permit 172.28.0.0 0.0.255.255
```

The first line puts the host at IP address 192.168.30.1 into the policy set, and the second line includes the host at 172.28.38.1. After this, we exclude all other hosts in the subnet 172.28.38.0/24. The fourth and last line includes the remaining hosts in network 172.28.0.0/16. Note that the sequence of entries is critical. If the second and third lines switch positions, host 172.28.38.1 is never included in the policy set. If the third and fourth lines are switched, the hosts in subnet 172.28.38.0/24 are never excluded from the policy set.

The Cisco configuration commands to set our policy are:

```
interface Ethernet1
    ip access-group 6 out
```

The first line specifies that we will modify the properties of interface Ethernet 1. The second line says that we apply the policy set defined by standard access list 6 to all IP traffic going out through router interface Ethernet 1 from the router.

Generic format of standard access lists

Now that we've seen some examples of the standard access list, we can define its format in some detail. The generic format of the standard access list entry is:

```
access-list [list number] [permit | deny] [IP address] [wildcard mask (optional)]
```

The arguments are:

list number
Access list number from 1 to 99.

permit | deny
Either permit or deny. permit includes a matching entry in the IP address set; deny excludes it.

IP address
An IP address used to match and determine the IP addresses that are included in a policy set.

wildcard mask
Optional wildcard mask that determines what bits of the IP address are significant when matching.

The first part of the standard access list entry is the keyword access-list, which declares the line to be an access list entry. The next part is the access list number, which identifies what access list the entry belongs to. The standard access list for IP uses numbers between 1 and 99, which gives us 99 possible standard access lists, more than enough for typical configurations. With Cisco routers, access list numbers specifically define an access list's type and the network protocol it uses. Standard access lists can't use extended access list numbers, while access lists associated with other network protocol suites (such as DECnet or IPX) can't use standard or extended IP access list numbers.

The argument following the list number is a keyword that determines whether an entry is included or excluded in a policy set. **permit** means to include all objects matching the entry, while **deny**, naturally, means to exclude all objects matching the entry. Another way to think of this keyword is that it either permits or denies a matching entry into a policy set.

The next part of the entry is the match portion, which consists of an IP address or network number followed by an optional wildcard mask. The mask is similar to a subnet mask, marking which parts of a set of IP addresses are constant and which are variable. Like an IP address, this access list wildcard mask is separated into four parts. Each part has a value from 0 to 255, representing a one-byte bit mask. A 0 bit in the mask indicates that this bit in an object must match exactly the same corresponding bit in the IP address, and a 1 bit means that any bit value matches in that position. Thus a mask of `255.255.255.255` matches all possible IP addresses, while `0.0.0.0` specifically matches the entire IP address.

Extended access lists

I mentioned in Chapter 1 that one policy tool network administrators have at their disposal is control over the type of packets that flow through a router. We looked at examples where it was necessary to restrict the kinds of packets passing through a router to specific protocols such as HTTP (web) or SSL packets. To implement this, we need to build a policy set that includes a variety of different kinds of IP packets. We can't do this with standard access lists because they deal with only IP addresses, sets of IP addresses, or network numbers, and not with the nature of the packets themselves. Although we saw how to use standard access lists to do packet filtering in the last example, there too we could only specify the hosts that are allowed to send IP traffic through a specific interface. There was no way to narrow down the kind of packets in a policy set to specific protocols such as TCP or UDP, specific protocol port numbers, or specific relationships between sets of IP addresses. Standard access lists allow all or nothing. To do packet filtering at a finer level of granularity, we need a way to extend the standard access list to include things like protocol, port number, and destination IP addresses.

One type of access list is designed to build policy sets for that type of control: the *extended access list*. This kind of access list extends the standard access list to include the ability to specify protocol type, protocol port, and destination in a certain direction. Of our three key motivations for building access policies, the main motivation for using extended access lists is security. It is often used for firewall purposes—specifying the packets that can pass through a router between networks of various degrees of trust. Thus, we'll speak in terms of allowing or denying packets through a router in our discussions of matching extended access lists.

Understanding TCP and UDP port numbers

Understanding TCP and UDP port numbers is fundamental to using extended access lists. To understand port number usage, you have to look at how hosts function together in networks. In a network environment, client processes on client hosts make requests to server processes on server hosts, which service the request and send back a response to the client process. With TCP, a connection is set up with the request, while with UDP, there is no connection setup. Many different services, such as Telnet or the Domain Name System (DNS), may reside on the server host. In order for a client to specify the service it wants to use, it addresses its request to a previously defined destination port number associated with the desired service. Ports are specified as 16-bit numbers. For example, the standard port for Telnet service is 23, the port usually used by HTTP (the World Wide Web protocol) is 80, and the standard port number for DNS service is 53. While there are standard port numbers, it is important to note that these services can use nonstandard ports. A client processes can use any of these services on other ports as long as it knows which port to use.

This is only half the process of servicing requests. The server needs to send back a response to the requesting client process. It is easy to identify where to send the response if all requests come from hosts with different IP addresses. But what if requests come to the same service from the same host? To deal with this scenario, the client process picks a unique source port on the client host for the destination of a particular request. The server sends responses back to the client's source port using the client source port as the response's destination port. The previously defined port for the service then becomes the source port for the response. In this way, a set of four values—source IP address, source port, destination IP address, and destination port—uniquely identify client/server relationships and enable clients and servers to talk to each other without confusion.

The port numbers below 1024 are called *well known ports*. The Internet Assigned Number Authority (IANA) defines the standard port numbers in this range for services such as Telnet, HTTP, and DNS (Table A-3 contains a list of the well known ports for a variety of services). Typically, source ports for both TCP and UDP are above 1023. This is the most common case, but there are some notable exceptions to both of these rules of thumb. DNS requests commonly use port 53 for UDP source and destination ports. In this case, a query ID is used to uniquely identify service requests. As mentioned previously, services can live on nonstandard ports as long as both client and server processes agree to use those ports.

Let's look at some examples to illustrate how the extended access list works. In Chapter 1, the second example demonstrated how to create a policy that permitted only web protocols to a web server with IP address 192.168.35.1 on an Ethernet interface of a router. Figure 2-3 shows how the web server and router connect. The web server lives on Ethernet 0. All hosts routing in through other interfaces (not on the same segment as Ethernet 0) are permitted only web access to the server.

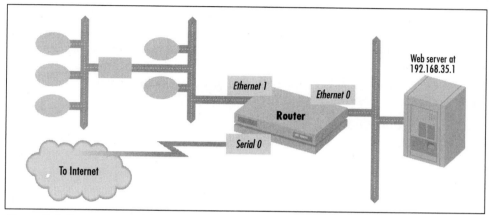

Figure 2-3. Restricting packets to a web server

To implement a policy allowing only web packets to the web server, we need to define a policy set that includes only packets for web protocols. The policy set specification looks like this:

Policy Set #101: HTTP packets to the host at 192.168.35.1

Policy Set #101: SSL packets to the host at 192.168.35.1

Policy Set #101: No other packets

How does this map into an extended access list? Here is the translation:

```
access-list 101 permit tcp 0.0.0.0 255.255.255.255 192.168.35.1 0.0.0.0 eq 80
access-list 101 permit tcp 0.0.0.0 255.255.255.255 192.168.35.1 0.0.0.0 eq 443
access-list 101 deny ip 0.0.0.0 255.255.255.255 192.168.35.1 0.0.0.0
```

Extended access lists begin with the **access-list** keyword, followed by a list number which must be between 100 and 199 (unlike standard access lists, which use numbers between 1 and 99). The number is followed by **permit** or **deny**, which means the same as it does for standard lists: either permit or deny packets matching the specification given in the rest of the line.

The next part is where things get different. After **permit** or **deny**, an extended access list specifies the IP protocol to which the list applies. In this example, we're interested in the HTTP and SSL protocols, which both use **tcp**. (The last line in this group denies access for all packets that haven't been matched previously. To make this as general as possible, we specify IP itself, rather than a specific IP protocol.)

Next, we have two address/mask pairs (rather than a single pair as we did with standard access lists). The first pair defines the source address; in this example, 0. 0.0.0 255.255.255.255 means "packet coming from any source address," as we'd expect. 192.168.35.1 0.0.0.0 means "packets going to the specific host 192.168.35.1." We thus allow traffic from any host to the specific host we named.

The access list ends with another protocol specifier: this time, the port number. HTTP uses port 80, so to allow HTTP access, we place "eq 80" at the end of the line, meaning "allow packets with the destination port 80." Likewise, we allow SSL access with "eq 443." You can also specify the port number for the packet source, as I will show later in this chapter. In this case, we didn't, meaning any source port was okay.

To be accepted into our policy set, a packet must match all parts of an entry. The source IP address, the destination address, the protocol, and any port or other IP protocol–specific condition all must match. To use an access list once the policy set is defined, we must apply it against a router interface. In the previous example, we applied our policy set with the following:

Ethernet interface 0: Apply Policy Set #101 to outgoing packets

The Cisco configuration commands to do the equivalent are:

```
interface Ethernet 0
ip access-group 101 out
```

The first line specifies that we will apply a policy to interface Ethernet 0. The second line says that we apply the policy set defined by IP access list 101 to all IP traffic going from the router out through router interface Ethernet 0. Note that our access list applies only to the IP protocol suite. If we had defined Ethernet 0 to handle IPX traffic, IPX packets would not be affected at all by access list 101. Protocols such as IPX and DECnet have their own access list syntax, which is beyond the scope of this book.

Some general properties of access lists

At this point, it is useful to note the similarities and differences between the standard access list and the extended access list. While an extended access list entry matches against two IP addresses as opposed to one IP address for the standard access list, both match each IP address against an IP address and wildcard masks combination in exactly the same way. Another syntactic difference is that masks of 0.0.0.0 are not optional with extended access lists. Remember that a router assumes a mask of 0.0.0.0, meaning to match the address exactly if a standard access list entry leaves off a mask from an IP address. Even with the standard access list use of an implied mask, IP address and mask matching is the same for both kinds of lists.

Another common feature of standard and extended access lists is that both have an implicit deny at the end. Thus we could have rewritten our access list 101 as:

```
access-list 101 permit tcp 0.0.0.0 255.255.255.255 192.168.35.1 0.0.0.0 eq 80
access-list 101 permit tcp 0.0.0.0 255.255.255.255 192.168.35.1 0.0.0.0 eq 443
```

The final access list entry that denied all other IP traffic to the web server is redundant.

IP address and wildcard mask matching and the implicit deny are common to all Cisco access list structures and are important concepts in understanding access lists. Other access list structures that we'll see later on use the same concepts.

Matching IP protocols

I mentioned earlier that other IP protocols can be specified in extended access lists. Here is an extended access list entry for building a policy set for packets of IP type 47 from the host at 192.168.30.5 to the host at 192.168.33.7:

```
access-list 102 permit 47 192.168.30.5 0.0.0.0 192.168.33.7 0.0.0.0
```

IP protocol 47 is GRE, the Generic Routing Encapsulation protocol. This protocol is used for tunneling non-IP protocols such as Novell IPX and AppleTalk through IP and by the PPTP protocol, a virtual private network protocol. The 0.0.0.0 mask means match the IP address exactly. Note that there are no "don't care" bit positions (1) in either the source or destination address wildcard masks. Because tunneling has a unique set of security hazards associated with it, it is usually a good idea to make policy sets involving tunneling as narrowly defined as possible. We will discuss tunneling in further detail in Chapter 7.

The following access list matches all IP packets sent from network 192.168.30.0/24 to host 192.168.33.5:

```
access-list 101 permit ip 192.168.30.0 0.0.0.255 192.168.33.5 0.0.0.0
```

The mask of 0.0.0.255 has all 1's in the last octet. This means that all IP packets from hosts in the network 192.168.30.0 destined for host 192.168.33.5 will be in the policy set. Again, this is similar to standard access lists except that the 0.0.0.0 wildcard mask is not optional. Specifying all IP between sets of addresses implies total trust by the destination from the source—any type of traffic can flow from the source to the destination.

More on matching protocol ports

We have created access list entries that have matched on the destination port of an UDP or TCP packet. We can also match on the source port. This is useful for preventing fraudulent or spoofed packets from entering. For example, the Network Time Protocol (NTP) uses UDP packets with both the source and destination port being 123. Any packet with the destination port of 123 and a source port of something other than 123 is likely not to be a real NTP packet. If we want to allow NTP packets to the web server in Figure 2-3, we add the following entry

```
access-list 102 permit udp 0.0.0.0 255.255.255.255 eq 123 192.168.35.1 0.0.0.0 eq 123
```

The source port is placed after the source IP address/mask pair.

So far, our examples have had only a single type of port operator: eq. This keyword forces matching packets to have a port *equal* to some value. There are other commonly used specifications; one of particular interest is gt. With this operator, a matching packet must have a port *greater than* some value. This comes up frequently as many UDP- and TCP-based applications use a source port greater than 1023. The following access list entry matches packets with source ports greater than 1023 and destination ports equal to 20:

```
access-list 101 permit tcp 0.0.0.0 255.255.255.255 gt 1023 192.168.35.1 0.0.0.0 eq 20
```

It includes in a policy set any packets coming from any host (0.0.0.0 255.255.255.255) with a source port greater than 1023 (gt 1023) going to the FTP server (192.168.35.1 0.0.0.0) with a destination port equal to 20 (eq 20). Because TCP port 20 is a well-known port used by File Transfer Protocol (FTP), this access list is commonly used when allowing FTP through a router.

The following access list entry matches packets that have a source port greater than 1023 and a destination port of 53:

```
access-list 101 permit udp 0.0.0.0 255.255.255.255 gt 1023 192.168.35.1 0.0.0.0 eq 53
```

This access list is commonly used when using the Domain Name System (DNS) protocol through a router. We'll talk more about these two access list entries when we go into more detail about using access lists for packet filtering in Chapter 3.

Let's look at a more complex example that demonstrates how to use extended access lists to tightly control packet flow. For this example, we have a router and hosts in a network configured as shown in Figure 2-4.

The host with IP address 192.168.35.1 is used to control medical diagnostic equipment. For patients' privacy and safety we wish to restrict who can access it and how it is accessed. The host 192.168.35.1 is isolated on Ethernet 0. All other hosts have routes via Ethernet 1.

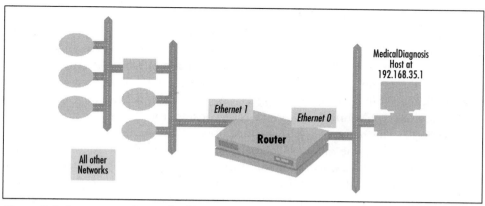

Figure 2-4. A more complex packet filtering example

We want to restrict access to the host to only those who need it. To do that, we have to look at what access requirements there are. In the first case, the system administrators of the diagnostic host access it from network 192.168.30.0/24. Hosts on this network should be trusted and should have complete TCP access to 192. 168.35.1. Next, the host runs an X Window application displayed on three different consoles. The X windows are displayed to a host with IP address 192.168. 31.1. In addition, doctors and lab technicians need to monitor the progress of a procedure and get the final results. These doctors and lab technicians use systems on network 192.168.32.0/24, and they use Telnet to access the host to check on diagnostic status. Also, since time must be very accurate, the host needs NTP access to an NTP time server. There are two time servers on the network, at 192. 168.50.10 and 192.168.50.11. Finally, we allow hosts on the system administration segment to "ping" 192.168.35.1 to check whether the machine is available. Ping is a utility that uses the ICMP protocol to send an echo request and expect a reply.

Let's implement an outbound access list that filters traffic from the router through Ethernet 0 to the segment where the medical diagnostic host resides. With the previously mentioned requirements, our access looks like the following:

```
access-list 101 permit tcp 192.168.30.0 0.0.0.255 192.168.35.1 0.0.0.0
access-list 101 permit tcp 192.168.31.1 0.0.0.0 192.168.35.1 0.0.0.0 range 6000
6002
access-list 101 permit tcp 192.168.32.0 0.0.0.255 192.168.35.1 0.0.0.0 eq 23
access-list 101 permit udp 192.168.50.10 0.0.0.1 eq 123 192.168.35.1 0.0.0.0
eq 123
access-list 101 permit icmp 192.168.30.0 0.0.0.255 192.168.35.1 0.0.0.0 echo
```

The first line of this access list allows TCP packets from all of network 192.168.30. 0/24 to the medical diagnostic host with IP address 192.168.33.5. The absence of any port operator and qualifer on either the source or destination IP address/mask pairs means that all TCP ports are allowed. The second line allows packets from host 192.168.31.1 to host 192.168.35.1 with destination ports 6000 through 6002. The diagnostic host has three consoles. For each console, the X Window protocol uses a different destination port, starting with port 6000 and incrementing for each console. The **range** option allows specification of a range of port addresses, cutting down the number of entries we need in our access list. The third line accepts Telnet packets from network 192.168.32.0/24. The Telnet protocol uses TCP destination port 23. The fourth line permits NTP packets from hosts 192.168.50.10 and 192.168.50.11. The mask of 0.0.0.1 includes both NTP servers in one IP address/mask pair. The fifth line allows ICMP echo requests from the system management network, 192.168.32.0/24, to the medical diagnostic host. ICMP doesn't have port numbers like TCP, but it does have different types of packets, such as **echo** or **echo-reply**. Allowing echo requests means that host 192.168.35.1 can receive ICMP echo requests and respond.

We've seen that extended access lists can be used to filter TCP packets on the basis of their source and destination ports. The same is true for UDP, which also uses the concept of ports (see the sidebar "Understanding TCP and UDP port numbers" earlier in this chapter). The ICMP protocol, which doesn't use ports, allows you to filter based on packet type; the most common ICMP packet types are **echo** and **echo-reply**. An example access list entry using echo is in access list 101 described earlier.

Text substitutes for commonly used ports and masks

Certain configurations are so common that Cisco has developed text substitutes instead of port numbers or address mask pairs. The IP address/mask pair:

```
0.0.0.0 255.255.255.255
```

matches any host or network address. It can be replaced with the single term **any**. The IP address/wildcard mask pair of the form:

```
<IP address> 0.0.0.0
```

can be replaced with the form:

```
host <IP address>
```

These text substitutes can be used in both standard and extended access lists.

Certain service ports are well defined and commonly used. In previous examples, we learned that the well known HTTP port is port 80, the NTP port is 123, and the Telnet port is 23. With this information, we could have rewritten our web server example as follows:

```
access-list 101 permit tcp any host 192.168.35.1 eq http
access-list 101 permit tcp any host 192.168.35.1 eq 443
```

Similarly, the common types of IP protocols have text values. We have already seen the common types of TCP, UDP, and ICMP used, but other IP protocols such as GRE have text values. We can rewrite the access list entry that allows GRE (IP protocol 47) as:

```
access-list 102 permit gre host 192.168.30.5 host 192.168.33.7
```

The more complex access list in the medical diagnostic equipment example can be rewritten as:

```
access-list 101 permit tcp 192.168.30.0 0.0.0.255 host 192.168.35.1
access-list 101 permit tcp host 192.168.31.1 host 192.168.35.1 range 6000 6002
access-list 101 permit tcp 192.168.32.0 0.0.0.255 host 192.168.33.5 eq telnet
access-list 101 permit udp 192.168.50.10 0.0.0.1 eq ntp 192.168.33.5 eq ntp
access-list 101 permit icmp 192.168.30.0 0.0.0.255 host 192.168.33.5 echo
```

Using these text substitutes makes for less typing and more readable access lists.

Generic format of extended access lists

Now that we have looked at a variety of extended access lists, let's define the generic format of extended access lists as they are typically used. Extended access lists take the following form:

```
access-list [list number] [permit | deny] [protocol] [source specification]
[destination specification] [protocol qualification][logging]
```

The arguments are:

list number
Access list number from 100 to 199.

permit | deny
Either permit or deny. permit includes a matching entry in the IP address set; deny excludes it.

protocol
Protocol of packet. This can be ip, tcp, udp, or icmp among other IP protocols, or it can be an IP protocol number.

source specification
A specification of the form [*IP address*] [*wildcard mask*] [*port number specification* (only for UDP and TCP)].

destination specification
A specification of the form [*IP address*] [*wildcard mask*] [*port number specification* (only for UDP and TCP)].

IP address
An IP address used for matching.

wildcard mask

> Optional mask for determining what bits of the IP address are significant in matching.

port number specification

> Optional specification determining some range of numbers for ports.

protocol qualifiers

> Optional specification defining a more specific instance of the protocol.

logging

> The logging keyword. If present, it turns on a log of all packet information every time the access list entry is matched.

As with standard access lists, the list number specifies an entry's access list number. For extended access lists, this number is from 100 to 199, allowing up to 100 IP access lists on a router. *protocol* is the type of IP protocol being matched. It can also be an IP protocol number or else one of the more common IP protocols such as icmp, tcp, udp, or ip (for all of IP). A complete table of the possible protocol values is included in Table A-1. Source and destination addresses and masks operate in the same way as the standard access list address and mask: the source address and mask apply to the source IP address of packets. The optional source port is the source TCP or UDP port of a packet matching against the list. Obviously, this applies only to UDP or TCP packets. The destination address, mask, and port function in the same way.

The optional protocol qualifier depends on the type of IP protocol specified. For ICMP, the protocol qualifier can be echo, echo-reply, or any of the other ICMP packet types. UDP and TCP typically use the port number specifications instead, but TCP has an additional qualifier called established. The established qualifier for TCP matches all TCP packets that are part of a TCP connection that is already set up, regardless of the source or destination port. This is a very useful qualifier, and we'll talk more about how to use it in Chapter 3. If no qualifier is specified, all packet types of the designated IP protocol that match the given source and destination criteria are matched and added to the policy set. Table A-2 includes all possible ICMP types and codes, while Table A-3 includes all port number qualifiers.

The final part of the extended access list entry is the logging keyword (you can abbreviate this by just using log). If the logging keyword is present, then every time that the access list entry is matched, a log entry is produced. This capability is available only with extended access lists. It is very useful for producing security alerts and for debugging, as we will see in Chapter 5.

Clearly, there are many possible values for various parts of extended access lists. Appendix A contains a number of tables that contain all the possible values for protocols and packet types used in extended access lists.

More on matching

Proper use of matching and masks can reduce the number of access list entries that a network administrator must write. As we discussed before, matching sets of IP addresses, whether for networks or hosts in standard access lists or for the source and destination definitions for an extended access list, always involves defining an IP address and a mask. Masks are bit masks that apply to the corresponding bit of the IP address. Remember that a 1 in a access list wildcard mask is a wildcard, meaning that the corresponding bit in the IP address is a match no matter what the value is in the IP address being compared. A 0 indicates that the corresponding bit must match the IP address exactly.

So far we have used only 1's in the last portion of a mask to match all the hosts in that network, like this:

```
192.168.30.0 0.0.0.255
```

In this and all previous examples, the 1's in a mask were on the right while the 0's were on the left, but we can mask on other portions of an IP address to consolidate access list entries, as we'll see here. Let's include four networks in a policy set: 192.168.32.0/24, 192.168.33.0/24, 192.168.34.0/24, and 192.168.35.0/24. The following access list entries accomplish this:

```
access-list 1 permit 192.168.32.0
access-list 1 permit 192.168.33.0
access-list 1 permit 192.168.34.0
access-list 1 permit 192.168.35.0
```

We can reduce the number of entries by looking at the network numbers and asking what these networks have in common. Clearly, the first two octets are the same: 192.168. Let's look at bit patterns for the third octet of the address in Table 2-1.

Table 2-1. Bit patterns for 32 through 35

Third octet decimal value	Binary equivalent
32	00100000
33	00100001
34	00100010
35	00100011

The first six bits are the same (001000), while the last two bit positions vary over the entire range of possible values (00, 01, 10, and 11) for a pair of bits. Any bit pattern in the two bit positions will match the mask. Thus we can consider those positions wildcards and use 1 in the mask at those positions. The bit pattern for the third octet mask is 00000011. This translates to 3 in decimal. Thus we can then write this access list as only one line:

```
access-list 1 permit 192.168.32.0 0.0.3.0
```

If we need to refer to those four networks again, either in a standard or extended access list, we can just refer to them as 192.168.32.0 0.0.3.0, a more terse and compact representation. Grouping networks together in this manner has other benefits as well, which we'll discuss later in the chapter.

Since the last two bits in the third octet are wildcards, we can use any of the following access list entries to match the four aggregated networks in addition to the previous entry:

```
access-list 1 permit 192.168.33.0 0.0.3.0
access-list 1 permit 192.168.34.0 0.0.3.0
access-list 1 permit 192.168.35.0 0.0.3.0
```

It is best to use our original aggregated entry, with the IP address/mask of `192.168.32.0 0.0.3.0`. This is the most intuitive entry, since the block of network starts with network 192.168.32.0/24 and has three more networks in the block. Using the other entries, while valid, can create confusion and make debugging problems harder because the IP address is not as intuitive.

Does the following access list entry create the same policy set as the previous aggregated entry?

```
access-list 1 permit 192.168.32.0 0.0.3.255
```

It seems to be equivalent. Networks 192.168.32.0/24, 192.168.33.0/24, 192.168.34.0/24, and 192.168.35.0/24 would be included in the policy set. I don't recommend using this as a mask, though. While the four networks we want are included, wildcarding the last octet includes other networks, like 192.168.32.128/25 and 192.168.32.64/26. In general, it is best to make access lists as specific as possible to prevent surprises like this in the future.

Let's look at another access list example:

```
access-list 101 permit ip 192.168.34.0 0.0.0.255 host 192.168.33.5
access-list 101 permit ip 192.168.35.0 0.0.0.255 host 192.168.33.5
access-list 101 permit ip 192.168.36.0 0.0.0.255 host 192.168.33.5
access-list 101 permit ip 192.168.37.0 0.0.0.255 host 192.168.33.5
```

This access list includes all IP packets from all the addresses in four networks going to host 192.168.33.5. As in the previous example, we have four consecutive networks. Each has a mask that matches all of the addresses in that subnet. Can we condense these entries into a single statement? No. To see why, let's look at Table 2-2, a mapping of the third octet to binary.

Table 2-2. Bit patterns for 34 through 37

Third octet value	Binary equivalent
34	00100010
35	00100011
36	00100100
37	00100101

The first address/mask pair that we might try is 192.168.34.0 0.0.3.255. As we saw in the previous example, an octet value of 3 (00000011) in the mask means that the two rightmost bit positions in the corresponding octet are wildcards. This implies that the leftmost six bits have a fixed value, in this case 001000. Since the two rightmost bits are wildcards, they can take on values from 0 to 3 (00, 01, 10, 11 in binary). Appending these bits to the unchanging bits leaves the bit patterns 00100000, 00100001, 0010010, and 00100011. These binary numbers, as we can see from Table 2-1, are 32, 33, 34, and 35. This address/mask pair does not work. It includes octet values 32 and 33, which we don't want, and excludes 36 and 37, which we do want.

Another address/mask pair that we might try is 192.168.34.0 0.0.7.255. With the third octet value being 7, the three rightmost bits are wildcards and thus range from 0 to 7. If we do a similar analysis to the one we did earlier, we end up with the possible values for the third octet being 32, 33, 34, 35, 36, 37, 38, and 39. While this includes 36 and 37, we still end up matching 32, 33, 38, and 39.

What happened here? When the rightmost bits of a mask are wildcards, the following are always true:

- The number of values matched is a power of 2. There are either 2, 4, 8, 16, 32, 64, 128, or 256 values that can be matched together.

- The starting address matched is a multiple of the number of values matched. If you match 2 addresses, then the first address matched is a multiple of 2 (even). If you match 4 addresses, then the starting address is a multiple of 4, and so on.

In the previous example, we tried to make the address/mask pair 192.168.34.0 0.0.3.255 match all the hosts in four networks: 192.168.34.0/24, 192.168.35.0/24, 192.168.36.0/24, and 192.168.37.0/24. This was an attempt to aggregate the numbers 34, 35, 36, and 37 in the third octet. By the first rule, we have to match a power of 2, in this case 4 since we are trying to match 4 addresses. The second rule states that the values matched start on a multiple of 4, and 34 is not a multiple of 4.

Since the closest multiple of 4 less than 34 is 32, the address/mask we used matched networks 192.168.32.0/24, 192.168.33.0/24, 192.168.34.0/24, and 192.168.35.0/24 instead of the ones we wanted. We then tried to use the address/mask pair `192.168.34.0 0.0.7.255` to aggregate the four networks. This clearly won't work, as the three wildcard bits match eight networks instead of four because of the first rule. The second rule says that the range of values matched must start at a multiple of 8. The nearest multiple of 8 less than 34 is 32, so the values 32 through 39 are matched, which is more than what we wanted.

Since 34 is not a multiple of 4, we cannot use a single set of wildcard bits to match 4 consecutive octet values. We can, however, use more than one set of wildcards. While 34 is not divisible by 4, it is divisible by 2. That means that a mask of 1 with 34 would incorporate both 34 and 35. The remaining two numbers, 36 and 37, can both also be matched by a mask of 1, since there are two numbers to match and 36 is divisible by 2. The access list can only be condensed to the following:

```
access-list 101 permit ip 192.168.34.0 0.0.1.255 host 192.168.33.5
access-list 101 permit ip 192.168.36.0 0.0.1.255 host 192.168.33.5
```

Here we have used a mask of 1 (00000001) as the third octet in each mask.

We have seen that we can use a mask such as `192.168.34.0 0.0.3.255` to match all the hosts in the networks 192.168.32.0/24, 192.168.33.0/24, 192.168.34.0/24, and 192.168.35.0/24. This mask is deceptive. At first glance, it may seem to match the hosts in networks 192.168.34.0/24 through 192.168.37.0/24. Starting the address/mask pair with address 192.168.32.0 is much clearer.

 Even if you do start a range with an address in the middle of the range, the router will store and display that particular access list entry with an address that starts the range. Using the previous example, the router would change `192.168.34.0 0.0.0.3.255` to `192.168.32.0 0.0.3.255`. This property could cause confusion later when you need to debug access list problems.

We can learn the following rules from our attempts to reduce our number of access list entries:

- For clarity, your matching rules should always give the base address of a range, followed by the mask. While any address within the range will work as the address, it is much more understandable to start with the base value.

- If you want to match some number of addresses that is not a power of 2 or that doesn't start at a multiple of a power of 2, you have to write two or more access list entries, each covering part of the range. An alternative is to include more addresses in the range, which, as we will see later, is often a good idea.

In general, you can condense a set of IP addresses by looking at the bit positions that would have fixed values over the entire set of IP addresses and those that could be wildcards. This can happen in the middle of an octet and not just those on the end. Consider the following access lists of networks:

```
access-list 10 permit 192.168.217.0
access-list 10 permit 192.168.221.0
```

These can be combined into:

```
access-list 10 permit 192.168.207.0 0.0.4.0
```

since the bit patterns of 217 and 221 (see Table 2-3) vary only in the sixth bit position. A 1 in the sixth bit position corresponds to a mask value of 4.

Table 2-3. Bit patterns for 207 and 211

Third octet value	Binary equivalent
217	11011001
221	11011101

It should be noted, however, that putting wildcard bits in the middle of octets does not make for easily readable access lists. Such unintuitive masks can make debugging problems more difficult. You should use masks like this only when your access-list lines are at a premium or if you are very sure that the octet values you are matching change very infrequently.

For your convenience, all possible octet values and their corresponding bit patterns is included in Table B-1. Table B-2 lists the most commonly used access list wildcard masks and what values they can match.

Good numbering practices

The way that IP addresses are assigned can save a network administrator significant amounts of time and network resources. Good numbering practices can reduce the number of access list entries, make the addition of hosts easier, improve performance, and even lessen network traffic. Factoring policy and access requirements into a network design at the beginning is lot easier than retrofitting policies later.

If you are assigning IP addresses to hosts and know that they have identical access list requirements, there are numbering practices that can reduce the number of access list entries you may need. To begin with, use blocks of addresses or networks in powers of 2. Start numbering at a multiple of that block size. For example, say that you are numbering four hosts that need permission to log into a router. You should get a block of four addresses and start numbering hosts at 4, 8, 12 or some other multiple of 4. That way, the block of IP addresses or networks can be matched in a single access list entry, in this case, with a mask of 3 in the

---

Why make access lists shorter?

Performance, stability, and ease of maintenance are the key reasons that access lists should be as short as possible. Remember, routers process access lists sequentially when checking to see if an IP address, network address, or packet is a member of a policy set. On each router interface with an inbound or outbound access list, the router needs to check each packet passing through the interface against the access list in each direction. Long access lists that force the router to parse and compare many entries consume the router's processing resources as the CPU costs increase with the number of interfaces that require attention.

Access lists can grow to the extent that they threaten a router's stability. If access lists are so large that the router's configuration no longer fits into flash configuration memory, only a partial configuration will be used when the router reboots. If the router crashes for any reason and reloads a partial configuration, the behavior of the router will be unpredictable. Although using configuration compression can help in this situation, there is still the risk of instability as a number of Cisco IOS versions have problems with configuration compression (discussed in Chapter 5).

Long access lists are also much more difficult to maintain. For example, if there is a problem with a 500-entry access list, a network administrator may have to examine each of the 500 entries to find the problem. Reducing access list length early on can save a lot of debugging work later.

In some situations, long access lists may be unavoidable. In later chapters, we'll talk more about how to deal with long access lists—how to debug them and how to lessen the impact of long access lists or many access lists.

---

proper octet. Since the IP addresses of the four hosts that need to access our router are 192.168.30.4, 192.168.30.5, 192.168.30.6, and 192.168.30.7, you could write the access list for them as follows:

```
access-list 1 permit 192.168.30.4
access-list 1 permit 192.168.30.5
access-list 1 permit 192.168.30.6
access-list 1 permit 192.168.30.7
```

But since we numbered them as we did, we could write a single access list entry for all four hosts:

```
access-list 1 permit 192.168.30.4 0.0.0.3
```

Our numbering work here is similar to how we reduced the number of access list entries by using masks. In this case, we allocate the numbers to create a mask that enables fewer entries in our access list.

When you know that you will have to add hosts that function identically to hosts already in access lists, a variation of this technique can save on future work. Let's say we have a web server at 192.168.30.16 and know that we may need to add more web servers later. We can create the access entry:

```
access-list 101 permit tcp any 192.168.30.16 0.0.0.15 eq http
```

and then reserve the block of addresses 192.168.30.17 through 192.168.30.31 for future web servers. That way, when another web server needs to be added, it can be added within the block of addresses already reserved. No access list changes required! We can add up to 15 more web servers without having to make access list changes. This can really save time, particularly if an organization allows router changes only during certain change windows. Although this technique does not efficiently use an address space, it is a tradeoff a network administrator can make on a case-by-case basis.

Allocating network numbers in a smart way can also improve router performance and even reduce network traffic. Like the example with hosts, if you have a number of networks that function similarly and need their routes distributed in identical ways, allocate network numbers that can be masked together easily. Let's look at a case where we need to advertise eight routes to the Internet. We could allocate eight consecutive networks that start on a multiple of 8, such as 192.168. 24.0 through 192.168.31.0. This allows us to express the networks in an access list with one entry instead of eight:

```
access-list 2 permit 192.168.24.0 0.0.7.0
```

Some routing protocols such as BGP and EIGRP can aggregate routing information so that a bigger aggregation of networks leads to smaller route updates and thus less network traffic. Smaller route updates reduce the amount of memory routers need for routing tables as well as the router CPU resources needed to manage routing updates.

Building and maintaining access lists

So far, we have seen many examples of access lists, but I have not shown how standard and extended access lists are entered into the router and maintained.

Access lists are part of the router's configuration; they are not some register values that we can set from the router's command line. That being the case, we enter access lists in the top level of configuration mode, and must have fully enabled access in order to do so. Access list entries are appended to the existing list in the order in which they are entered. For example, here is how to enter the access lists implementing the first example in Chapter 1 on a router called RouterA:

```
RouterA# conf term
RouterA(config)# access-list 1 permit 192.168.30.1
RouterA(config)# access-list 1 permit 192.168.33.5
```

This creates the following access list with two entries:

```
access-list 1 permit 192.168.30.1
access-list 1 permit 192.168.33.5
```

If we exit the router's configuration mode and then reenter and type the following access list entries:

```
RouterA# conf term
RouterA(config)# access-list 1 permit 192.168.30.2
RouterA(config)# access-list 1 deny 192.168.30.1
```

we end up with the following access list:

```
access-list 1 permit 192.168.30.1
access-list 1 permit 192.168.33.5
access-list 1 permit 192.168.30.2
access-list 1 deny 192.168.30.1
```

It is critical to understand how new access list entries affect an access list. If you want to delete or change an individual access list entry, you have to delete the entire access list and reenter it with the changed or deleted access list entry. Again, this is because any new access list entries are appended to the list. In our example, we entered *deny 192.168.30.1* after `permit 192.168.30.1`. The `deny` entry does not "cancel" the `permit` entry; it only makes the access list bigger. Moreover, it is never even evaluated. As I mentioned earlier in the chapter, access lists are evaluated sequentially. The `permit` entry for host 192.168.30.1 is always evaluated before the `deny` entry for host 192.168.30.1. Thus the `deny` entry is superflous.

You should note that while access lists may be deleted, references to those access lists do not disappear. If an access list is deleted and then rebuilt, policy settings that refer to it will use it in the same way as before. In our first example, we used access list 1 to control login access. We used the following configuration commands:

```
line vty 0 4
access-group 1 in
```

If we delete access list 1 (using the `no access-list 1` configuration command), the reference to access list 1 still remains. How does a standard access list behave when it is applied to a `vty` line or interface but has no entries? You might expect that since access lists have an implicit deny at the end, an access list without entries would deny everything. In fact, the opposite is true. The empty access list behavior is to permit everything. For standard access lists, this becomes:

```
access-list 1 permit any
```

Similarly, an extended access list without entries permits everything:

```
access-list 101 permit ip any any
```

The easiest way to create and maintain access lists is to keep them all in a single file on a host and read them in via Trivial File Transfer Protocol, or TFTP. (Most Unix systems have TFTP implementations, and software to implement a TFTP service is available on operating systems from Windows 3.1, 95, and NT to VAX/VMS.) To maintain access lists this way, precede every access list with the statement no access-list *n*, which deletes list *n* and allows you to create a new list from scratch. Here is an example using the access list associated with our very first example:

```
no access-list 1
access-list 1 permit 192.168.30.1
access-list 1 permit 192.168.33.5
```

When this file is read into the router, access list 1 is deleted. A new access list 1 is then constructed from the entries of access list 1 that follow. With this technique, a network administrator can edit individual access list entries offline from the router. An entire access list does not need to be typed in just because a few individual entries were changed. Once access lists are ready, the configuration file can be loaded in over the network.

Note that this technique, while convenient, can have risks. Under some versions of IOS, reusing an access list number after deleting it can result in some or all of the same entries still being there. Test your version of the IOS for ACL "ghosts" before using this technique.

Another benefit of maintaining access list entries in a file is the ability to insert comments. As an access list grows in length, inserting comments can make it much easier to read, modify, and maintain, especially if someone other than yourself needs to change it. Even if you are the original author of an access list, you may forget why you created a particular entry. Lines in the configuration file that have an exclamation mark (!) or hash (#) as the first character are comments. For example, let's document our previous example:

```
# access list 1 - policy set of addresses allowed
# to log into router A
#
! cancel old access list
no access-list 1
! permit Ted's workstation
access-list 1 permit 192.168.30.1
! permit Mary's workstation
access-list 1 permit 192.168.33.5
```

The comments make it easier to understand and remember the purpose of access list 1 and its entries and are ignored by the router.

To load a configuration file over the network, the file has to be placed in an area that is accessible via TFTP from the router. It needs to be made readable by everyone on the host. Once the file is ready, we need to configure the router over the network. As an example, let's configure (we have to be fully enabled) a router from a file called *routera-access* on a host with IP address 192.168.30.1:

```
RouterA# copy tftp://192.168.30.1/routera-access system:running-config
Configure using routea-access from 192.168.30.1? [confirm] y
Loading routera-access from 192.168.30.1 (via Ethernet 0): !!!!!!!
[OK - 12052 / 128975 bytes]
RouterA#
```

On most implementations of TFTP, a file has to be "world readable" to be read from the network. This makes your access lists viewable to everyone on the host and potentially everyone on your network. This is problematic. You do not want to make a cracker's life easier by giving him your access lists. In addition, you probably do not want to make all the files on the host accessible to the world either. To avoid these security problems, you can do the following. First, configure TFTP to limit read access to a specific directory. This prevents other people on your network from reading files on your host that are not in the directory you specify for access list configuration. It also does not allow anyone to substitute their version of access lists into the directory and have those loaded into your routers. Second, configure your TFTP software to allow only your router access to the configuration files. Third, delete the configuration file or change its read permissions to not be world-readable after you are done configuring the router.

Generally, performing the following steps every time you configure a router with TFTP will greatly reduce security exposure:

1. Make access lists readable only by the router

2. Configure router via TFTP

3. Make access lists unreadable from the network and to other users on the TFTP server

There are many ways to implement Step 3. One of the simplest ways is to delete the access list file from the TFTP accessible area. Other ways include changing the read permissions on the access list file or turning off the TFTP service. Whatever you choose, performing these steps, either through automation or manually, will reduce any potential vulnerability.

Risks of deleting access lists as an update technique

Our approach to maintaining access lists (using *no access-list*) has its drawbacks. As mentioned earlier, if we refer to an access list and then that access list is deleted with a *no access-list* command, the default behavior is to allow everything. When reading in a configuration, there is a brief period between the time that the *no access-list* command is executed and the first access list entry is accepted. During this period, there is no access list, and everything is permitted. Once the first entry is accepted, the implicit deny takes effect and only specifically permitted entries are accepted into a policy set. When you are updating standard access lists, someone could use a previously restricted resource, or routing information once controlled could leak. When you are updating extended access lists, packets previously stopped could get through during that small window of time. For some denial-of-service attacks, all that is needed to crash a host is one packet.

Fortunately, the risk is small, and there are ways to mitigate this risk. To find out how, let's look at this issue in more detail. First, the period of vulnerability is much smaller than a second. Routing updates have a frequency of 30 seconds for routing protocols such as RIP, 90 seconds for IGRP, and as needed for protocols such as EIGRP and BGP. For any routing information to leak inadvertently, the window of vulnerability must occur during a routing update. Second, there are ways to configure a network so that there is always at least one filtering barrier between potentially hostile areas and a protected area. We will talk about this in Chapter 7 in a firewall case study.

If the risk is still unacceptable, there are maintenance techniques to eliminate it. Instead of using *no access-list* at the start of the configuration file, build any new access list versions using a different access list number. In our previous example, we build access list 2:

```
access-list 2 permit 192.168.30.1
access-list 2 permit 192.168.33.5
```

We then read in access list 2 via TFTP (note that we can define and maintain access lists on a router even if they are not used). When we are ready to cut in the new access list version, we use access list 2 as a new access group:

```
line vty 0 4
access-group 2 in
```

If you reserve two access list numbers per access list, you can switch back and forth between access list numbers every time you update the list. This will help conserve access list numbers in the unlikely event that you are close to running out. It does limit you to 50 different access lists, and you have to change access list numbers every time you change access lists. Another method is to reserve at least one access list number for transition purposes. With this technique, you can load in a new access list with the reserved number and then use the old access list number as the new reserved number. Also, although the example uses a standard access list, we can configure interfaces similarly with extended access lists.

Displaying access lists

We have discussed building and entering access lists, but not how to examine the access lists on a router. To see a router's access list, you can use the command *show access-list*. This command shows all of the access lists in the router, both simple and extended. If you follow the *show access-list* command with an access list number, you see only an individual access list. Here is an example listing for a standard access list:

```
access-list 1
     permit 192.168.30.1
     permit 192.168.33.5
```

Here is example output for an extended access list:

```
access-list 101
     permit tcp any host 192.168.30.1 eq www
     permit tcp any host 192.168.35.1 eq 443
```

Notice that the output of *show access-list* has a different syntax from the format used to create access list entries. The output is not legal syntax for entering access list entries, so cutting and pasting the entire output of the *show access-list* command into a file will not produce an immediately usable configuration. Also, *show access-list* does not show any comments you may have created in the configuration file. The router doesn't save comments in its configuration; they are ignored when the router sees them. You don't need to be fully enabled in order run the *show access-list* command.

Storing and saving configurations

If you have been working extensively on access lists by using the `configure terminal` mode of the router, the access lists configured on the router may not be synchronized with the access list stored offline. One way to capture the current access lists is to write them to a file via TFTP. Here is the router command (which requires fully enabled access) to save your configuration:

```
RouterA# copy system:running-confg tftp://192.168.30.1/RouterA-access
Write file RouterA-access on host 192.168.30.1? [confirm] y

Writing RouterA-access !!!!!!!!!!!! [OK]
RouterA#
```

In this example, we copy the configuration of RouterA to a file called *RouterA-access* on host with IP address 192.168.30.1. The file now contains the entire configuration of the router (stuff other than access lists), but the current access lists can be edited out of the file.

Older versions of the IOS use the command *write network* instead of *copy*.

To save a configuration via TFTP, you have to make an area on your TFTP server available to the router for writing files. This leaves a potential security vulnerability, especially if you use the configuration file you have saved to configure this or other routers. A cracker could potentially overwrite the router configuration with a configuration that suits the cracker's purposes. If you are not careful about making what you leave writable, the cracker can write malicious files and programs to the TFTP host. To reduce your risk, the steps you should take are similar to those for configuring a router by TFTP: limit write access to a specific directory and configure your software so that only the router can write to that specific directory. After saving the configuration, move the file out of the directory or change its permissions to be unwriteable and unreadable. Performing the following steps whenever you save configurations via TFTP should greatly reduce potential security exposure:

1. Make area writeable by router

2. Save configuration via TFTP

3. Make configuration file unwriteable and unreadable from the network and to other users on the TFTP server

As mentioned previously, Step 3 can be implemented in many ways, such as changing file permissions on the configuration file, shutting down the TFTP service, or moving the file to another directory.

You can avoid many of the problems of writing configurations over the network by making all configuration changes in a file. This configuration file gets loaded in over the network when you need to configure your router. In this case, use the *copy tftp* command only as a way to archive router configurations or to check if someone has changed the router's configuration without your knowledge (by comparing your configuration file with what you have saved). Another advantage of this approach is that since Cisco routers ignore comments when reading in configurations over the network, any comments you make will be lost when you write your configuration via TFTP into a file. Making all of the changes to the router in a file and then loading that file preserves your comments and keeps your file and configuration on the router synchronized.

Using the implicit deny for ease of maintenance

Certain practices make maintaining access lists easier. Take advantage of the implicit deny at the end of access lists, which is particularly useful for standard access lists. If you don't put an explicit deny at the end of an access list, you can add more IP addresses and routes to that list quickly by entering them in configuration mode. You don't have to upload a file. This is very helpful when debugging problems, and it can become critically useful when you are working on a problem and lose connectivity with the host storing your access list configuration files. This convenience does come at some cost. Inserting an explicit deny at the end of an access list serves as a marker for the end of the access list. When used with the logging, it can determine what traffic is trying to violate an access policy. Also, the explicit deny makes it harder for network administrators to make rapid changes simply by adding entries. This tends to reduce the number of hasty, ad hoc, not-well-thought-out changes. Any new entries added after the explicit deny are ignored.

Named access lists

In the examples so far, access lists are identified and classified by numbers. I mentioned that there are limits on the number of standard and extended access lists available for use in a router configuration. In addition, a number is not a very descriptive way to illustrate an access list's function, as compared to a generic string like "network-management-hosts" or "valid-company-routes." To increase the number of access lists available and to provide better, more descriptive names, more recent versions of the Cisco IOS provide a facility called *named* access lists. Named access lists use character strings instead of numbers as identifiers.

Named access lists are usable only under more recent versions of IOS (11.2 and later), and not under all possible applications of access lists. Under some versions, using a named ACL will stop forwarding on an interface. Test your use of named access lists before using them in any kind of production environment.

They are used exactly the same way as numbered, standard, and extended access lists. For example, here is a named access list called **network-admin-hosts** used to restrict router logins:

```
line vty 0 4
 access-class network-admin-hosts in
```

Here's a named access list called `incoming-web-traffic` used for packet filtering:

```
interface Ethernet0
 Ip access-group incoming-web-traffic in
```

Named access lists differ from numbered access lists in how they are created. When creating a named access list, you first need to declare the name and type. After that, individual entries are put in. Unlike numbered access lists, you don't need the access list name with every entry. Here is an example of a standard access list being configured:

```
RouterA# conf terminal
RouterA(config)# ip access-list standard network-admin-hosts
RouterA(config-std-nacl)# permit 192.168.30.1
RouterA(config-std-nacl)# permit 192.168.33.5
```

There are a few key features of named access lists to note here. First, the keyword `ip` needs to be used, along with the type of access list, `standard` or `extended`. Next, notice that after the access list name is declared, the configuration prompt changes to `RouterA(config-std-nacl)#`, indicating the named access list configuration mode has been entered. Finally, the access list keyword and access list name are not needed with each access list entry. This feature of named access lists reduces the size of named access lists compared to numbered access lists. Converting numbered access lists to named can reduce the storage requirements of access lists, particularly for long access lists.

Since named access lists are available only on the more recent versions of the Cisco IOS, I use numbered access lists for most of the examples in this book. Still, they are worth mentioning, because if you do use an IOS with named access lists, they are a convenient and useful feature.

In this chapter:
• *Router resource control*
• *Packet filtering and firewalls*
• *Alternatives to access lists*

Implementing Security Policies

In Chapter 1, you learned that security, robustness, and business drivers are the primary motivations for implementing network traffic policies, and in Chapter 2 you learned how to format, build, and maintain standard and extended access lists. With this background, you are now ready to implement policies for the first key motivation: security. There are three sections in this chapter. Since security policies most often use two different tools in the network administrator's policy tool kit—router resource control and packet filtering—there is a section on each. These router resources include services on the router, such as Telnet or SNMP access that should be closely managed by any network administrator. Packet filtering, or regulating what kind of packets can flow through the router, is commonly used in firewall applications. Since access lists consume resources on the router, I have included a third section in this chapter, which describes some alternatives to access lists you might want to consider when implementing security policies.

Router resource control

As I have said, creating router resource policies requires building policy sets of host IP addresses and giving those policy sets permission to use a router resource. The most common examples, discussed later in this chapter, are policy sets of hosts allowed to log into a router, but other examples might include controlling SNMP access to router information or permission to use the router as a network time server. To implement router resources, we will create sets of IP addresses using the standard access list described in Chapter 2.

Controlling login mode

As you may know, Cisco routers can have different levels of login access, each with different security privileges. You can configure the router to have user accounts with different levels of privilege. The default configuration provides a general restricted login, known as *user EXEC* level access, with a specific login password used for initial entry. Once logged in, a user can look at router statistics, such as routing tables and interface traffic counts, and telnet to other hosts (if permitted; we'll talk about how to control this later), but he or she *can't* configure the router or examine its configuration. Router configuration commands do not exist at that initial login level of privilege. If someone who has gained login access to the router wants to configure the router, he must request to do so. At that point, another password is required to gain the necessary privilege level, known as *privileged EXEC*.

While it may seem that the initial login mode is not particularly useful, this is not true. Having multiple levels of privilege can be very useful. From basic login access, a network technician or administrator can still debug problems and monitor key router information, such as interface statistics, without risking critical services or the security of the router and the organization and business needs it serves. Particularly in large organizations, this separation of function and responsibility can be a key component of a smoothly operating network infrastructure, all the more so when different groups manage different parts of it. This is shown in Figure 3-1.

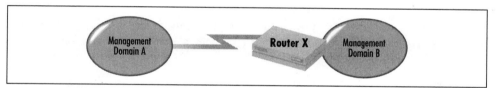

Figure 3-1. Different management domains bordering each other

Network administrators from one management domain may give network administrators in another management domain login access, but not privileged access, to routers. In Figure 3-1, Domain B may allow Domain A to have login access to Router X. This allows Domain A to debug problems but not to change the configuration. One real-world example of this is with Internet service providers (ISPs) and their high-speed leased-line customers. Some ISPs offer an Internet connectivity service with a router that they manage on the customer's premise. Customers are given the user EXEC mode password, but they cannot change the router's configuration because they are not given the privileged EXEC password. In the context of Figure 3-1, the ISP would be Domain A, and the customer would be Domain B.

As mentioned earlier, login access lets users telnet to other hosts. This is a capability of login mode that a network administrator may want to control, particularly in situations where login access is granted to people in other organizations. We'll use access lists to do this shortly.

Router login permission

An administrator who has access to the privileged mode password can control the resources available to the user logins and should pay close attention to how those resources are managed. Let's revisit the router access example from Chapters 1 and 2. Figure 3-2 shows a router and the hosts that can access it.

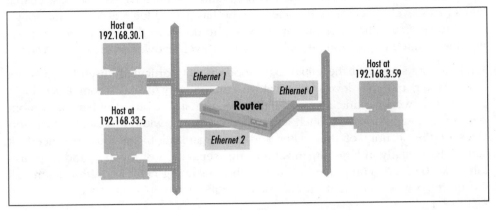

Figure 3-2. A router and hosts that can potentially access it

We wish to establish a policy that allows logins only from hosts at IP addresses 192.168.30.1 and 192.168.33.5. We first create a policy set with these two addresses:

```
access-list 1 permit 192.168.30.1
access-list 1 permit 192.168.33.5
```

Then we configure the login permissions on the router by saying only hosts in the policy set we just defined can use the virtual terminals of the router:

```
line vty 0 4
  access-class 1 in
```

The *access-class* command does not consider what interface is used to telnet into the router, so all interfaces are protected by this command. If host 192.168.30.1 or 192.168.33.5 have a route to the router through interface Ethernet 0, they can continue to use that interface to gain access to the router. Similarly, the host at 192. 168.3.9 cannot telnet to the router no matter which interface it uses. If the hosts at 192.168.30.1 and 192.168.33.5 have a route to the router over the Internet, then they can also use that route. This is an important lesson about router resource controls: although we control what hosts have access, we also need to be careful about the route taken by packets from those hosts. We can control our router resources by combining control over routing with resource access lists. I'll talk more about controlling routes in the next chapter.

To turn off Telnet access to the router from any host, we define an access list of:

```
access-list 1 deny all
```

This forces all router logins to take place from the router's console. Alternatively, we can simply not define any virtual terminals. Defining virtual terminals and then denying access to them is useful if you need to permit Telnet access at some point in the future. In that case, Telnet access can be enabled by defining access list 1 to include the proper IP addresses in its policy set, although leaving the service enabled leaves it vulnerable to potential exploitation.

Addresses reachable from the router

Consider the concerns of Domain A in Figure 3-1. Domain A has access to Router X for debugging, but Domain A should not be able to use Router X as a platform for probing or attacking Domain B's network. Although Telnet access to Domain B may seem innocuous, it really isn't. Since the *telnet* command on Cisco routers allows users to specify the port they want to connect to, Telnet access can be used to access any service using TCP, from web services to electronic mail services, which dramatically increases the security risk to Domain A.

 It is worth noting that restricting outgoing Telnet access does not affect the other debugging utilities on a router. Utilities such as *ping* and *traceroute* still work despite any constraints on outgoing Telnet.

There are other reasons to restrict the addresses reachable from a router. If a router login password is compromised, restricting access can trap the intruder and make it impossible for him to get any further (of course, if the enable password is compromised, the intruder can simply reconfigure the router to let him through). Also, network administrators may wish to prevent their user communities and network technicians from using a router as a Telnet proxy to get around firewalls, and an unscrupulous person could use the router as a way to perform activities that cannot later be traced by firewall logs.

Let's expand on the management domain example from Figure 3-1 to illustrate how to implement policies restricting access from a router. Figure 3-3 shows a more detailed picture of the situation.

Figure 3-3 again shows two companies, Organization A and Organization B, connected by a dedicated serial line. Router X is controlled by Organization B. To help Organization A obtain visibility of the serial line and to aid in debugging when there are problems, Organization B has given Organization A the login password to Router X. The enable password is withheld. Organization B carefully

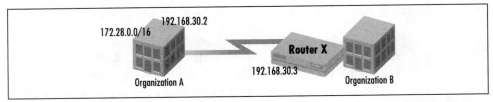

Figure 3-3. Controlling Telnet access from routers that share access between organizations

chooses what access type of to permit to Organization A. It does not want anyone from Organization A to use Router X as a point from which to attack its network.

Keeping in mind these policy goals, how do we implement this? First, we need to identify the IP addresses that people in Organization A should be able to access. The IP addresses used on the serial link, 192.168.30.2 and 192.168.30.3, should be accessible from Router X to assist in debugging line problems. Organization A's network of 172.28.0.0/16 should also be available from Router X. Everything else should be forbidden. Thus we have IP addresses 192.168.30.2 and 192.168.30.3 in our policy set, along with all of the hosts in network 172.28.0.0/16. The following access list builds the appropriate policy set:

```
access-list 2 permit 172.28.0.0 0.0.255.255
access-list 2 permit 192.168.30.2 0.0.0.1
```

Once we have defined our policy set, we declare that only those addresses are accessible from Router X:

```
line vty 0 4
 access-class 2 out
```

The first line applies the statements that follow to virtual terminal sessions. The second line assigns the policy set defined by access list 2 as the IP addresses available from people logged on to Router X.

As with controlling incoming Telnet using the **in** qualifier, the *access-class* command's **out** qualifier does not specify the interfaces that outgoing Telnet may use. If there is a route for a destination IP address through an interface, then outgoing Telnet traffic will go out that interface. In the next chapter, we'll look into controlling individual routes to and from a router.

Organization B could completely eliminate all Telnet access from Router X using the following access list:

```
access-list 2 deny 0.0.0.0 255.255.255.255
```

Although limiting Telnet access from a router has security benefits, it also limits the usefulness of Telnet as a debugging tool. We talk more about using Telnet for debugging in Chapter 5.

Restricting SNMP access

Because Simple Network Management Protocol (SNMP) is used to manage network equipment, SNMP and the Management Information Base (MIB) are resources a network administrator must control carefully. SNMP uses UDP and not TCP for transport, making it a lightweight way to examine or modify a router's state.

As with Telnet access, security, robustness, and traffic preferences are concerns with SNMP. And like Telnet access, SNMP has two modes: a read-only mode useful for debugging and a write-enabled mode that allows changes to the router. Passwords (called *community strings* in the SNMP context) for Version 1 of SNMP (the default) are sent in clear text. They are also designated either *read-only*, allowing the router's state to be read, or *read-write*, allowing the router's state to be both read and modified.

To restrict SNMP access, we include in a policy set all the hosts who can potentially access the router via SNMP and restrict those hosts to known SNMP network management stations in our organization. Even hosts that have Telnet access to a router typically do not require SNMP access unless they are network management systems. Let's say that we have two network management stations at IP addresses 192.168.57.3 and 192.168.57.18. We then put these two stations in a policy set:

```
access-list 5 permit 192.168.57.3
access-list 5 permit 192.168.57.18
```

This is applied to SNMP access with:

```
snmp community string public ro 5
```

This particular configuration command sets a read-only (`ro`) community string to `public` and restricts access to hosts included in access list 5.

If we want to permit only the host with IP address 192.168.57.3 SNMP read-write access, we would build a different policy set with only 192.168.57.3 in it:

```
access-list 6 permit 192.168.57.3
```

Then we apply access list 6 to the list of hosts with SNMP read-write access:

```
snmp community string MyRWPass1 rw 6
```

This configuration command permits only hosts in the policy set defined in access list 6 to have both read and write access to the router's SNMP MIBs using the community string `MyRWPass1`. Again, note that there are no explicit restrictions on the interfaces used for these transactions.

It's good idea to either disable SNMP or change the default community strings when you first configure a router.

The default access list for router resources

The generic SNMP command does not require an access list specification, just as the generic **vty** definition does not require access list specifications for outgoing or incoming Telnet. As we mentioned in Chapter 2, Cisco routers have a default access list of:

```
access-list <access list number> permit any
```

"Anything and everything" is the default policy set for commands that have optional access lists arguments, such as *snmp community* or *tftp-server.* For example, if the *access-group* commands are not specified in the **vty** definition, the generic access list is the default access list for both in and out directions. This is important to keep in mind when using these commands.

I mentioned in Chapter 2 that if you have an access list defined for a router resource, such as this:

```
line vty 0 4
  access-class 1 in
```

and access list 1 has no entries, then the default behavior access list again is:

```
access-list <access list number> permit any
```

An access list that is referenced but has no entries allows everything. This behavior is counterintuitive, but this is how Cisco routers behave. Do not assume that simply because a router resource access list is referenced, there is an implicit deny that denies everything. Using the last SNMP example, if you left access list 6 applied but turned off all SNMP read-write access with the following:

```
no access-list 6
```

you would actually allow all hosts to have read-write SNMP access.

Packet filtering and firewalls

Firewalls are systems that regulate and monitor services passing between two networks, usually one that is trusted and the other untrusted. Extended access lists are the typical method of implementing firewalls with Cisco routers, since they are the preferred mechanism for filtering packets through the interfaces of two networks. In this section, we start with our simple example that controls access to a web server by packet filtering with an extended access list. We then continually expand the example, gradually including functionality and features to our small firewall to demonstrate how to build robust security policies.

A simple example of securing a web server

The first example of packet filtering demonstrates how to limit access to a web server to prevent the kinds of attacks described in Chapter 1. Before deciding what access lists are needed, it is often helpful to draw a diagram of network connectivity. Figure 3-4 shows the layout of the web server's connectivity.

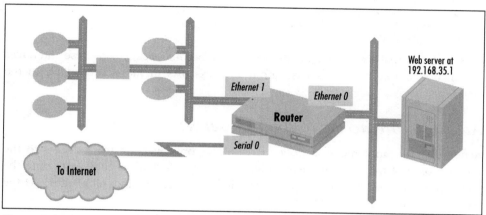

Figure 3-4. Restricting packets to a web server

We have a serial line to the Internet on the router interface serial 0. The web server lives on segment 192.168.35.0/24, with IP address 192.168.35.1 and uses the well-known web port, 80, and the well-known SSL port, 443, for delivering web services. Other hosts within the organization are connected to the router through interface Ethernet 1.

The policy set we need here, as with all extended access lists, contains the type of packets that can pass through the interface of a router. The policy that needs to be applied in this case limits access to the web server to just web protocols:

```
access-list 101 permit tcp any host 192.168.35.1 eq www
access-list 101 permit tcp any host 192.168.35.1 eq 443
```

The policy set specified by access list 101 is then applied to the interface Ethernet 2, the interface used to connect the web server to the router:

```
int Ethernet 2
 access-group 101 out
```

Only TCP packets with a destination port of 80 or 443 are allowed "out" onto the Ethernet interface where the web server is connected. Since the web server uses the well-known web ports 80 and 443, access to the web server from the Internet and other hosts within the organization is limited to just the two web protocols.

Recall that with access lists, "out" means out of the router, and "in" means into the router. In this example, we control access to the web server by filtering packets out of the interface leading to the web server. We could have implemented the same policy by filtering packets with an inbound list applied to the other two interfaces of the router, serial 0 and Ethernet 1:

```
int Ethernet 1
access-group 101 in
int serial 0
access-group 101 in
```

This assumes that the router needs no other inbound packets on these interfaces to function correctly. I'll discuss inbound access lists in more detail later in the chapter.

Adding more access to the web server

Access list 101 implements a policy that allows only web protocol access to the server. Some of the web site users might feel uncomfortable if they can't ping the web server. If we amend our policy to allow web traffic and ping traffic to the web server, the access list becomes:

```
access-list 101 permit tcp any host 192.168.35.1 eq www
access-list 101 permit tcp any host 192.168.35.1 eq 443
access-list 101 permit icmp any host 192.168.35.1 echo
```

This is a very restrictive configuration. Users can reach the server only via the two open web ports, and they can also ping the server to see if it is alive, but that is it. We want to guard against what we saw in the first scenario in Chapter 1: a cracker changing the web server's content.

While a cracker will have a hard time modifying the web server's contents, so will the server's administrator. With the network access extremely restricted, the administrator must log into the server's console and change content either by hand-editing it or by bringing in new content on a physical medium like a tape or CD-ROM. Some administrators may choose to have this level of control over their Internet web presence. For other administrators, the convenience of network updates might outweigh any security concerns. If the web server administrator wants to use the FTP to load content onto the server, there are two ways to update the web server over the network: with FTP sessions initiated from another host to the web server or from the server to another host. The first method has the advantage of convenience. Content providers for the web server can transfer their content from hosts in the network without having to log on to the web server console, but this convenience has a price in security since FTP uses passwords that go over the network in clear text. The second approach initiates FTP from the web server to hosts in the network. In this case, the web server administrator no longer has to move content onto physical media for transfer but still has to log on to the server console to do the operations. From a security standpoint, web server passwords never appear in the clear, so they cannot be listened for and later reused by an attacker. However, a potential downside is that now the content hosts' passwords appear in the clear.

Since both methods have their tradeoffs, I'll show how to implement each one. First, let's take a look at having FTP sessions initiated from the web server. We can define the access policy as follows:

Allow any host to get web pages from the web server

Allow any host to ping the web server

Allow web server to FTP files from other hosts in the organization's network (172. 16.0.0/16)

We have already implemented the first two policy declarations, so let's focus on implementing the third.

Allowing FTP access to other hosts

The FTP protocol has a number of unusual properties that complicate writing access lists for it, as shown in Figure 3-5.

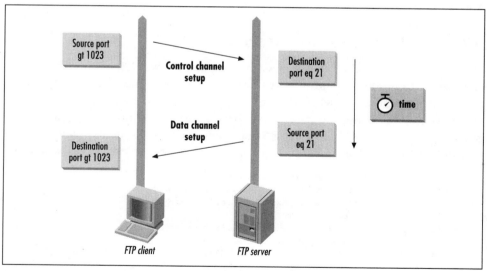

Figure 3-5. Connection setup and port usage with the FTP protocol

When an FTP client connects to an FTP server, it connects to port 21 on the server. This connection becomes the FTP session's control channel. Commands and command parameters (like filenames) are sent over this channel. When a data transfer for a directory listing or for copying a file needs to take place, the FTP client sends the request to the server along with a destination port greater than 1023 for a data connection. The FTP server then sets up a new TCP connection from source 20 to the destination port on the client specified by the client.

Since the web server is acting as an FTP client, we need to allow two types of packets into it: packets associated with the FTP control connection and packets associated with any data connections that are needed. FTP control connection packets going to the web server will have a source port of 21 and a destination port greater than 1023. Data connections will have a source port of 20 and a destination port greater than 1023. If you look up the protocol identifiers for TCP ports 20 and 21 in Table A-2, you can see that port 20 is the `ftp-data` port, and port 21 is the `ftp` port. The access list then becomes:

```
! Allow any host to get web pages from the web server
access-list 101 permit tcp any host 192.168.35.1 eq www
access-list 101 permit tcp any host 192.168.35.1 eq 443
! Allow any host to ping the web server
access-list 101 permit icmp any host 192.168.35.1 echo
! Allow web server to FTP files from other hosts in the company
access-list 101 permit tcp 172.16.0.0 0.0.255.255 eq ftp-data host 192.168.35.1 gt
1023
access-list 101 permit tcp 172.16.0.0 0.0.255.255 eq ftp host 192.168.35.1 gt 1023
```

And we're done.

Allowing FTP access to the server

Now let's implement the other policy, the one that allows FTP connections to the web server from any host in the organization's network. The source and destination port information is switched in this case to allow access to the web server: incoming control connection packets will have a destination port of 21 with source ports greater than 1023. Incoming data connection requests use source ports greater than 1023 with a source port of 20. For this policy, access list 101 would be:

```
! Allow any host to get web pages from the web server
access-list 101 permit tcp any host 192.168.35.1 eq www
access-list 101 permit tcp any host 192.168.35.1 eq 443
! Allow any host to ping the web server
access-list 101 permit icmp any host 192.168.35.1 echo
! Allow any host to FTP to the web server
access-list 101 permit tcp 172.16.0.0 0.0.255.255 gt 1023 host 192.168.35.1 eq
ftp-data
access-list 101 permit tcp 172.16.0.0 0.0.255.255 gt 1023 host 192.168.35.1 eq ftp
```

This version of access list 101 allows any host in the organization to FTP files from the web server if they have a valid password. In practice, for the purpose of uploading content to a web server, we would probably be better off permitting FTP only between specific hosts and the web server, since we would know in advance which hosts would need to upload content. If we designate host 172.16.30.1 as a content upload machine, we would change the last two entries in access list 101 to:

```
access-list 101 permit tcp host 172.16.30.1 gt 1023 host 192.168.35.1 eq ftp-data
access-list 101 permit tcp host 172.16.30.1 gt 1023 host 192.168.35.1 eq ftp
```

Passive mode FTP

At some point, we might decide to distribute files via *anonymous FTP* on the web server, letting anyone transfer certain files without a password. This is a common way to distribute files on the Internet. If we choose to do this, we have to deal with a commonly used feature of FTP called PASV ("passive") mode. When FTP is set to passive mode, the FTP client and server set up data connections differently, as shown in Figure 3-6.

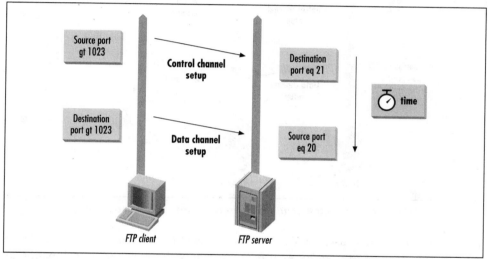

Figure 3-6. Connection setup and port usage using FTP passive mode

Instead of the data connection set up from the server to the client, the client in PASV mode sets up the data connection from a source port greater than port 1023 to server port 20. The access list 101 we built previously:

```
! Allow any host to get web pages from the web server
access-list 101 permit tcp any host 192.168.35.1 eq www
access-list 101 permit tcp any host 192.168.35.1 eq 443
! Allow any host to ping the web server
access-list 101 permit icmp any host 192.168.35.1 echo
! Allow any host to FTP to the web server
access-list 101 permit tcp any gt 1023 host 192.168.35.1 eq ftp-data
access-list 101 permit tcp any gt 1023 host 192.168.35.1 eq ftp
```

covers this case. PASV mode has a number of advantages over FTP's standard method for managing data connections. With PASV mode, all TCP connections are initiated from the client to the server. The client does not have to permit any connections to it at all. Also, the destination port for the data connection is fixed at 20. The client does not have to leave open a large number of ports (ports greater than 1023), as must be done in standard FTP mode.

Unfortunately for network administrators, many web browsers in use today on the Internet do not implement PASV mode correctly. Figure 3-7 shows how these browsers behave.

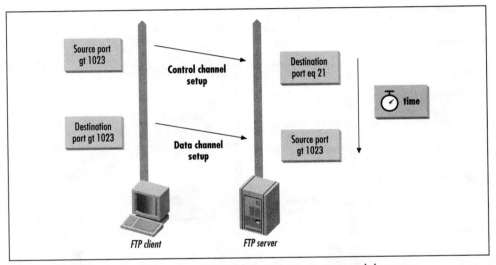

Figure 3-7. PASV mode connection setup and port usage on some web browsers

These browsers, when used as FTP clients, connect to ports greater than 1023 on the server instead of to port 20. As a result, to allow the web server to function as an anonymous FTP server in the manner requested by most web browsers, we need to add an additional line to access list 101:

```
! Allow any host to get web pages from the web server
access-list 101 permit tcp any host 192.168.35.1 eq www
access-list 101 permit tcp any host 192.168.35.1 eq 443
! Allow any host to ping the web server
access-list 101 permit icmp any host 192.168.35.1 echo
! Allow any host to FTP to the web server
access-list 101 permit tcp any gt 1023 host 192.168.35.1 eq ftp-data
access-list 101 permit tcp any gt 1023 host 192.168.35.1 eq ftp
access-list 101 permit tcp any gt 1023 host 192.168.3.1 gt 1023
```

This exposes the host providing an anonymous FTP server to many possible attacks on many ports, but this is a risk associated with providing anonymous FTP service.

Allowing DNS access

If we want our web server to use FTP to transfer files, it's also reasonable to allow DNS through the router so that the server's administrator can use hostnames instead of IP addresses. None of the access lists that we have developed so far allow DNS traffic. To allow DNS through our router, we need to understand the port behavior of DNS. Queries from most DNS daemons use UDP port 53 as source and destination ports. Queries from DNS tools such as *dig* and *nslookup* use a UDP source port greater than 1023 and a destination port of 53. If the responses to queries are very large, the DNS client, whether a DNS daemon or a tool, will initiate a TCP connection to destination port 53. Since having DNS capability will make the web server administrator's job much easier, we modify the access policy to be the following:

```
Allow any host to get web pages from the web server
Allow any host to ping the web server
Allow web server to FTP files from other hosts
Allow the web server to do DNS queries
```

With this policy change, the access list becomes:

```
! Allow any host to get web pages from the web server
access-list 101 permit tcp any host 192.168.35.1 eq www
access-list 101 permit tcp any host 192.168.35.1 eq 443
! Allow any host to ping the web server
access-list 101 permit icmp any host 192.168.35.1 echo
! Allow web server to FTP files from other hosts
access-list 101 permit tcp any eq ftp-data host 192.168.35.1 gt 1023
access-list 101 permit tcp any eq ftp host 192.168.35.1 gt 1023
! Allow the web server to do DNS queries
access-list 101 permit udp any eq domain host 192.168.35.1 gt 1023
access-list 101 permit udp any eq domain host 192.168.35.1 eq domain
access-list 101 permit tcp any eq domain host 192.168.35.1 gt 1023
```

We used the port designator **domain** for DNS port 53.

Preventing abuse from the server

Now our web server is locked down tightly while still offering many services. But just to be sure, let's ask: what if a cracker did manage to penetrate the web server? What if the evil or inept system administrator of the web server decides to attack systems on the Internet or within the organization? What kind of damage could they do? How can we protect the rest of the world from our web server machine, as well as protect our machine from the world? With the current access list, the web server can still be used to generate denial-of-service attacks that crash systems by sending strangely formatted packets. No return response is necessary, as would be required if a TCP connection needed to be set up to conduct the attack. One packet-based denial-of-service attack is called "ping of death." This attack sends peculiarly formatted ICMP packets that are designed to crash a host. With the access lists like those configured previously, anybody can launch the ping of death against a machine on the Internet or within the organization because we have placed no restrictions on what can be sent out through the serial line or through Ethernet interface 1. While the policy we have been defining and implementing does not explicitly permit attacks from being launched from the web server, we have no mechanism in place to enforce that.

To remedy this situation, we first need to define a policy that explicitly deals with potential attacks from the web server. Keeping this requirement in mind, let's implement the following policy with the addition of the final line to our previous web server policy:

> Allow any host to get web pages from the web server
>
> Allow any host to ping the web server
>
> Allow web server to FTP files from other hosts
>
> Allow the web server to do DNS queries
>
> Disallow any packets from the web server not needed to implement the allowed services

This policy allows all of the services we have specified so far, but doesn't allow attacks to be sent from the web server. To implement our policy, we need additional access lists that we can apply to the outgoing serial line and the other Ethernet connection going to the rest of the organization (Ethernet interface 1):

```
! Allow web server to respond to HTTP requests
access-list 102 permit tcp host 192.168.35.1 any established
! Allow web server to reply to ICMP echo requests
access-list 102 permit icmp host 192.168.35.1 any echo-reply
! Allow web server to FTP files from other hosts
access-list 102 permit tcp host 192.168.35.1 any eq ftp
! Allow the web server to send DNS queries
access-list 102 permit udp host 192.168.35.1 any eq domain
access-list 102 permit tcp host 192.168.35.1 any eq domain
! Disallow any packets from the web server that are not needed
! to implement the services allowed above with implicit deny
```

The first line with protocol TCP and the **established** qualifier is used to implement the policy rule that lets clients in the Internet and within the organization connect to the web server. The **established** qualifier matches packets that are part of a TCP connection already set up between a client and a server. Figure 3-8 shows how the **established** qualifier works.

When a host establishes a TCP connection to another host, it sends a connection set up packet to that host. The packet has the SYN flag (for *synchronize*) set in the TCP header, instructing the second host to synchronize TCP packet sequence numbers for connection set up (sequence numbers are used to determine if

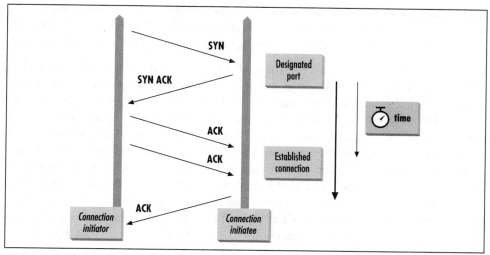

Figure 3-8. The established qualifier and TCP connection setup

packets arrive out of order and check if the correct amount of data has been received). If the host can honor the connection request, it responds by sending a packet with both the SYN and ACK bits set. The ACK bit (for *acknowledge*) flags the packet as being part of an established TCP connection. All other packets in the connection from both hosts have the ACK bit set. The `established` qualifier matches packets with an ACK bit set, and thus includes (or excludes) in a policy set packets that are part of an TCP connection already set up.

How does an access list entry with `established` enable web traffic to the web server? Since web service requests use TCP, a connection needs to be set up for each request. Requests go to the web server through Ethernet 0, where access is controlled by access list 101. Return packets go out through either serial 0 or Ethernet 1 with their ACK bit set. Since the ACK bits are set, the `established` entry includes the packets of requests made to the web server in the policy set of packets allowed out. Note what the line doesn't include. It doesn't allow connections to be set up from the web server to systems on the Internet or within the organization. Since connection request packets set only the SYN bit and not the ACK bit, the `established` access list entry does not include them in the policy set.

Using an `established` access list entry at the start of an access list has a number of benefits. First, it allows most packets of a TCP connection to match the first line of the access list. This can significantly save router CPU because the router doesn't have to process entire access lists for most of the packets it sees. Second, it spares the access list writer from having to specify the source ports of return packets of TCP connections for different applications allowed through an interface. For example, if we added a new service on TCP port 23 of the web server, we would only need to add a line to access list 101 to permit this service. Return packets of the TCP connection would match the `established` line. This can save significant amounts of time as more and more TCP protocols are allowed through an interface.

Let's look at the rest of access list 102 and see how it implements our policy. The next policy entry needs to be implemented to allow users to ping the web server. Ping uses ICMP echo packets coming into the web server. The web server replies with ICMP echo-reply packets. We explicitly allow only `echo-reply` ICMP packets out to the Internet and the rest of the organization. The next line allows the web server to set up FTP connections to other systems on other hosts. As we mentioned, connection setup packets are not included in the first line that uses `established`, so we have to allow it explicitly. Recall that FTP sets up its control channel to port 21 on the target server host, so we allow TCP connections from the web server out on port 21. What about FTP's data connection? Do we explicitly need to allow outgoing connections to port 20? For normal (not PASV) FTP transfers, we do not, because the host acting as the FTP server initiates the connection from a port greater than 1023 to port 20 on the web server. Return packets are matched by the first line with `established`. The final two lines implement DNS access for the web server. Outgoing DNS requests uses UDP port destination 53. If the answer to a DNS requests is large, TCP port 53 (going out) needs to be open. How do we stop all other outgoing services? We will put an access list on interfaces Ethernet 1 and serial 0; all other services are prohibited by access list 102's implicit deny from going out.

We apply this access list to the serial interface to the Internet and to the Ethernet interface leading to the rest of the company with the following:

```
interface Serial 0
  access-group 102 out
interface Ethernet 1
  access-group 102 out
```

Direction of packet flow and extended access lists

In the previous example, the decision to tightly control packets flowing both in and out of a segment resulted in the need for inbound and outbound access lists. For every service we add, we need to think about the IP protocol used by the service, such as ICMP, UDP, TCP, or some other IP protocol number, and the source and destination ports (if any) of packets flowing to and from client and server. To make this easier for you, Table C-1 in Appendix C lists the source and destination ports for common services you may need to control. Let's look at a few more examples of working with IP protocols and source and destination to illustrate a few more important points. Let's require that the web server at 192.168.35.1 be able to get Network Time Protocol (NTP) service from the Internet. NTP is a protocol used for synchronizing system clocks over a network. If you look at Table A-3, you can see that NTP uses UDP and port 123, which we can specify as port `ntp` in our access list for both source and destination. To add NTP packets to the policy sets of packets allowed through to the web server, we need to add the following access list entries:

```
access-list 101 permit udp any eq ntp host 192.168.35.1 eq ntp
access-list 102 permit udp host 192.168.35.1 eq ntp any eq ntp
```

Note that access list 101 filters traffic going to the web server, while access list 102 filters traffic leaving the web server.

While the following access list entries will also work:

```
access-list 101 permit udp any host 192.168.35.1 eq ntp
access-list 102 permit udp host 192.168.35.1 any eq ntp
```

the first set of entries are preferred because they define permissions more narrowly. In general, it is best to declare permissions as narrowly as possible so you don't permit any packets or services that aren't needed or that might cause problems. In the previous example, if you use the following access list entry to allow DNS:

```
access-list 102 permit udp host 192.168.35.1 any eq domain
```

you permit potentially damaging packets with source port 123 and destination port 53. Another problem is with how widely we have allowed NTP access. We have allowed any host on the Internet to send NTP packets to the web server. While this might be intended as a public service, if it is not, access should be limited to the Internet NTP hosts you want to use as servers.

To control TCP-based services, you need to know the direction of the connections that will be set up between a client host and a server host, and what port numbers will be used. Although FTP is more complicated, with most other TCP-based services the client sets up a connection to the server on a set port. So for this example, let's have our web server offer a service for people on the Telnet port. From Table A-3, you can see that Telnet uses a single connection with TCP port 23 as the destination port on the server and source ports greater than 1023. If you add the following access entry:

```
access-list 101 permit tcp any host 192.168.35.1 eq telnet
```

Telnet is enabled. What about the packets for this service that need to go from the web server back to the client? These are taken care of by the access list entry with **established** in access list 101 (as I pointed out earlier, the **established** keyword is very useful in reducing the number of access list entries needed). Recall that there are a number of TCP services we permitted that require connections initiated from the web server to hosts on the Internet and within the organization. If we add the following entry to access list 101:

```
access-list 101 permit any host 192.168.35.1 established
```

we can eliminate the access list entries that specifically allow TCP packets back to the web server after connections have been set up. Access list 101 then becomes:

```
! Allow any host to get web pages from the web server
access-list 101 permit tcp any host 192.168.35.1 eq www
access-list 101 permit tcp any host 192.168.35.1 eq 443
! Allow any host to ping the web server
access-list 101 permit icmp any host 192.168.35.1 echo
! Allow the web server to FTP files from other hosts
access-list 101 permit tcp any host 192.168.35.1 established
access-list 101 permit tcp any eq ftp-data host 192.168.35.1 gt 1023
! Allow the web server to do DNS queries
access-list 101 permit udp any eq domain host 192.168.35.1 gt 1023
access-list 101 permit udp any eq domain host 192.168.35.1 eq domain
```

We have replaced the entries that specifically allowed packets back from FTP sessions and from DNS queries that required TCP. Since the web server initiates the TCP connections, all of the packets coming back to the web server are matched by the access list entry that uses established.

Using the established keyword to optimize performance

The established keyword is also useful in improving packet forwarding performance through an access list. If you put in an access list entry with established at the start of an access list (as we did in access list 102), most of the packets checked by the access list will match the first entry. This is because most packets in FTP and HTTP (web) requests are sent after a connection is established. To optimize access list 101, move the established access list entry to the beginning of the list:

```
! Allow in established connections
access-list 101 permit any host 192.168.35.1 established
! Allow any host to get web pages from the web server
access-list 101 permit tcp any host 192.168.35.1 eq www
access-list 101 permit tcp any host 192.168.35.1 eq 443
! Allow any host to ping the web server
access-list 101 permit icmp any host 192.168.35.1 echo
! Allow web server to FTP files from other hosts
access-list 101 permit tcp any eq ftp-data host 192.168.35.1 gt 1023
! Allow the web serverto do DNS queries
access-list 101 permit udp any eq domain host 192.168.35.1 gt 1023
access-list 101 permit udp any eq domain host 192.168.35.1 eq domain
```

Most of the valid TCP packets going through interface Ethernet 2 will be matched by the first entry. We still filter other TCP-based services by permitting only those services we allow to set up connections with the web server.

Exploring the inbound access list

Before you start using inbound access lists, you need to understand how they work compared to outbound access lists. When a Cisco router filters packets passing through it, it has two places where it can filter: at the interface where the packets come into the router or at the interface where they go out. Cisco routers match packets against an outbound access list when packets come into one interface of the router and then exit through the interface against which the outbound extended access list is applied. In the web server example, the router checks access list 101 when packets come in from either the serial line interface or the Ethernet interface 1, and are destined for Ethernet interface 0. The router also checks packets against access list 102 when packets come into the router via one of the Ethernet interfaces and go out the serial line interface. The important thing to remember here is that an outbound access list does not filter packets originated by the router. This means that all the packets that might go out of an interface and that originate from a router (such as with routing update packets, outgoing Telnet session packets, NTP service packets, and various broadcast packets such as ARP requests) cannot be checked against an outgoing access list. This also means that packets going into a router that are not forwarded are never checked by an outbound access list. It may seem that inbound access lists must be long and not very useful. Their usefulness comes from the fact that they do look at everything coming into a specific interface. There are instances when you want to control such actions as routing updates and packets coming in just from a specific interface. We'll see this later in the chapter.

Implementing a policy with inbound access lists

Let's look at some examples of how to use inbound and outbound access lists together. I'll use the network configuration in Figure 3-9 for the next example.

In this network configuration, Company C wants to share information and do business with Company A and Company B. To do that, Company A has set up a web server that is accessible by both Companies A and B. Companies A and B connect into Company C's web server via serial lines into Router X. The web server lies on an Ethernet connected to Router X. Company A uses network 192.168.28.0/24, and Company B uses network 192.168.29.0/24.

Company C wants to share certain information with both companies A and B through the web server. It also wants to run secure business transactions only with Company B. As a result, Company C wants to allow regular web traffic from both Company A and Company B, but allow SSL traffic for secure business transactions exclusively from Company B. Both companies should be able to ping the web server, which uses the standard well-known ports of HTTP and SSL (TCP ports 80

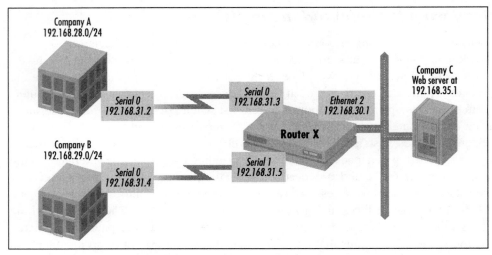

Figure 3-9. Network diagram for inbound/outbound access list issues

and 443, respectively). To summarize, Company C needs to implement the following policy:

> Network 192.168.28.0/24 needs HTTP (TCP port 80) access to 192.168.30.2
>
> Network 192.168.28.0/24 needs to be able to ping 192.168.30.2
>
> Network 192.168.29.0/24 needs HTTP (web) access to 192.168.30.2
>
> Network 192.168.29.0/24 needs SSL access to 192.168.30.2
>
> Network 192.168.29.0/24 needs to be able to ping 192.168.30.2

Let's implement this with inbound and outbound lists applied to the serial lines. First, we need to permit traffic in HTTP and incoming pings from Company A to the web server:

```
access-list 101 permit tcp 192.168.28.0 0.0.0.255 host 192.168.30.2 eq www
access-list 101 permit icmp 192.168.28.0 0.0.0.255 host 192.168.30.2 echo
```

Next, we permit traffic from the web server to Company A for the return packets of HTTP connections and responses to pings:

```
access-list 102 permit tcp host 192.168.30.2 192.168.28.0 0.0.0.255 established
access-list 102 permit tcp host 192.168.30.2 192.168.28.0 0.0.0.255 echo-reply
```

Access list 103 permits HTTP, SSL, and ping for Company B to the web server:

```
access-list 103 permit tcp 192.168.29.0 0.0.0.255 host 192.168.30.2 eq www
access-list 103 permit tcp 192.168.29.0 0.0.0.255 host 192.168.30.2 eq 443
access-list 103 permit icmp 192.168.29.0 0.0.0.255 host 192.168.30.2 echo
```

Access list 104 permits traffic from the web server back to Company B:

```
access-list 104 permit tcp host 192.168.30.2 192.168.29.0 0.0.0.255 established
access-list 104 permit icmp host 192.168.30.2 192.168.29.0 0.0.0.255 echo-reply
```

We apply these access lists against the interfaces as follows:

```
int serial 0
access-group 101 in
access-group 102 out
int serial 1
access-group 103 in
access-group 104 out
```

Implementing the same policy with outbound access lists

Now we'll implement the policy with only outgoing access lists. First we define the policy set of packets going to the web server out through the Ethernet interface:

```
access-list 101 permit tcp 192.168.28.0 0.0.1.255 host 192.168.30.2 eq www
access-list 101 permit tcp 192.168.29.0 0.0.0.255 host 192.168.30.2 eq 443
access-list 101 permit icmp 192.168.28.0 0.0.1.255 host 192.168.30.2 echo
```

The first access list entry permits HTTP traffic both from Company A's network 192.168.28.0/24 and Company B's network 192.168.29.0/24. The second entry permits SSL for Company B. The third access list entry allows pings from both companies.

Next, we'll define the access list for packets going out to Company A and Company B. For Company A:

```
access-list 102 permit tcp host 192.168.30.2 192.168.28.0 0.0.0.255 established
access-list 102 permit icmp host 192.168.30.2 192.168.28.0 0.0.0.255 echo-reply
```

We allow the return packets for HTTP and the ping replies; we do the same for Company B:

```
access-list 103 permit tcp host 192.168.30.2 192.168.29.0 0.0.0.255 established
access-list 103 permit icmp host 192.168.30.2 192.168.29.0 0.0.0.255 echo-reply
```

All three access lists are applied to interfaces as follows:

```
int Ethernet 2
access-group 101 out
Int serial 0
access-group 102 out
Int serial 1
access-group 103 out
```

Comparing the inbound and outbound access list implementations

Now that we've implemented the policy two different ways—one using inbound access lists and another using outbound access lists—let's look at how the implementations differ. Are the two implementations, one using inbound access lists and one using outbound access lists, really equivalent from a policy standpoint? Imagine if Company A and Company B, while seeking to maintain good relations with Company C, are very hostile competitors. Company A, learning somehow that

Company B is doing secure transactions using SSL, tries to slow down Company B by spoofing TCP packets to the web server's SSL port from Company B's network 192.168.29.0. This is an attempt to bog down the processing of Company B's transactions by overwhelming the web server's SSL routines. With the inbound access list implementation, such an attack would be prevented. Spoofed packets from Company A posing as Company B's 192.168.29.0/24 packets would be stopped by the implicit deny of access list 101. With the outbound access list implementation, this attack would be successful. Since outbound access lists do not differentiate between the interfaces where packets originate, there is no way to stop the forged packets from coming in.

The inbound access lists consisted of four different access lists and a total of nine access list entries. The outbound access list consisted of three different access lists and seven access list entries. Why did the outbound access list have fewer entries and access lists? As I mentioned earlier in this section, outbound access lists do not need to consider the interface a packet came in from. In the inbound access list case, we had to have separate rules for allowing in HTTP and ping traffic for both Company A and Company B. With outbound lists, we used masking to combine those entries, since networks 192.168.28.0/24 and 192.168.29.0/24 can be combined as `192.168.28.0 0.0.1.255`, and we are filtering traffic going out to the web server on Ethernet 0. By using outbound access lists exclusively, you can usually have shorter access list configurations, which really makes a difference if you start to run out of nonvolatile memory for storing configurations on a router.

Other differences come into play when considering how the companies would monitor and maintain their network connectivity. For instance, what happens if Company A or Company B cannot reach the web server? With the outbound access list implementation, Company A may ping the serial interface address 192. 168.31.3 to see if the serial link is running. If the interface is down, then Company A can conclude that the reason the web server is unreachable is that the line is down. If the interface is up, the problem is most likely at Company C. In a similar fashion, Company B may ping the serial interface 192.168.31.5 and make similar conclusions about network connectivity. With the inbound access list implementation, ping will not work. Since the inbound access lists 101 and 103 do not explicitly allow ICMP echo packets coming in to the interface address, Company A and Company B lose visibility into the network, since they can't see if the other sides of the serial lines are up.

Similarly, if Company A or Company B wants to provide routing information to Company C via a dynamic routing protocol, the outbound access list implementation would allow the protocol to work while the inbound access list implementation would not. If Company A and Company B wants to use BGP as the routing protocol, the inbound access list would have to add the following access list entries:

```
access-list 101 permit tcp host 192.168.31.2 host 192.168.31.1 eq bgp
access-list 103 permit tcp host 192.168.31.6 host 192.168.31.5 eq bgp
```

BGP uses TCP, and we have to allow it explicitly on the inbound access lists.

From our explorations of the differences of using inbound and outbound extended access lists, we can draw some conclusions about what tradeoffs are involved when deciding between inbound and outbound access lists. Outbound access lists are generally more permissive and tend to result in fewer access list entries. With outbound access lists, you don't have to worry about specifically permitting functions like routing updates, ARP, and ping. This results in less work for the router. Inbound access lists require the access list author to specify many more entries. Inbound access lists are the router's only defense against packet spoofing. Outbound access lists cannot stop packet spoofing. I generally recommend using outbound lists as much as possible, and using inbound lists to stop spoofing and making them as simple as possible. For our outbound implementation, let's add the following inbound access lists:

```
access-list 104 permit ip 192.168.28.0 0.0.0.255 host 192.168.30.2
access-list 104 permit icmp 192.168.28.0 0.0.0.255 host 192.168.31.1 echo
access-list 105 permit ip 192.168.29.0 0.0.0.255 host 192.168.30.2
access-list 105 permit icmp 192.168.29.0 0.0.0.255 host 192.168.31.5 echo
```

These would be applied as follows:

```
interface serial 0
access-group 104 in
interface serial 1
access-group 105 in
```

The first line of access list 104 includes only packets from Company A in the policy set of permitted packets. The first line of access list 105 does the same. We can allow the category of the protocol to be as broad as IP because we have further filtering being done by outbound access lists. The second entries in access lists 104 and 105 permit ping requests into the router. If we need to use BGP between the three companies, we have to add access list entries explicitly allowing BGP like we did earlier. We don't have to worry about permitting responses to pings of the serial interfaces in an access list because we are using outbound extended access lists, which do not filter the packets of ping responses generated by the router itself.

Using inbound access lists to prevent IP address spoofing

As I mentioned earlier, spoof prevention is an important use of inbound access lists. Many denial-of-service attacks use source address spoofing as a method of entry. Spoofing often works because many security mechanisms trust packets that have a source address from a trusted network. In Chapter 1, I described a scenario where a disgruntled ex-employee caused damage by sending spoofed packets from the Internet into the network of his former employer. Such attacks can be stopped with inbound access lists. Figure 3-10 shows how organizations typically connect to the Internet.

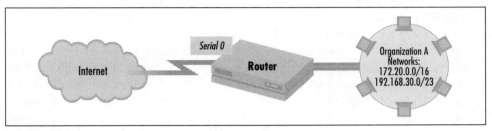

Figure 3-10. Typical Internet connectivity for an organization

In this configuration, we see Organization A with two networks, 172.20.0.0/16 and 192.168.30.0/23. The organization connects to the Internet through serial link 0. The organization needs to protect against packets from the Internet that have source IP addresses from its own two networks. Packets originating from networks 172.20.0.0/16 and 192.168.30.0/23 from other interfaces should be okay, but packets using the organization's networks as source IP addresses through serial 0, the Internet interface, are spoofed addresses that should be blocked. We can take care of this problem by setting up an inbound access list on serial 0:

```
access-list 100 deny ip 172.20.0.0 0.0.255.255 any
access-list 100 deny ip 192.168.30.0 0.0.1.225 any
access-list 100 permit ip any any
```

This access list is applied against incoming packets on the serial interface to the Internet:

```
interface serial 0
access-group 100 in
```

The first two entries in access list 100 stop packets that are forged as being from IP addresses within the company. The third entry permits any other packet to go inside the company. An added benefit of using inbound access lists in this way is that as long as the serial interfaces do not use IP addresses that are inside the company, we do not need an extra entry to allow routing updates. While permitting all IP traffic in after the two **deny** entries is very broad, it is implicit in these access lists that further filtering is done by outbound access lists on other interfaces.

> # *Inbound access lists and the address resolution protocol*
>
> The Address Resolution Protocol (ARP) is used by hosts on a shared medium such as Ethernet to determine the MAC address belonging to a particular IP address. The MAC (Media Access Control) address is a way of specifying the device address at layer 2 of the network stack. Without some way of learning the MAC address of other systems, there would be no way that hosts could communicate with each other. With inbound access lists, you need to be careful to allow ARP into an interface. For example, if you have a router with interface 192.168.35.1 connected to a network 193.168.35.0/24, the following access list entry allows ARP into the interface:
>
> ```
> access-list 101 permit ip 192.168.35.0 0.0.0.255 host 192.168.35.1
> ```
>
> You basically need to allow all IP from systems on the network to the interface IP address. It is unfortunate that there is no narrower way to define access, but that is the nature of ARP.
>
> An alternative to permitting so broad a range of packets into an interface is to explicitly define the ARP address of hosts you want to reach into the router. This technique saves access list lines at the expense of lines of hardcoded ARP entries and a lack of flexibility. In the previous comparison between inbound access lists, we assumed that the ARP entries were hardcoded.

Making routing protocols go through an inbound access list

I have mentioned that when using inbound access list on an interface, if you want to receive routing information on that interface, you need to specifically allow packets for those protocols. In this section, I go through a list of common routing protocols and access list entries that allow any host to send in routing updates for that protocol through an inbound access list. For the purpose of these examples, the interface we are filtering and receiving updates on has IP address 192.168.31.3 and allows updates from hosts on 192.168.31.0/24. Access list 101 is an incoming access list on this interface.

Here are the access entries for a number of routing protocols:

RIP

RIP uses UDP port 520:

```
access-list 101 permit udp 192.168.31.0 0.0.0.255 host 192.168.31.3 eq 520
```

IGRP

IGRP has its own special IP protocol type that needs to be specifically allowed:

```
access-list 101 permit igrp 192.168.31.0 0.0.0.255 host 192.168.31.3
```

EIGRP

EIGRP is notable in that it uses multicast hellos. This means that you have to allow special multicast addresses into the interface. Like IGRP, it has its own special IP protocol type:

```
access-list 101 permit eigrp 192.168.31.0 0.0.0.255 host 224.0.0.10
access-list 101 permit eigrp 192.168.31.0 0.0.0.255 host 192.168.31.3
```

OSPF

Like EIGRP, OSPF uses multicast hellos and has its own IP protocol type:

```
access-list 101 permit ospf 192.168.31.0 0.0.0.255 host 224.0.0.4
access-list 101 permit ospf 192.168.31.0 0.0.0.255 host 192.168.31.3
```

BGP

BGP is straightforward to implement because it uses TCP to a well-known port. Access to the TCP must be bidirectional for each peer for BGP to function.

```
access-list 101 permit tcp 192.168.31.0 0.0.0.255 host 192.168.31.3 eq bgp
access-list 101 permit tcp 192.168.31.0 0.0.0.255 eq bgp host 192.168.31.3 gt
1023
```

Session filtering using reflexive access lists

Reflexive access lists are available on IOS Versions 11.3 and up.

Reflexive access lists can be used to exercise a tight level of control over individual client and server sessions. Let's look at the network in Figure 3-11 to show how they can be used.

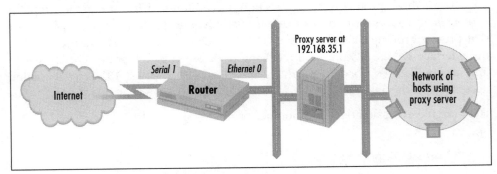

Figure 3-11. A proxy server with Internet access

This network diagram shows a proxy server with Internet access. A proxy server is a system that makes connections and service requests on behalf of other hosts and forwards the results back to the requesting hosts. Let's say that this proxy server requires full access on all TCP ports to the Internet. The following access lists and interface statements implement this policy:

```
! access list out to the proxy server from the Internet
ip access-list extended out-to-server
  permit tcp any host 192.168.35.1 gt 1023
! access list out to the Internet from the proxy server
ip access-list extended out-to-Internet
  permit tcp host 192.168.35.1 any
! interface statements
interface Ethernet 0
ip access-group out-to-server out
interface serial 1
ip access-group out-to-Internet out
```

While these access lists implement our policy, it leaves the proxy server vulnerable to probes of ports greater than 1023. A cracker could check these ports for services that can be exploited. Since a number of proxy services default to ports greater than 1023, an open proxy port could be used by an intruder to access hosts on the other side of the proxy server or to attack other systems on the Internet.

Using the **established** qualifier can help with this problem:

```
! access list out to the proxy server from the Internet
ip access-list extended out-to-server
  permit tcp any host 192.168.35.1 established
! access list out to the Internet from the proxy server
ip access-list extended out-to-Internet
  permit tcp host 192.168.35.1 any
! interface statements
interface Ethernet 0
ip access-group out-to-server out
interface serial 1
ip access-group out-to-Internet out
```

Changing the access list **out-to-server** eliminates the direct probes, but crackers can still pump in traffic to the proxy server as long as they set the ACK bit on packets.

Reflexive access lists take care of this problem by automatically creating an access list entry for each TCP connection that is established. We would configure the access list in the following way:

```
! access-list out to the Internet
ip access-list extended out-to-server
  permit tcp any host 192.168.35.1
  evaluate tcp-connections
ip access-list in-from-Internet
  permit tcp any any reflect tcp-connections
! interface statements
interface serial 1
  ip access-group out-to-Internet out
  ip access-group in-from-Internet in
```

The `evaluate` access list entry in the access list `out-to-server` says that when a TCP connection is created, the router creates a reflexive access list entry in the reflexive access list `tcp-connections` that specifically allows only traffic for that particular connection. The `reflect` entry in the access list `in-from-Internet` makes the access list compare the packet against the reflexive access list entries in `tcp-connections` that are created. As an example, let's say that the proxy server sets up a TCP connection from source port 3456 to port 80 on host 172.30.45.1. In response to this connection, the router would set up the following access list entry on the reflexive access list:

```
permit tcp host 172.30.45.1 eq www host 192.168.35.1 eq 3456
```

The *show ip access-list* command would yield:

```
Extended IP access list Out-to-server
  permit tcp host 192.168.35.1 any
  evaluate tcp-connections
Extended IP access-list in-from-Internet
  permit tcp any any reflect tcp-connections
Reflexive IP access list tcp-connections
  permit tcp host 172.30.45.1 eq www host 192.168.31.1 eq 3456 (6 matches) (time
left 119 seconds)
```

The only way to get packets into the proxy server is to use these specific source and destination ports and source and destination IP addresses. This access list entry disappears when the TCP connection is shut down. The router looks for the FIN packets requesting that a TCP connection be shut down and then removes the entry. If a TCP connection is shut down before FIN packets can be sent, then the entries disappear after a timeout interval. The default timeout period is 300 seconds (five minutes), but it can be set with the global configuration command `ip reflexive-list timeout`.

Reflexive access lists are created in the opposite direction of the extended access list that activates it. In our example, the reflexive list was created as an inbound access list of the serial interface connecting to the Internet. Let's implement the policy with inbound access lists:

```
! access-list in from the server
ip access-list extended in-from-server
  permit tcp any host 192.168.35.1 any
  evaluate tcp-connections
ip access-list extended out-to-server
  permit tcp any any reflect tcp-connections
! interface statements
interface Ethernet 0
  ip access-group out-to-server out
  ip access-group in-from-server in
```

The reflexive access list entries created would be outbound access lists going to the proxy server. For our previous example, the reflexive access list entry created would have been the same, only evaluated on an outgoing access list.

UDP client/server sessions can also be filtered with reflexive access lists. Figure 3-12 shows a server that makes DNS requests and ICMP echo requests to name servers in the Internet.

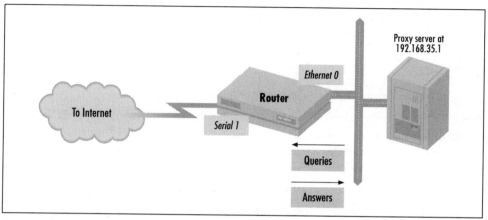

Figure 3-12. A server that makes DNS queries

We can limit access to the server with the following access lists:

```
! access list out to the server from the Internet
ip access-list extended out-to-server
  permit udp any eq 53 host 192.168.35.1 eq 53
  permit udp any eq 53 host 192.168.35.1 gt 1023
  permit icmp any host 192.168.35.1 echo-reply
  permit tcp any any reflect tcp-connections
! access list out to the Internet from the server
ip access-list extended out-to-Internet
  permit udp host 192.168.35.1 gt 1023 any eq 53
  permit udp host 192.168.35.1 eq 53 any eq 53
  permit icmp host 192.168.35.1 any echo
  permit tcp host 192.168.35.1 any eq 53
  evaluate tcp-connections
! interface statements
interface Ethernet 0
ip access-group out-to-server out
interface serial 1
ip access-group out-to-Internet out
```

While this does limit access to the server, an intruder can still probe for UDP ports over 1023 by using a source port of 53. Since UDP is a connectionless protocol, there is no equivalent to **established** for filtering session startup packets. Reflexive access lists can fix this problem:

```
! access list out to the server from the Internet
ip access-list extended out-to-server
  permit icmp any host 192.168.35.1 echo-reply
  permit tcp any any reflect tcp-connections
  permit udp any any reflect udp-sessions
```

```
! access list out to the Internet from the server
ip access-list extended in-from-Internet
  permit udp host 192.168.35.1 gt 1023 any eq 53
  permit udp host 192.168.35.1 eq 53 any eq 53
  permit icmp host 192.168.35.1 any echo
  permit tcp host 192.168.35.1 any eq 53
  evaluate tcp-connections
  evaluate udp-sessions
! interface statements
interface Ethernet 0
  ip access-group out-to-server out
  ip access-group in-from-server in
```

Since UDP is connectionless and doesn't have the equivalent of a FIN packet marking the end of a session, the router maintains the access list entry as long as it sees traffic within the reflexive access list timeout interval. A query from the name server that uses source port 1234 to host 172.30.45.60 then creates the entry:

```
permit udp host 172.30.45.60 eq 53 host 192.168.35.1 eq 1234
```

Reflexive access lists have a number of limitations. You cannot use them on protocols that do not have source ports, such as ICMP. In the previous entry, we needed to put in specific entries to allow ICMP echo replies to the server. You cannot use reflexive access lists with protocols that change ports during a session or that have sessions set up in two directions. A good example is active mode FTP. A control connection is set up from client to server with a source port greater than 1023. When a file needs to be copied or a directory listing is needed, a data connection is set up from the server to the client. If a reflexive access list is used, the entry created for the control connection prevents the data connection from being set up. Passive mode FTP would work, however, since data connections are set up in the same direction. Reflexive access lists also require named access lists. If you are using an older version of the Cisco IOS that does not support named access lists, then you can't use reflexive access lists.

An expanded example of packet filtering

Let's look at a more complex example of packet filtering. For this example, I use the configuration shown in Figure 3-13.

This configuration is known as a screened subnet firewall. The goal of this architecture is to allow the hosts in Organization X to access and provide Internet services without directly exposing those hosts to attack. The hosts that we want to protect strongly are connected to Ethernet 1 in networks 192.168.32.0/24 through 192.168. 39.0/24. The Internet is connected to the serial interface, and all packets from that serial interface are considered potentially hostile. Hosts in networks 192.168.32.0/24 through 192.168.39.0/24 do not access the Internet directly. All contact with the Internet is proxied through hosts in network 192.168.30.0/24. The combination of

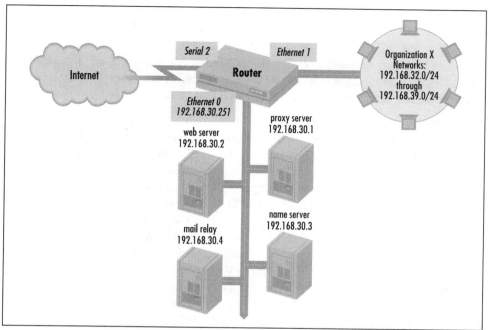

Figure 3-13. A screened subnet firewall

protecting a set of hosts while proxying all Internet access through another subnet makes packet filtering in the screened subnet firewall more complex.

Let's see how proxy access works, and how it affects packet filtering. Hosts in networks 192.168.32.0/24 through 192.168.39.0/24 access web servers outside the Organization X through the proxy server. Web requests are sent to the proxy on TCP port 911, which gets the requested web pages and sends them back to the requestor. Incoming and outgoing electronic mail is relayed through a mail relay. Mail destined for inside Organization X is sent to the mail relay, which forwards it to Organization X's internal mail servers. Mail from Organization X to the Internet is sent first to the mail relay, which then forwards it on to its final destination. Network services that Organization X provides the Internet, like web and name services, are offered through dedicated web and name servers. Hosts in network 192.168.30.0/24 on do not have full access to Organization X's networks 192.168.32.0/24 through 192.168.39.0/24. They are given only enough access to the internal networks to carry out their proxy functions.

The network 192.168.30.0/24 is called a DMZ, for De-Militarized Zone. The rationale behind this design is that hosts we want to protect must not have direct Internet access. All Internet access is done through hosts in the DMZ, which protects the internal hosts from direct attack. When a significant security weakness in hosts or software is found, Organization X can concentrate first on fixing the weakness in DMZ systems (which typically have far fewer systems). Once the DMZ systems are hardened against the security weakness, crackers on the Internet cannot exploit the weakness against Organization X. If a DMZ system is compromised, access into Organization X's internal networks is controlled. An additional benefit is that Organization X has a central location for tracking its Internet use because all Internet access is proxied through DMZ systems.

In addition to the goals of the screened subnet architecture, let's make other policy decisions that will affect how we define the extended access lists. Internet hosts 192.168.10.4 and 192.168.12.5 will be DNS secondaries for Organization X's domains. This means that these two hosts, existing somewhere out on the Internet, will also provide DNS queries for Organization X's domain. To make that possible, they must be able to copy all of the DNS data about Organization X from the name server on the DMZ, a process known as a *zone transfer*, so our access lists need to permit zone transfers by only those two nodes. Another policy decision is that Organization X will give relatively small answers to DNS queries. As you may recall, a DNS client that receives a large answer to a DNS query starts a TCP connection to get all of the answer. Keeping DNS answers small eliminates the need for allowing all Internet hosts TCP port 53 connectivity into its name server and speeds response time to queries, since fewer packets are sent for each answer, and no TCP connection is needed. Note that Organization X must implement this policy by being disciplined about the DNS resource records that it creates. In most cases, there is no reason to have extremely large DNS resource records. An exception is for large web sites that do load balancing to large numbers of servers with DNS round robin, a technique that assigns a number of IP addresses to the hostname of a web server.

What about routing? We know exactly which networks are connected to which interface. Network 192.168.30.0/24 is on Ethernet 0, networks 192.168.32.0/24 through 192.168.39.0 are on Ethernet 1, and everything else on the Internet is reached through serial 2. It is easy to use static, hardcoded routes on the router, so for this example, we won't use dynamic routing protocols. In firewall designs, you should avoid using dynamic routing protocols as much as possible, since they add complexity to access lists, and routing updates can also be spoofed. I'll talk about this in more detail in Chapter 4.

With all the information we have gathered about policy and the screened subnet architecture, let's define how IP packets should flow through Organization X's router:

Deny packets from the Internet that have a source address within an organization (prevent spoofing)

All hosts on the screened subnet can be pinged from all networks

DNS queries should be permitted from the name server to the Internet and vice versa

Internet hosts 192.168.10.4 and 192.168.12.5 should be able to do DNS zone transfers from name server

Web access is permitted to the web server from all networks

FTP, Telnet, and web access out to the Internet is permitted from the proxy server

FTP, Telnet, and web proxy access on TCP port 911 from the internal networks is permitted to the proxy server

The mail relay has SMTP access to all networks and can receive SMTP connections from all networks

No direct connectivity is permitted between the Internet and the internal networks

Defining what access lists are necessary

The first policy entry states that packets from the Internet with the organization's address as the source IP address are denied entry. This policy rule is designed to stop source IP address spoofing, and as I mentioned in a previous section, inbound access lists are the network administrator's tools for spoof protection. Access list 100, shown below, implements the anti-spoof policy:

```
access-list 100 deny ip 192.168.30.0 0.0.0.255 any
access-list 100 deny ip 192.168.32.0 0.0.7.255 any
access-list 100 permit ip any any
```

Organization A uses networks 192.168.30.0/24 in its DMZ and networks 192.168. 32.0/24 through 192.168.39.0/24 in the core of its network. The first entry in access list 100 denies packets from the Internet that have source addresses of the DMZ network 192.168.30.0/24. The next line denies packets from internal networks 192. 168.32.0/24 through 192.168.39.0/24. We can express this in a single statement by using a network mask. After spoofing is stopped, everything else is permitted through the interface (outbound access lists will be used to do the rest of the filtering). Access list 100 is applied as an inbound access list to the interface facing the Internet:

```
interface serial 2
access-group 100 in
```

Are there any other interfaces that require inbound access lists? Any system that exchanges packets directly to the Internet is a possible point of compromise. What if a DMZ system, which does exchange packets directly with the Internet, were compromised by crackers? That system could be used as a base for launching attacks against other Internet sites or against the internal networks. To prevent a DMZ from potentially being used for spoofing attacks, we can create access list 101 that permits only DMZ packets from that segment:

```
access-list 101 permit ip 192.168.30.0 0.0.0.255 any
```

The implicit deny of access list 101 stops spoofed packets. This access list is applied to interface Ethernet 0 with:

```
interface Ethernet 0
access-group 101 in
```

You might question whether we need to put an incoming access list on Ethernet 1 to prevent spoofing attacks from Organization X's employees. Since we are going to prevent the internal networks from talking directly to the Internet, it may not seem necessary. But attacks by disgruntled insiders are a real threat. Hosts on the internal network could potentially spoof packets with addresses from the DMZ in order to get them out onto the Internet. To take care of spoofing attacks on the DMZ and stop accidental traffic, we can build another very simple inbound access list 102:

```
access-list 102 permit ip 192.168.32.0 0.0.7.255 any
```

which allows packets from the internal networks only into the router. This is then applied with:

```
interface Ethernet 1
access-group 102 in
```

Although we made a decision not to use dynamic routing protocols, the way that I have used inbound access lists for anti-spoofing purposes in this example allows us to use dynamic routing protocols on the serial interface without changing our access lists. In other words, as long as the IP addresses on both ends of the serial link do not use the internal IP addresses or DMZ addresses, the router allows routing updates into the serial interface. Similarly, as long as the routers off Ethernet 1 use internal IP addresses, route updates are permitted on that interface. Using inbound access lists for anti-spoofing purposes gives us this flexibility.

Now that we are done with the inbound access lists, we need to work on the outbound access lists. Since we have policies applying to networks attached to all three interfaces of the router, let's define outgoing access list numbers as follows:

- 103—Outgoing access list on interface serial 2 (to the Internet)
- 104—Outgoing access list on Ethernet 0 (to the DMZ)
- 105—Outgoing access list on Ethernet 1 (to internal networks)

With access list numbers defined, we can start creating access lists entries for each of the packet-forwarding rules:

Deny packets from the Internet that have a source address within an organization (prevent spoofing)

We handled this policy with our inbound access lists.

All hosts on the screened subnet can be pinged from all networks

To implement this policy statement, we need to allow `ICMP echo-reply` packets out to the Internet and internal user networks. For the outgoing serial interface access list, we have:

```
access-list 103 permit icmp 192.168.30.0 0.0.0.255 any echo-reply
```

We need the same leading into the internal segments:

```
access-list 105 permit icmp 192.168.30.0 0.0.0.255 192.168.32.0 0.0.7.255
echo-reply
```

The DMZ segment itself needs to receive ICMP echo requests:

```
access-list 104 permit icmp any 192.168.30.0 0.0.0.255 echo
```

DNS queries should be permitted to and from the name server

We need to allow DNS packets in and out of the DMZ segment for DNS queries. As I mentioned in our web server example, DNS queries come into a name server with a UDP destination port of 53 and a source port of either 53 or greater than 1023. Large queries use TCP on destination port 53. With this information, we generate the following access lists:

```
! access list out to the Internet (serial 2)
access-list 103 permit udp host 192.168.30.3 eq domain any eq domain
access-list 103 permit udp host 192.168.30.3 gt 1023 any eq domain
access-list 103 permit udp host 192.168.30.3 eq domain any gt 1023
access-list 103 permit tcp host 192.168.30.3 any eq domain
! access list out to the DMZ (Ethernet 0)
access-list 104 permit tcp any host 192.168.30.3 established
access-list 104 permit udp any eq domain host 192.168.30.3 eq domain
access-list 104 permit udp any eq domain host 192.168.30.3 gt 1023
access-list 104 permit udp any gt 1023 host 192.168.30.3 eq domain
```

The name server at IP address 192.168.30.3 can send any DNS query out to the Internet because the first line and second lines of access list 103 permit UDP packets with a destination port of 53 and a source port of 53 or greater than 1023. Should the name server require TCP to get a large DNS answer, the fourth line of access list 103 permits that type of connection. The first line of access list 104 allows return packets from that TCP connection, and the second and third lines of access list 104 permit responses to the name server's queries to go back to the name server.

The name server also needs to answer queries from the Internet The second and third lines of access list 104 permit the name server to receive any DNS query. The first and third lines of access list 103 permit responses to DNS queries. Since we explicitly decided that all DNS answers about Organization X would be small, connection to TCP port 53 is not allowed.

Internet hosts 192.168.10.4 and 192.168.12.5 should be able to do DNS zone transfers from name servers

We implement this policy statement by first setting up an established TCP access list entry on the outgoing serial interface to the Internet:

```
access-list 103 permit tcp host 192.168.30.0 0.0.0.255 any established
```

We make it generic to all of the DMZ so we can also catch all TCP connections going out of the DMZ that have already been set up. Hosts 192.168.10.4 and 192.168.12.5 are permitted to do zone transfers from the name server. Zone transfers use TCP port 53. So in the access list going to the DMZ, we have:

```
access-list 104 permit tcp host 192.168.10.4 host 192.168.30.3 eq domain
access-list 104 permit tcp host 192.168.12.5 host 192.168.30.3 eq domain
```

Since both zone transfers and DNS queries with large answers use TCP port 53, we'll have to require all DNS answers from those name servers small enough to not require a TCP connection. Otherwise, there would be no way to allow zone transfers from only the designated secondary DNS servers as we would have had to allow TCP port 53 to be open to all on the Internet.

Web access is permitted to the web server from all networks

We need to allow web protocols to have access on port 80 into the web server at 192.168.30.2. This is done with:

```
access-list 104 permit tcp any host 192.168.30.2 eq www
```

Return packets to the Internet are covered by the **established** access list entry in list 103. We need a similar entry going into the internal networks (list 105):

```
access-list 105 permit tcp 192.168.30.0 0.0.0.255 192.168.32.0 0.0.7.255
established
```

FTP, Telnet, and web access out to the Internet is permitted from the proxy server

We add an **established** statement to list 104 to handle return traffic on a connection set up from the proxy server to the Internet. Since the other servers on the DMZ will be making and receiving connections to the Internet too, it is safe to make the established connection apply to the rest of the DMZ:

```
access-list 104 permit tcp any host 192.168.30.0 0.0.0.255 established
```

Since web servers can live on a number of ports, we need to add generic TCP access going out to the Internet from the proxy server:

```
access-list 103 permit tcp host 192.168.30.1 any
```

To make FTP work, we need TCP ports greater than 1023 going to the proxy server from source port 20:

```
access-list 104 permit tcp any eq ftp-data host 192.168.30.1 gt 1023
```

FTP, Telnet, and web access from the internal networks is permitted to the proxy server

This is similar to the previous policy statement, but we can be much more specific about what networks can talk to the proxy server:

```
access-list 105 permit tcp host 192.168.30.1 eq ftp-data 192.168.32.0 0.0.7.
255 gt 1023
```

We need to permit the proxied services of FTP, Telnet, and Web into the proxy server from the internal segments:

```
access-list 104 permit tcp 192.168.32.0 0.0.7.255 host 192.168.30.1 range
ftp-data ftp
access-list 104 permit tcp 192.168.32.0 0.0.7.255 host 192.168.30.1 eq telnet
access-list 104 permit tcp 192.168.32.0 0.0.7.255 host 192.168.30.1 eq 911
```

The mail relay has SMTP access to all networks and can receive SMTP connections from all networks

SMTP uses port 25 as a destination port. We already have established statements, so we need the following statements:

```
access-list 103 permit tcp host 192.168.30.4 any eq smtp
access-list 104 permit tcp any host 192.168.30.4 eq smtp
access-list 105 permit tcp host 192.168.30.4 192.168.32.0 0.0.7.255 eq smtp
```

No direct connectivity is permitted between the Internet and the internal networks

This is taken care of by the explicit **permit** entries and implicit deny entry at the end of the access lists.

Optimizing the order of access list entries

We now have a large collection of access list entries. What is the best way to arrange them? You want to have the most frequently used access list entry at the top, followed by the next most frequently used entry, and so on. As mentioned earlier, doing this minimizes the impact that access lists have on a router. The most frequently used access list entry in environments that use TCP-based services such as HTTP, SMTP, and FTP is the **established** entry. It is almost always a good idea to put a very general **established** entry at the top of a list because the vast majority of traffic will match the first line of an access list and the router will not have to process other access list entries. Next, you typically want to use DNS statements since most Internet services use hostnames and not just IP addresses, thus requiring a DNS lookup. After DNS access list entries, ICMP **echo** and **echo-reply** entries should go next because ping is used frequently on the Internet. Finally, the other permit entries for TCP services and other services should be covered. Bear in mind, these are general guidelines, and utilization of access list entries may be different, depending on your needs and traffic patterns. Whatever order you choose, be careful about moving deny entries in an access list or permit statements ahead of deny entries. This kind of movement in particular can completely change the policy you are trying to implement, denying entries you did not intend to deny or permitting services you did.

In this case, the final version of access list 103, the outbound access list going to the Internet, becomes:

```
! access list out to Internet through serial interface 0
access-list 103 permit tcp host 192.168.30.0 0.0.0.255 any established
access-list 103 permit udp host 192.168.30.3 eq domain any eq domain
access-list 103 permit udp host 192.168.30.3 gt 1023 any eq domain
access-list 103 permit udp host 192.168.30.3 eq domain any gt 1023
access-list 103 permit tcp host 192.168.30.3 any eq domain
access-list 103 permit icmp 192.168.30.0 0.0.0.255 any echo-reply
access-list 103 permit tcp host 192.168.30.1 any
access-list 103 permit tcp 192.168.32.0 0.0.7.255 host 192.168.30.1
access-list 103 permit tcp host 192.168.30.4 any eq smtp
```

while access list 104, the access list leading to the DMZ segment, is as follows:

```
! access list out to DMZ through Ethernet interface 0
access-list 104 permit tcp any 192.168.30.0 0.0.0.255 established
access-list 104 permit udp any eq domain host 192.168.30.3 eq domain
access-list 104 permit udp any eq domain host 192.168.30.3 gt 1023
access-list 104 permit udp any gt 1023 host 192.168.30.3 eq domain
access-list 104 permit icmp any 192.168.30.0 0.0.0.255 echo
access-list 104 permit tcp any host 192.168.30.2 eq www
access-list 104 permit tcp 192.168.32.0 0.0.7.255 host 192.168.30.1 range ftp-data
ftp
access-list 104 permit tcp 192.168.32.0 0.0.7.255 host 192.168.30.1 eq telnet
access-list 104 permit tcp 192.168.32.0 0.0.7.255 host 192.168.30.1 eq 911
access-list 104 permit tcp any eq ftp-data host 192.168.30.1 gt 1023
access-list 104 permit tcp any host 192.168.30.4 eq smtp
access-list 104 permit tcp host 192.168.10.4 host 192.168.30.3 eq domain
access-list 104 permit tcp host 192.168.12.5 host 192.168.30.5 eq domain
```

(I have moved the entries that permit zone transfers toward the end since the zone transfer operations are specific to certain hosts and are not part of the generic DNS functionality offered to the whole Internet and thus are used less frequently.)

Finally, access list 105, the access list leading to the internal networks, becomes:

```
! access list to internal networks through Ethernet 1
access-list 105 permit tcp 192.168.30.0 0.0.0.255 192.168.32.0 0.0.7.255
established
access-list 105 permit icmp 192.168.30.0 0.0.0.255 192.168.32.0 0.0.7.255 echo-
reply
access-list 105 permit tcp host 192.168.30.1 eq ftp-data 192.168.32.0 0.0.7.255 gt
1023
access-list 105 permit tcp host 192.168.30.4 192.168.32.0 0.0.7.255 eq smtp
```

We apply all our access lists (including all inbound lists) as follows:

```
int serial 0
 access-group 100 in
 access-group 103 out
```

```
interface Ethernet 0
  access-group 101 in
  access-group 104 out
interface Ethernet 1
  access-group 102 in
  access-group 105 out
```

Figure 3-14 shows how the access lists are applied.

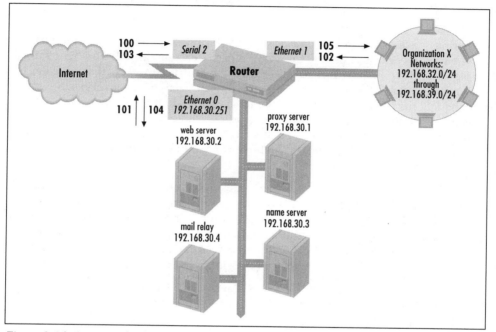

Figure 3-14. A screened subnet firewall with access lists

Alternatives to access lists

The CPU costs incurred by access lists can be quite high. For this reason, Cisco routers offer a number of alternatives to using access lists for security. I'll discuss them here.

Routing to the null interface

Occasionally, you may encounter a network or a single host that you absolutely do not trust. In a company, this could be a segment where known outsiders and potentially hostile people are working, or perhaps a lab network that has different Internet access. It could also be a DMZ or a system on the DMZ such as a dial-in terminal server, where you may have some doubts about the security on that network or who is on that system. In any case, the systems and data that you want to

---

Limitations of packet filtering

While packet filtering with extended access lists can be very useful for implementing security policies, it has some notable limitations. Static packet filtering (i.e., not reflexive lists) does not maintain a protocol state. This means that nonreflexive access lists filter packets without caring whether those packets are valid in the sequence of a protocol. For example, the access list entry:

```
access-list 100 permit tcp any host 192.168.35.1 range 20 21
```

permits packets for an FTP data session (TCP port 20) whether or not the necessary FTP control session (TCP port 21) has been established. Another example is the TCP qualifier `established`. It allows all TCP packets that have flags set for an established connection, even if the connection has never been established. Some crackers use this feature to scan hosts behind an access list. They send a TCP FIN packet to a particular port on a host, which responds in a certain way if there is a service on that port. While the crackers may not be able to directly exploit any services that they find, the information may be of use to them for identifying targets.

Another key limitation of packet filtering, even with reflexive lists, is that it cannot stop in-protocol attacks. This means that if there are weaknesses that can be exploited within a protocol, packet filtering cannot stop it. Examples of this are exploits using HTTP that allow remote users to execute commands on a host simply by issuing coded HTTP requests. A packet filter can only allow or disallow HTTP traffic, not check for holes in a server's HTTP implementation.

Another example is a SYN flood attack. An extended access list can allow TCP SYN packets, but it cannot stop a flood of SYN packets that are designed to disable a host.

---

protect may be so sensitive that you don't want to take any chances with traffic or data flowing to the untrustworthy network or host. One tactic you can use for absolute certainty is to route all traffic to a null device with a static route. Here, I use a static route to drop all traffic going to network 192.168.29.0/24:

```
ip route 192.168.29.0 255.255.255.0 null0
```

This static route configuration command sends all traffic to network 192.168.29.0 on to a null device, effectively throwing away all packets going to that network. This is a succinct way to completely eliminate traffic going to a given network. Dropping all traffic to a host is much more common. If we were to drop all traffic going to host 192.168.29.1, we would use the route command:

```
ip route 192.168.29.1 255.255.255.255 null0
```

You need to be careful of a number of things when using the null route as an access list replacement. All of the router is affected by such a command, not just particular interfaces. With this technique, you can't drop traffic from some hosts or network to the hosts while permitting others; all traffic going out of the router to this host is dropped. Also, just because you can't send traffic to a network or a host doesn't mean they can't send traffic to you.

Stopping directed broadcasts

It is possible to send a broadcast directed at a specific network through a router without being on that network. For example, a Network Time Protocol (NTP) server can send a directed broadcast to update the clocks used by the hosts on a given segment. This could be done with a single packet, resulting in considerably less traffic than the typical polling used by NTP. While the directed broadcast can be useful, it is very dangerous. Directed broadcasts are the basis of a number of denial-of-service attacks. A cracker on the Internet sends a packet into a corporation's network broadcast address with a spoofed source address. All the machines on that network reply to the broadcast by sending packets to the attacked host, which crashes under the load. Typically, ICMP is used, since many hosts respond to it.

You can explicitly permit or deny directed broadcasts with extended access lists. To match a directed broadcast into network 192.168.30.0/24, you can use an entry like this:

```
access-list 101 deny ip any 192.168.30.255 0.0.0.0
```

A directed broadcast has all 1's in the host portion of the address, which is in this case 255. This particular entry denies all directed broadcasts because it uses `ip` as the protocol, but you can specify individual IP protocols like UDP if you prefer. However, in firewall situations, you should turn off any directed broadcasts for which you don't need to use an access list, since you can do this on an interface basis with the command *no ip directed-broadcast.* For example, if you want to turn off directed broadcasts going out of interface Ethernet 0, use the following:

```
interface Ethernet 0
no ip directed-broadcast
```

This saves you from having to worry about adding an extra entry to the outgoing access list on that interface or inbound access lists on other interfaces and also reduces the size of the router's configuration.

Removing router resources

To manage a router, a network administrator must log in through an untrusted network. Figure 3-15 shows a diagram of this kind of situation.

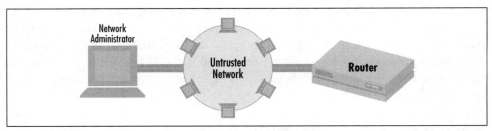

Figure 3-15. Managing a router through untrusted networks

One possible scenario is when a network administrator at a network trade show logs into one of his routers through an untrusted network. Since Telnet sessions into routers are unencrypted, the administrator's password is stolen. There are less dramatic instances in which this situation comes up: managing a router reachable only through DMZ segments, for example, where you know machines are exposed to attack from the Internet, or segments populated by people you do not trust, such as a segment with hosts run by multiple organizations.

If the situation depicted in Figure 3-15 applies to you, and you still maintain physical security of your router, you can manage the router from the console and simply not define any router resources like SNMP and virtual terminal lines, as opposed to dealing with access lists. This may seem extremely obvious, but sometimes you may forget about router configurations like virtual terminal lines that you may have added in the past to make configuration easier. Since you have physical security with your router, managing the router from the console is extremely secure and doesn't expose any passwords to anyone who may be eavesdropping. A variation of this strategy is to put a terminal server on the console port of the router and make the terminal server accessible only from trusted networks. This is a good solution if you manage routers connected to a DMZ.

4

Implementing Routing Policies

A key policy decision that network administrators need to make is how to route packets. Application performance, security, and cost can all be affected by these decisions. Routers, in addition to forwarding and receiving data packets, send routing messages that describe where to send those packets. Network administrators use two policy tools to manipulate these routing messages: route filtering and filtering based on characteristics of routes. The first section of this chapter talks about the general issues of implementing routing policies—how filtering the routes distributed by routing protocols can affect network stability and business goals, and the following section goes into the details of making networks robust. After that, we discuss how to implement traffic preferences according to specific objectives and look at the costs incurred when implementing routing policies. Finally, we briefly examine some alternatives to using access lists. This chapter focuses mainly on routing within smaller networks and intranets, but the concepts discussed here are applicable to routing in the Internet and in very large networks, which we'll talk about in Chapter 6.

Fundamentals of route filtering

In Chapter 3, we saw how access lists can be used to filter packets moving through a router. Packets are not the only types of information that can be monitored by access lists. Routing information, which instructs routers how to forward data packets to their proper destination, are often critical to control. Let's talk a little about routing basics and the reasons for building router filtering policies for our networks and organizations, which will prepare us for implementing access lists to control the flow of routing information later in the chapter.

Routing information flow

When networks grow past a certain size, there is no way that administrators can manually update every router with information about the best way to route packets. Network links change capacity, routers go up and down, and traffic conditions vary. To ensure that all of the routers in a network know about changing network conditions, routers pass routing information between each other in a series of packets called routing updates or route advertisements. *Routing updates* provide information about the paths going to individual networks so that routers can decide how to forward packets to those networks. Routing information can include the number of router hops to a network, path delay, network congestion, or other information such as flags that routers attached to the routing information. With this information, routers make decisions about the best path to a given network.

In a similar manner to the control of packets we examined in Chapter 3, a router can forward and filter routing information, as shown in Figure 4-1.

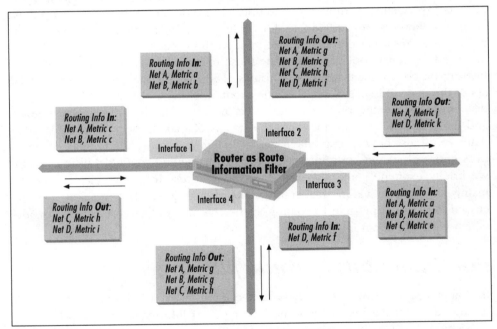

Figure 4-1. Routing information is forwarded and filtered through a router

Routing information comes into the router from several different interfaces, using a routing protocol with a single metric whose values are shown. Routing updates about Networks 1 and 2 come into Interfaces 1 and 2. The updates from Interface 1 have c as the value of the metric for both networks. The updates coming into interface 2 have the metric for Network 1 as a and the metric for X as b. Interface

3 sees routing information that gives Network 1 a metric of a, Network 2 a metric of d, and Network 3 a metric of e, while Interface 4 sees that Network 4 has a metric of f. The router then distributes routing information about the networks that it received. Network 1 is then advertised out of Interfaces 2 and 4 with a metric of g, but it is advertised out of Interface 3 with a metric of j and not advertised at all out of Interface 1. Network 2 is advertised with a metric of g out of Interfaces 2, 3, and 4. Network 3 is advertised with a metric of h out of Interfaces 1, 2, and 4, while Network 4 is advertised with a metric of i out of Interfaces 1 and 2 and advertised with a metric of k out of Interface 3.

As you can see, there are similarities to the flow of information to packet control. Routing information flow differs from packet information flow most significantly in that the router can substantially change the contents of routing information flowing through it.

Elements in a routing update

Let's talk more about routing information itself. Let's look at the key elements in any routing information update:

Network number and mask
> The network number and mask determine what network the route information applies. It is also the part of the routing information most commonly used to determine whether a routing update is included in a policy set for further processing.

Routing protocol and version
> The routing protocol is another key piece of information about routing updates. There are a number of different routing protocols for IP, and a router can be configured to listen to more than one. Dealing with different routing protocols and distributing routing information between them is a common thing that network administrators must deal with, and it is one of the most common uses of access lists.

Next hop
> The next key piece of information, next hop, is the IP address where the router is advised to send packets bound for the network advertised. If the router accepts the routing update as the best path to that network, all packets destined to that network are sent to the next hop IP address.

Source of routing information
> Closely related to next hop is the source of routing information. This is the IP address of the router sending the routing update. This router is usually (but not always) the next hop. A network administrator may choose to add routes to a policy set based on next hop information or on the source of routing

information. This is an instance of the last network administrator tool mentioned in Chapter 1: controlling routes based on a characteristic of those routes.

Metric information

Metric information is the information used by a routing protocol to determine the optimal route. There can be a single numerical value, or there can be a series of other values used as metrics, not all of them numeric. Metric information can be used as criteria for placement into a policy set. Once a policy set of routes has been established, a network administrator can manipulate the metric values of the routes in the policy set.

Other information

Other information is nonmetric information that is in a routing update for the purpose of setting routing policies. Some routing protocols do not have this kind of information. I will talk more about using other information in routing updates in the Chapter 6, when we talk about route maps and the BGP-4 routing protocol.

It is important to keep these elements separate and distinct when thinking about routing updates. Filtering a route to Network A (the network number) is different from filtering routes from routers on Network A (the source of routing information). You can receive routes to Network A from routers that are not directly connected to Network A. In particular, the network number of a route described in a routing update should not be mistaken for any other elements.

Once the policy sets you build based on the elements above are established, a network administrator can program routers to act on them through four actions. First, the administrator can choose to reject routing updates in a policy set so the router ignores the information from those updates. Second, the router can be programmed not to forward the routing updates in a policy set. In this case, the router knows how to send packets to the networks specified, but it does not let other routers know this information. Third, a router can change any of the elements contained in incoming routing updates, so that its own routing table differs from the routing information that it receives. Finally, the router can send out routing information that is different from the routing information in its own routing table.

Network robustness

A desirable property of a network is robustness. A problem in one part of the network shouldn't affect all of the network, and the network as a whole should keep running even if parts of it are broken. Maintaining network robustness is about modularity and problem isolation. As networks scale in size, different parts of the network are usually run by different organizations. Those parts should be *modular*: self-contained and thought of and managed as a unit. Breaking down a large network into smaller self-contained units makes a network much more manageable.

Once a network has become organized into smaller units, a routing problem or misconfiguration in one unit should not impact everyone in the network, as the problem will be more easily isolated to one modular unit. Let's look at an example. Figure 4-2 shows a network made of different sites connected through a single router.

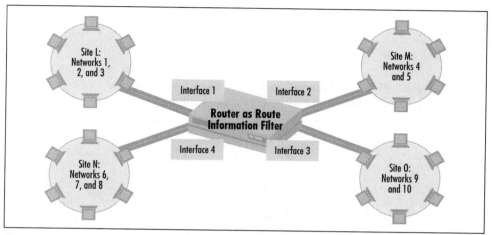

Figure 4-2. Network robustness in a multi-domain/organization network

In this network, the router in the center connects four different sites. Site L, connected through Interface 1, uses Networks 1, 2, and 3. Site M, connected through Interface 2, uses Networks 4 and 5. Site N, connected through Interface 3, uses Networks 6, 7, and 8, while Site O, connected through Interface 4, uses Networks 9 and 10.

The network administrator managing the router wants to make sure that a routing problem in one site doesn't impact the other sites. For example, if Site O started advertising routes to Site L's Networks 1, 2, and 3, the router should not accept these routes and should not forward traffic bound for Site L's networks to Site O. To provide some modularity in routing and make the network more robust in the case of misconfiguration, the router should only accept a site's designated routes. Routes for 1, 2, and 3 should be accepted only through Interface 1. Routes 4 and 5 from Site M should only be accepted through Interface 2. Similarly, routes 6, 7, and 8 from Site N should only be accepted through Interface 3, and routes 9 and 10 from Site O only through Interface 4. In this way, sites can advertise any routes they want, but only their designated routes are accepted.

Static routes do not scale

In the previous example, we knew what routes were expected from each site, and that enabled us to make the network much more robust. You might argue that since we had that knowledge, we could have set up static routes to each of the sites, eliminated the use of dynamic routing protocols, and avoided route filtering entirely. *Static routing* is the practice of explicitly configuring how a router sends traffic. Once the routing is set, the router forwards traffic according to those rules no matter how a network might change. Indeed, *static routing* is an alternative for simple networks, and I will talk about this alternative later in this chapter. Still, there are reasons you might want to use static routing with dynamic route filtering. If Site L had problems and Networks 1, 2, and 3 became totally unavailable, Site L would signal that problem by not advertising these routes. Traffic for network a would cause a network unreachable message to be sent from the central router instead of being forwarded into Site L, as would be done with static routes. In addition, pure static routing becomes difficult to maintain when a network becomes more complex. Take, for example, a version of the network shown in Figure 4-3.

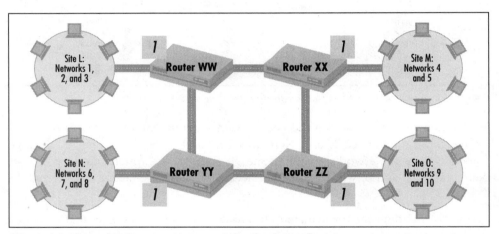

Figure 4-3. Network robustness in a more complex network

In the network shown in Figure 4-2, one central router forwards all traffic between all four sites, and thus the router itself becomes a critical point of failure. If the router fails, no traffic can be sent between any sites. The network in Figure 4-3 solves this problem, because there are multiple paths between sites. If one router fails, then the site attached to it is cut off from the others, but the rest of the sites can still communicate between each other. Similarly, if one path between routers fails, there are alternate paths that can route traffic. If static routing is used, each of the four routers need to have explicit knowledge about all the paths from that router to each of the networks. That's a lot of data to manage, and dynamic routing protocols are designed to learn and manage this kind of information automatically.

Implementing network robustness through route filtering

No matter how complex your organization, with dynamic routing protocols, we make networks robust in the same manner. For instance, in the case of Figure 4-3, we know what networks should be advertised from each site into Interface 1 on the site's adjacent router. Router WW should allow in route updates only for Networks 1, 2, and 3; Router XX should allow updates only for 4 and 5; Router YY should only allow in updates for Networks 6, 7, and 8; and Router ZZ should only allow in updates for Networks 9 and 10. If any one of the sites advertises a network that it does not own, the bad routing information is not propagated across the network.

So far, I have only talked about filtering incoming routing updates, where the router listening for route updates takes responsibility for making sure the correct routing information is received, accepted, or dropped as necessary. However, senders of routing information can also take responsibility for making sure the proper routing information is distributed. Cisco routers, for example, have the ability to restrict the routes that they send out. Let's look at an example coming from the network in Figure 4-3. Consider the situation if all of the sites connected to the network of routers via serial lines and Routers WW, XX, YY, and ZZ are managed by different groups than any of the sites they connect. Each site connects to the central network of routers with a configuration similar to that shown in Figure 4-4.

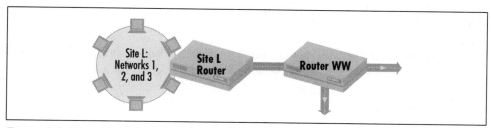

Figure 4-4. Connecting a site to wide area network

Here's the problem: Site L knows that it should only send routes to Router WW for Networks 1, 2, and 3. If someone makes a configuration error within Site L, routes other than those for Networks 1, 2, and 3 could be sent to Router WW. Since a different organization maintains Router WW, Site L's network staff has no assurances that Router WW correctly filters routes. With a situation like this, Site L should restrict route updates sent to Router WW to include only Networks 1, 2, and 3. If Router WW accepts only these routes from Site L, routing still functions properly. If Site L makes a mistake and tries to propagate a route to a network that it doesn't own, and if for some reason Router WW doesn't filter incoming route updates, the outgoing route filter will stop the bad route from being advertised. Although it may seem redundant that Site L is ready for the worst from Router WW while Router WW is ready for the worst from Site L, mistakes do happen. Rather than have network traffic totally disrupted if a route is advertised incorrectly, a little paranoia can go a long way to making sure a network stays up and running.

To summarize, the key to ensuring network robustness is to enforce what you know about how routing updates should take place with routing filtering. Don't accept routes you know you should not accept. Don't send out routes that you know that you should not send. Don't assume that the router you are listening to or sending route updates to will do the right thing, especially if that router is controlled by another organization. I'll show examples later in this chapter that demonstrate how to use access lists to implement routing policies that will help make your network fault-tolerant.

Business drivers and route preferences

Left alone, routing protocols decide what the best path network traffic will take based on network topology metrics such as bandwidth and router hops. But organizations often want to have more control over the path the traffic takes to get its final destination. In this section, we'll talk about implementing route preferences driven by an organization's business goals.

Why would an organization choose traffic preferences different from the ones selected by routing metrics? I discussed a number of the reasons in the scenarios described in Chapter 1. Some paths are more secure than others. Paths over internal networks tend to be more secure than paths over the open Internet. Some paths may be cheaper than others, while some may have more bandwidth and better performance. Whatever the reason, path selection and failover preferences are completely up to the organization, and it falls on network administrators to enforce those policies.

You can picture the general problem of route preferences and business goals as a path selection problem. Figure 4-5 shows two networks, Network 1 and Network 2. There are several ways to get between the two networks through a mesh of routers—Path A is one way, Path B is another, and so on.

While routing metrics may indicate that traffic between Network 1 and Network 2 should use one path, an organization may prefer that traffic go in another direction. For example, let's say that routing metrics prefer that traffic from Network 1 to Network 2 go through Path A. If Path A is unavailable, traffic will go through Path B. If Path B is unavailable, traffic will go through Path C, and so on for Paths D and E. The failover sequence is (A, B, C, D, E). Alternatively, the organization may prefer traffic from Network 1 and Network 2 to flow through Path B. It may prefer that the failover sequence be (A, C, D, E, B) or even (B, D, E), which does

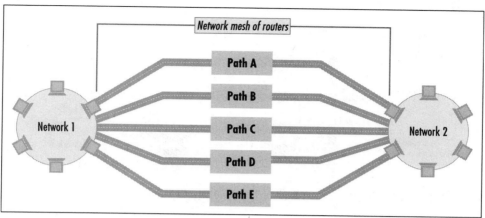

Figure 4-5. Path selection and business goals

not allow Paths A or C to be used at all. The organization, in its wisdom, may even decide that no traffic whatsoever should pass between Networks 1 and 2.

I mentioned earlier in the chapter that routers have four possible actions to control routing information: reject routing information, accept but not forward routing information, modify incoming routing information, or modify outgoing routing information. Route preferences are most commonly implemented by rejecting routes or modifying incoming or outgoing routing information.

I'll start with the first method, rejecting routing information. As in our previous example, we want to specify how traffic flows between Network 2 to Network 1. Figure 4-6 shows routing information for Network 1 coming into a router with a path to Network 2.

There are five possible paths, A, B, C, D, and E, from Router X to Network 1. We want traffic to go over Path A, C, or E, but not B or D. To do this, Router X rejects routing information about routes going over Paths B and D. Router X will have no information about Paths B and D at all.

The next two options for route preferences modify routing information after it reaches the router. We can do this as routing information comes in or goes out. Figure 4-7 shows how to do this by modifying incoming route information.

Here, we are trying to control the path that traffic from Network 2 takes to Network 1. In our example, routing metrics in all of the incoming routing updates, before we modify them in Router X, are numerical value a. This indicates that the path from Router X to Network 1 can take either Path A, B, or C with equal preference. We want to change the path selection preference so that traffic to Network 1 first goes through Path A. If Path A is unavailable, traffic should go through Path B, and then if B is unavailable, through Path C.

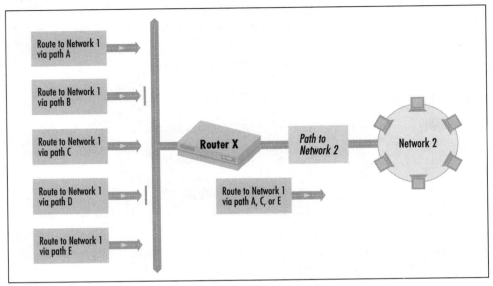

Figure 4-6. Rejecting routes to implement traffic preferences

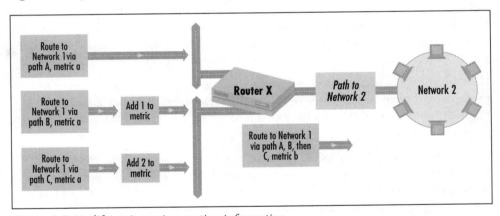

Figure 4-7. Modifying incoming routing information

To make this happen, we alter the routing metric values of each routing update after each comes into Router X. The metric for the route to Path B is increased by 1. The metric for the route to Path C is increased by 2. Since the original unaltered metrics for the three routes were equal, the metric for the route through A is the lowest, followed by the metric for the route via B and finally by the metric for the route through C. Since routing protocols take the path with the lowest metric, the most preferred Path is A, followed by B and then C.

Similarly, we can alter routing metrics as they go out of the router. This is shown in Figure 4-8.

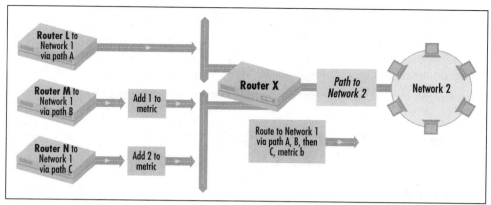

Figure 4-8. Modifying outgoing route information

In this figure, we manipulate Routers L, M, and N, and not Router X. As in Figure 4-7, the metrics advertised to Router X for the path to Network 1 are the same for Paths A, B, and C. We want to make traffic prefer routes in the order A, B, then C. To do this, we add 1 to the routing metric of the routing updates from router M, which has Path B to Network 1. We add 2 to the routing metric of the routing updates from router N, which has Path C to Network 1. When the routing information to Network 1 arrive at router X, the path through A has the lowest metric, followed by B then C. Traffic to Network 1 then prefers Path A, B, and then C.

When should you use these different techniques for implementing route preferences? It usually depends on what you want to achieve and what routers you administer. The technique of rejecting incoming routes is best used when you want to completely reject some routes and allow others. It does not allow for explicitly picking failover preferences. Modifying route information must be done when you have to set up a specific order of preferences for route failover. For instance, you would modify incoming routing information when you have control over a router receiving routing updates. On the other hand, if you only have control over the routers' advertising paths, then you need to modify routing information that is sent out.

Implementing routing modularity

So far, we have been looking at the concepts of implementing routing policies. In this section, we'll start implementing real routing policies using access lists, focusing on routing policies that implement routing modularity.

Minimizing the impact of local routing errors

Let's revisit the scenario we saw in the first chapter, where a typographical error caused a route to be incorrectly advertised, making two sites unreachable on an organization's intranet. Figure 4-9 shows a network topology for that scenario.

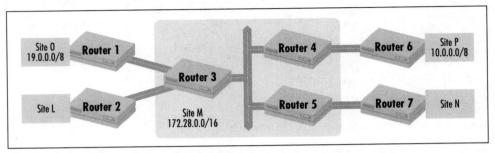

Figure 4-9. Routing modularity in a large intranet

In Figure 4-9, we see a network where four sites, L, N, O, and P, connect to each other through a central hub Site M. Network 19.0.0.0/8 belongs to Site O, and network site 10.0.0.0/8 belongs to Site P. Network 172.28.0.0/16 belongs to Site M. In our failure scenario, a typographical error causes Site O to advertise a route to network 10.0.0.0/8 from Router 1 instead of network 19.0.0.0/8. (This is an easy typo to make since the number 9 is close to the number 0 on the computer keyboard.) The typo causes Sites L, M, and N to see two routes to network 10.0.0.0/8 and no routes to network 19.0.0.0/8. Just to make things interesting, let's also say that the serial link between Routers 1 and 3 has much greater bandwidth than the serial link between Routers 4 and 6. That makes the route from Router 3 to Site O the preferred route to network 10.0.0.0/8 for Sites L, M, and O because of the more favorable network.

This scenario is a problem because network 19.0.0.0/8 is no longer advertised in the intranet, and no one in Sites L, M, N, or P can reach Site O. Conversely, no one in Site O can use the services of any other network since the return packets for a connection (or for server responses) have no route back to Site O. In addition, since the preferred route to Site P's network 10.0.0.0/8 goes to Site O, no packets ever reach Site P either.

How can we minimize the impact of this kind of typographical error? We know which routes should be sent from each site and which should be received. If we enforce a policy that says that only the well known and previously agreed upon routes should be sent and received from each site, then a route mistakenly advertised from a site will not get propagated. Let's spell out the policy so we can translate it into access lists:

Only network 19.0.0.0/8 should be accepted from Site O

To implement this policy with access lists, we build a policy set with network 19.0. 0.0/8 in it, and then accept only the routes in that policy set from Site D. Here is the access list:

```
access-list 1 permit 19.0.0.0
```

For this example, let's say that Router 3 is connected to Site O via serial interface 1, and the routing protocol used is EIGRP. We then apply access list 1 on Router 3 with the following:

```
router eigrp 1000
  distribute-list 1 in Serial 1
```

This first line says that we will modify the EIGRP routing protocol for Autonomous System 1000. The second line says that only the routes defined in access list 1 will be permitted in from serial 1.

How does this access list deal with our typographical error scenario? When Site O broadcasts a route to network 10.0.0.0/8 instead of a route to network 19.0.0.0/8, the route will be rejected by Router 3 and not propagated to the rest of the network. While the route to network 19.0.0.0/8 has disappeared, the route going to Site P's network 10.0.0.0/8 is unaffected. In this way, routing problems in Site O affect only Site O. We have gained routing modularity because bad route advertisements by Site O will not propagate across the intranet.

Since Site M cannot control what routes Site O broadcasts to it, Site M needs to limit the routes it hears from Site O. Although we have just implemented a policy that permits only routes in from Site O that belong to O, we cannot depend on that policy because Site M may be administered by a different organization than Site O, or because of any of the other reasons discussed before. To make sure that bad routes do not propagate, Site O should filter outgoing route updates to ensure that inappropriate routes, whether caused by typographical errors or other reasons, do not propagate. On Router 1, we build a policy set of Site O's routes:

```
access-list 2 permit 19.0.0.0
```

If we say that Router 1's connection to Site M is through serial interface 0, we apply the access list on Router 1 as follows:

```
router eigrp 1000
distribute-list 2 out Serial0
```

The **distribute-list out** command allows only the routes defined in access list 2 to be sent out of the serial interface going to Site M.

Site P and Site M have a relationship similar to the relationship between Site O and Site M. We can make routing robust between the sites in the same way. Let's say that Routers 4 and 6 both use serial interface 2 to talk to each other. Since Site E uses network 10.0.0.0/8, we would set up the following on Router 4:

```
access-list 4 permit 10.0.0.0
! routing process section
router eigrp 1000
 distribute-list 4 in Serial 2
```

This configuration fragment permits only the route to 10.0.0.0 in through serial interface 2 of Router 4, thus permitting only network 10.0.0.0/8 to come in from Site O. Router 6 should have the following:

```
access-list 5 permit 10.0.0.0
! routing process section
router eigrp 1000
 distribute-list 5 out Serial 2
```

This fragment of router configuration prevents Site P from advertising any route other than network 10.0.0.0/8. Put together, these two applications of access lists make it much more unlikely that a bad route will escape from Site P.

Managing routing updates to stub networks

Intranets typically have what are called *stub networks.* These are networks or administrative domains that send all traffic not destined for a host on that network out through a single router or small set of routers. There is no transit traffic through these networks; any traffic that is on the network is either to or from the network. External traffic typically goes to some central network that has connectivity to all other networks on that intranet.

The host segments shown in Figure 4-10 are stub networks, and the router connecting them to the backbone segment is a stub router. The stub router has several Ethernet segments with hosts connected to it and one connection to a fast Ethernet backbone segment. The function of the router is to connect the hosts to the backbone segment. The host segments do not need to hear routing updates because no other routers are on the segments. Hosts can easily be configured to default all traffic not bound for their segment to the router. At the same time, no routing updates should be accepted from the host segments. Any routing updates heard on the segment must be from misconfigured hosts or another router that has been mistakenly connected to one of the host segments.

To reduce unnecessary traffic on the segments and to prevent any spurious routing updates from injecting bad routing information, we need to enforce the policy:

Do not send routing updates to the host segments

Do not accept routing updates from the host segments

Advertise on the backbone segment only the routes for the networks connected to the router

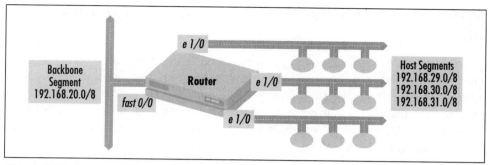

Figure 4-10. A router with a single backbone connection

To implement the policy, we need an access list with no routes in it:

```
access-list 1 deny all
```

This access list permits nothing into a policy set and can be used to deny all routes. We will use this kind of access list for the first and second policy statements. To implement the third policy statement, we will build an access list of the networks connected to the router:

```
access-list 2 permit 192.168.29.0
access-list 2 permit 192.168.30.0 0.0.1.0
```

The access lists are then used to define the routes sent out of specific interfaces. Let's say we are using the routing protocol EIGRP in this network:

```
router eigrp 10
 network 192.168.20.0
 network 192.168.29.0
 network 192.168.30.0
 network 192.168.31.0
 ! no routes to the host segments
 distribute-list 1 out Ethernet 1/0
 distribute-list 1 out Ethernet 1/1
 distribute-list 1 out Ethernet 1/2
 ! no routes from the host segments
 distribute-list 1 in Ethernet 1/0
 distribute-list 1 in Ethernet 1/1
 distribute-list 1 in Ethernet 1/2
 ! advertise only connected routes
 distribute-list 2 out fast 0/0
```

The policy implementation takes place in the **distribute-list** commands. The first three **distribute-list out** statements stop any routes from being advertised to the host segments. The next three statements stop the router from believing any route updates form the host segments. The last distribute list prevents the router from distributing anything but the three networks directly connected to it.

Redistributing routing information between routing protocols

Another key border where routing policies often need to be enforced is the interface where routing information is redistributed from one routing protocol or routing protocol administrative system to another. Each routing protocol has its own unique properties that network administrators want to either take advantage of or avoid. Let's look at an example where we send routing information in a certain routing protocol but refuse to listen to it.

In Figure 4-11, three routers are connected via their Ethernet 1 interface to an Ethernet segment containing a number of hosts. The routers also have a serial line (serial interface 0) connecting them to other networks. The routers broadcast RIP updates to the hosts, so they know which router to use for the best path to whatever networks the routers know about. Note that although most host systems come configured to understand only RIP, RIP has many limitations as a routing protocol, so the routers actually talk to each other using IGRP. So in this case, we want to make sure that we send out RIP routing updates (from the routers to the hosts) but have the routers ignore all RIP information received.

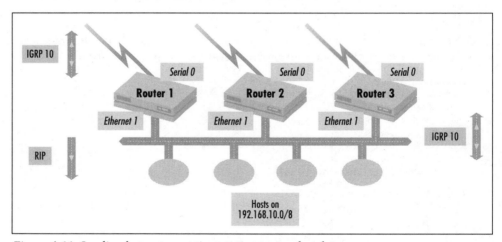

Figure 4-11. Sending but not accepting routing protocol updates

To implement this, we use the deny all access list defined in the previous example:

```
access-list 1 deny all
```

We use this access list to get an empty policy set, which is the set of all the routes we accept in via RIP. Next, let's define the RIP routing process:

```
router rip
network 192.168.10.0
redistribute igrp 10
distribute-list 1 in
```

The network statement here says that we broadcast RIP on all interfaces connected to network 192.168.10.0/8. The next statement says that we will redistribute all routes learned from IGRP process 10 into RIP. The final **distribute-list** statement restricts what routes are accepted in by RIP. Since no interface is specified, all RIP routing updates accepted by the router must be in the policy set defined by access list 1. Since access list 1 denies all routes, all routes advertised via RIP are ignored, regardless of what interface they come in on.

Minimizing routing updates to stub networks using default networks

In Figure 4-9, all the sites except for Site M are stub networks. Since Site M uses network 172.28.0.0/16, any traffic going between sites needs to go through that network first, making the network an ideal *default network*. A default network is a destination where a router sends all packets that have no explicitly defined routes in its routing table. For example, if a router has only network 10.0.0.0/8 and default network 172.28.0.0/16 in its routing table, and it was asked to forward a packet to network 198.168.30.0/8, the router forwards the packet to the same path as to 172.28.0.0/16, the default network. Note that a default network is different from a default route. A default route is where a router sends a packet if it does not have explicit routing information for the packet's destination. It is a route as opposed to a network, although the route to the default network becomes the default route.

Default networks are very useful in reducing the load and complexity of routing and route filtering. They reduce the router resource impact by reducing the number of routes that routers need to know about. In some cases, such as the interface between the Internet and an intranet, using a default network can spare routers from having to process tens of thousands of routes.

Let's look in detail at a section of Figure 4-9, the interface between Site O and Site M. This is shown in Figure 4-12.

Router 1 only accepts traffic for network 19.0.0.0/8 since Site O is a stub network and does not transit traffic through it. We can reduce the number of networks that Site O has to see and propagate within itself by using the following configuration in Router 1:

```
default-network 172.28.0.0
access-list 1 permit 172.28.0.0
router rip
 distribute-list 1 in Serial 0
```

The first statement declares that network 172.28.0.0/16 is the default network. Access list 1 defines a policy set consisting only of the default network. The next

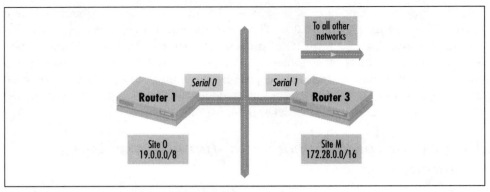

Figure 4-12. A stub network and its default network

two statements define the properties of the RIP routing process, saying that only the default network 172.28.0.0 is allowed into Router 1 (and thus Site O) because only the routes in the policy set defined by access list 1 are accepted in through serial interface 0.

How does this reduce the processing of routing updates in Site O's network? Since we accept only one route, to network 172.28.0.0/16 as the default network to other networks, Router 1 doesn't have to accept route 10.0.0.0/8 from Site O or any other route from other sites within the intranet. Because only one route is accepted, Site O has fewer routes to broadcast within its internal routing updates, which reduces the size of routing updates sent and the amount of network bandwidth used by those routing updates within Site O. Recall that Site O can have its own internal network structure with routing updates; as a stub network it doesn't transit traffic from other sites. Fewer routes also means that routers within Site O have fewer routes to examine when using routing access lists and building routing tables, thus reducing the CPU load.

Using default networks can also reduce the bandwidth used for routing updates on the serial line between Site M and Site O. If the administrator of Site M knows that all other sites use 172.28.0.0/16 as a default network, Routers 3, 4, and 5 can send only the default network to other sites during routing updates (see Figure 4-9). For example, Router 3 would use a configuration like this:

```
access-list 2 permit 172.28.0.0
router rip
 distribute-list 2 out Serial 1
```

to limit the routing updates sent to Site O. In this way, more bandwidth is reserved for user data.

Default networks do have some tradeoffs that must be acknowledged. Traffic to networks not defined anywhere within an intranet will travel to a default network

The costs of using access lists for route filtering

Using access lists for route filtering consumes critical resources on routers. Overuse can slow the flow of packets or even cause some of them to be dropped. You need to understand the costs of using route filtering in order to weigh the benefits against decreased router performance.

To gain this insight, you need to understand how routers handle tasks. A router has different switching modes for different tasks. Packet switching can be done through what is called optimum switching, or through modes like netflow switching or fast switching. The fastest switching modes are done by a number of specialized processors in the router. The slowest mode, process switching, is done by the router's central CPU. A router typically has only one CPU available for process switching at a time. General router "housekeeping" chores are done with process switching: handling interactive logins, answering SNMP requests, and managing router resource access control.

Handling of route updates and processing routing filter lists is also done with process switching. Since there is usually only one CPU doing process switching, this can easily bog down the entire router if you are not careful. For instance, protocols such as IGRP and RIP regularly broadcast entire routing tables, meaning that every 30 or 90 seconds respectively (or whatever interval you set), a router may be required to process through the access lists of the entire routing table of several other machines. Although small access lists are usually not a problem, when the CPU requirements of an access list are multiplied by processing large numbers of routes from a large number of routers, CPU loading can have a significant impact on router performance. When this happens, interactive sessions on the router itself become slow to unusable. Other system tasks, such as answering SNMP requests, also slow down.

How can we avoid having access lists for routing negatively affect router CPU? The key factors we need to look at are the access list length, the number of routes received in an update, and the number of updates received. Reducing any of these will reduce the CPU impact of router access lists. Another method is to use access list alternatives. I'll talk about how to reduce the impact of routing access lists and alternatives later in the chapter.

before getting dropped by a router on the default network. That means the bad traffic ends up taking more resources because more time goes by before they are rejected. In considering this tradeoff, you have to consider how much traffic will be sent to unreachable networks and how much of that you want to tolerate.

Filtering routes distributed between routing processes

So far, I have only shown how to filter routes sent out of interfaces, but Cisco routers have another option for filtering routes that allow network administrators to reduce the impact of route filtering. In the previous example, we filtered routes going out of Router 3 and all of the routes learned by the RIP routing protocol were compared to an access list every time a routing update was sent from Router 3's serial interface, creating a potentially dangerous CPU load.

Even if we used the IGRP routing protocol with AS 5 instead of RIP, where the configuration on Router 3 would look something like this:

```
access-list 2 permit 172.28.0.0
! igrp definition
router igrp 5
network 172.28.0.0
! rip definitions
router rip
redistribute igrp 5
distribute-list 2 out Serial 1
```

the CPU load problem would remain because the chief difference in the RIP routing definition is the **redistribute igrp** 5 line, which serves only to send all of the routes in IGRP 5 into RIP.

An an option of the **distribute-list** statement that lets us reduce the impact of filtering routes when they are distributed from one routing process to another. If we specify a routing process instead of an interface, routes are received only when they are updated by that routing process. We can rewrite the example as follows:

```
access-list 2 permit 172.28.0.0
router igrp 5
network 172.28.0.0
! rip definition
router rip
distribute-list 2 out igrp 5
redistribute igrp 5
```

Routes are filtered and sent to the RIP process every time the IGRP routing protocol sends updates. This happens every 90 seconds (the IGRP default). Since the RIP process receives the default route only when IGRP is updated, it does not need to filter routes when it sends routing updates, and the router needs to filter the route only every 90 seconds, as opposed to every 30 seconds with RIP. If there were many interfaces the router needed to send RIP updates out from, the CPU savings would be substantial. Generally, when filtering routes directly from one route process into another, it is best to send routes from the least frequently updated process into the more frequently updated routing process. This saves the most CPU by conserving processing time.

Implementing route preferences

Earlier in this chapter, I talked about the strategy of implementing route preferences. In this section, I discuss and show examples of how to implement them. I start with the basic example of simply eliminating routes and move on to more complex examples of using `offset-list` statements to alter routing metrics and altering route administrative distances based on the sources of routing updates.

Eliminating undesired routes

The simplest way to prefer routes is to prevent the routes that are not preferred from being accepted by a router at all. Let's look at Figure 4-13 for an example.

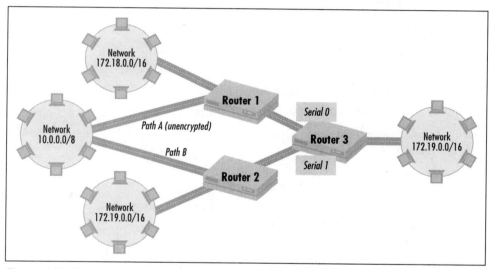

Figure 4-13. Ignoring routes through an unencrypted path

In this part of an intranet, Routers 1 and 2 send routing updates for the networks 172.18.0.0/16, 172.19.0.0/16, and 10.0.0.0/8 to Router 3 through Router 3's serial interfaces 0 and 1. Both Router 1 and Router 2 have routes to network 10.0.0.0/8, Router 1 via Path A and Router 2 via Path B. In this intranet, the network administrators try to encrypt all of the serial links between networks wherever they can to safeguard their intranet from eavesdropping. They generally succeed except for the paths leading to network 172.18.0.0/16, such as Path A, which is in one of a number of countries where encryption is heavily controlled. The network administrators accept this fact by setting the following policy:

Only traffic to and from 172.18.0.0/16 should go through Router 1

Traffic between networks 10.0.0.0/8 and 172.20.0.0/16 should not go through
Router 1. Traffic between network 10.0.0.0/8 and network 172.19.0.0/16 (in case
Path B goes down) also should not go through Router 1. What are the implica-
tions for Router 3? Router 3 needs to make sure that traffic to networks 10.0.0.0/8
and 172.19.0.0/16 does not go over the unencrypted Path A. Thus, traffic from
Router 3 to network 10.0.0.0/8 should use Path B, and traffic to network 172.19.0.
0/16 should never go out of serial 0.

We can implement this policy on Router 3 by making sure that it never learns a
route to network 10.0.0.0/8 via Router 1. Since routing updates from Router 1
come in through serial interface 0, we can build a policy set of everything except
networks 10.0.0.0/8 and 172.19.0.0/16 and apply it to serial interface 0. Access list
1 creates such a policy set:

```
access-list 1 deny 10.0.0.0
access-list 1 deny 172.19.0.0
access-list 1 permit any
```

However, we can shorten this particular access list since we know that only traffic
to 172.18.0.0/16 should go through serial 0:

```
access-list 1 permit 172.18.0.0
```

Traffic to networks 10.0.0.0/8, 172.18.0.0/16, and 172.19.0.0/16 are acceptable
through serial 1. Access list 2 defines the appropriate policy set:

```
access-list 2 permit 10.0.0.0
access-list 2 permit 172.18.0.0 0.1.0.0
```

We then apply both access lists with the following, assuming we are using routing
protocol EIGRP with autonomous system 10:

```
router eigrp 10
distribute-list 1 in Serial 0
distribute-list 2 in Serial 1
```

With this configuration, traffic between networks connected to Router 3 and network 10 never travel over unencrypted paths. We achieved this by ignoring
routing updates leading to the path that we did not prefer, accepting only updates
for routes using the preferred path. Our usage of `distribute-list` statements is
similar to how we implemented routing modularity earlier but differs in that we
received routing updates for network 10 through serial 0. This is not incorrect; we
have simply set up an arbitrary policy that prevents all traffic flowing that way.

Route preferences through offset-list

Often, a network administrator wants to prefer certain routes but not eliminate the
possible use of the less-preferred routes. One technique for doing this uses the
`offset-list` statement. In this section, I'll discuss why using `distribute-list`

Local and global distribute-list interactions

I have shown examples of the local `distribute-list` statement, one that is assigned to a specific interface, and the global `distribute-list` statement, one that is used for all routing updates. You may wonder how global and local `distribute-list` statements interact if both are defined. They are applied sequentially, with the local `distribute-list` applied first and the global applied after. That means that if a network is in a policy set defined by a local `distribute-list` statement, it also needs to be in the policy set defined by the global `distribute-list` before it is accepted by the routing process. As an example, consider the following configuration:

```
access-list 1 permit 192.168.10.0
access-list 1 permit 192.168.13.0
access-list 2 permit 192.168.10.0
router rip
distribute-list 1 in Ethernet 0
distribute-list 2 in
```

Routes for network 192.168.10.0/24 would be accepted in Ethernet 0 because it is in each of the policy sets defined by access lists 1 and 2. Routes for 192.168.13.0/24 would be rejected, since although it is in the local `distribute-list` policy set, it is not in the global one.

statements can be problematic for implementing certain kinds route preferences, followed by sections on how you can use `offset-list` statements to prefer routes and how to select the metric offsets.

Limitations of using distribute-list for preferring routes

Using `distribute-list` to prefer routes has limitations. Figure 4-14 shows an example of this.

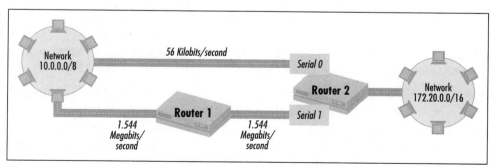

Figure 4-14. Preferring routes without eliminating routes

In this figure, there are two paths between network 172.20.0.0/16 and network 10. 0.0.0/8. One path goes directly between the two networks over a 56 kilobits per second (Kb) link. The second path has one router hop through Router 1 but goes over two 1.544 megabits per second (Mb) links. In this network, the RIP routing protocol is used. RIP uses one metric for routing: router hops. Given this partic- ular property of RIP, the routers calculate that the routing metric through the 56- Kb path is 1 (one router hop away) while the path through the 1.544-Mb link has a routing metric of 2 (two router hops away). The router then decides that the best path between network 172.20.0.0/16 and network 10.0.0.0/8 is the 56-Kb link, even though the other path has 30 times the bandwidth. A reasonable policy for this intranet might be the following:

> Prefer the 1.544-Mb path first.
>
> If the 1.544-Mb path is down, use the 56-Kb path as a backup link.

Let's first try to implement this policy with `distribute-list` statements, as we did in the previous section. On Router 2, we define three access lists, two with only one network in it, and one that has no networks in it:

```
access-list 1 permit 10.0.0.0
access-list 2 permit 172.20.0.0
access-list 3 deny any
```

We use the policy sets defined to accept only network 10.0.0.0/8 in through serial 1 and advertise only network 172.20.0.0/16. We then refuse to advertise or accept routes out of serial interface 0, so traffic isn't sent through that interface:

```
router rip
  distribute-list 1 in Serial 1
  distribute-list 2 out Serial 1
  distribute-list 3 in Serial 0
  distribute-list 3 out Serial 0
```

Since no routing advertisements for network 172.20.0.0/16 are sent over the 56-Kb path, no traffic from network 10.0.0.0/8 to network 172.20.0.0/16 is sent out that way. Since no route advertisements for network 10.0.0.0/8 are received over the 56-Kb path, no traffic from network 172.20.0.0/16 to network 10.0.0.0/8 is sent through that path. Routes are sent and received only through serial interface 1, so all traffic between the two networks goes only over the higher-speed path.

This implements the first part of the policy, but what happens if the 1.544-Mb path goes down? Since there are no route updates through the slow path, traffic will not go over that link if the faster path goes down. Using `distribute-list` for route preference only allows or disallows routes. There is no way to specify a sequence of preferences: Path A preferred first, then Path B, then Path C.

Using offset-list statements to prefer routes

In the previous section on routing theory, I showed that the way to implement routing preferences is by changing the metrics in routing updates coming in or out of the router. One way that Cisco routers can do this is through `offset-list` statements. These statements modify the value of routing metrics for some policy set of routes when routers send or receive route updates. Let's see how we would use them in our example. First, let's define a policy set with network 10.0.0.0/8 and another with network 172.20.0.0/8 in it:

```
access-list 1 permit 10.0.0.0
access-list 2 permit 172.20.0.0
```

We then use `offset-list` in the following way:

```
router rip
offset-list 1 in 3 Serial0
offset-list 2 out 3 Serial0
```

The first `offset-list` statement says that when updates for the routes in the policy set defined by access list 1 are heard through serial interface 0, 3 will be added to the metric of those routes. When routing updates for network 10.0.0.0/8 come into Router 2 over the 56-Kb link, the route metric to network 10.0.0.0/8 over that path becomes 4. Since the route metric coming in over serial interface 1 remains 2, the "best" path for the packets becomes the 1.544-Mb path, since it has the lower routing metric. Now if the 1.544-Mb path fails for some reason, routing updates are still being received through the other path, so traffic to network 10.0.0. 0/8 can go that way.

The second `offset-list` statement takes care of traffic in the other direction, from network 10.0.0.0/8 to network 172.20.0.0/16. Routing updates for network 172.20.0. 0/16 get 3 added to them, so network 10.0.0.0/8 sees that the route metric for the path to 172.20.0.0/16 over the 56-Kb link is 4. The route metric over the 1.544-Mb path remains 2, so that path becomes preferred. If the higher bandwidth path is unavailable, traffic from 172.20.0.0/16 to 10.0.0.0/8 will go over the 56-Kb link.

`offset-list` statements are useful with default networks in implementing the preferred order of default paths. Figure 4-15 shows a stub network with a number of possible routes to a default network.

Network 10.0.0.0/8 is a stub network that sends all of its traffic to other networks through a default network of 172.20.0.0/16. The three paths between the two networks have equal routing metric values, and the network uses the IGRP routing protocol in AS 172. Network administrators want network 10.0.0.0/8 offsite traffic to first go through Router 1, then Router 2, and then Router 3. To implement this, let's build policy sets that contain each route:

```
access-list 1 permit 10.0.0.0
access-list 2 permit 172.20.0.0
```

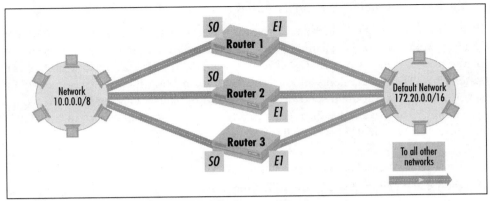

Figure 4-15. Stub network with multiple paths to a default network

On Router 1, which is the most preferred, we can define the routing as follows:

```
default-network 172.20.0.0
router igrp 172
```

The first statement defines the default network. For the IGRP process, since Router 1 is on the preferred path, we don't have to add any bias to routing metrics.

On Router 2, we define routing with the following:

```
! build policy sets
access-list 1 permit 10.0.0.0
access-list 2 permit 172.20.0.0
default-network 172.20.0.0
! router definition
router igrp 172
offset-list 2 out 1000 Serial 0
offset-list 1 out 1000 Ethernet 1
```

The first `offset-list` adds a bias of 1000 to the route advertisements for network 172.20.0.0/16. The second `offset-list` statement adds 1000 to the route advertisements for network 10.0.0.0/8, making it less attractive then the path through 1. In this way, we make the path through Router 2 to and from network 10.0.0.0/8 less attractive then the path through Router 1. Note that with IGRP, the possible range of metric values is much larger than with RIP, so we have used the larger offset of 1000 here. I will talk more about selecting offset values later.

On Router 3, we define routing as follows:

```
! build policy sets
access-list 1 permit 10.0.0.0
access-list 2 permit 172.20.0.0
default-network 172.20.0.0
! router definition
router igrp 172
offset-list 2 out 2000 Serial 0
offset-list 1 out 2000 Ethernet 1
```

The biases added with these `offset-list` statements are bigger than the biases added on Router 2. That makes the path through Router 3 less preferred than the one through Router 2, and even less preferred than the one through Router 1.

Selecting metric offsets

While extremely useful, `offset-list` statements need to be applied with care. It is easy to make networks unreachable if you select metric offsets that are too large. What would happen if, to be extra certain that traffic uses the faster path, we added an even bigger bias to the example in Figure 4-14, like this:

```
router rip
  offset-list 1 in 15 Serial 0
  offset-list 2 out 15 Serial 0
```

The effect of this application of `offset-list` would be to make the 56-Kb path unused even if they the 1.544-Mb line went down. Why? RIP has a maximum metric size of 15. If you add 15 to the metric value, it exceeds the maximum metric limit, and any routes with a metric like this is considered unreachable. In general, you have to make sure that the bias value you select is not so large that it makes the route unreachable in parts of the network. For this example, using an offset of 8 would be okay as long as there are no more than seven router hops in network 172.20.0.0/16 and other networks using RIP. In the example we used with Figure 4-15, we cannot use a metric greater than 65536, since the maximum metric size in IGRP is 65536. Table 4-1 contains a list of some routing protocols and the maximum possible values of their routing metrics.

Table 4-1. Routing protocols and their maximum metric values

Routing protocol	Maximum metric value
RIP	15
IGRP	65535
EIGRP	4294967295

The dynamic nature of routing protocols needs to be considered when you use `offset-list` statements. A topology change can make the route you are trying to have preferred become unpreferred. Let's look again at Figure 4-15. Router 1 connects to network 10.0.0.0/8 at some point in that network, but at a different point than Router 2 or Router 3. If there is a network topology change so the route within network 10.0.0.0/8 to Router 1's connection point becomes much longer, then the path through Router 1 may no longer be the most preferred path. This kind of problem can happen when you add biases to route advertisements you send into organizations you don't control. Some routing protocols, like IGRP and EIGRP, change routing metrics based on network delays and bandwidth utilization. Transient changes in traffic can affect routing metrics to the point where any biases you place may be overcome, so you need to make sure that any bias you use is high enough to override any increases in metrics caused by any possible change in network topology or traffic flow.

Routing policies and OSPF

You may have noticed that there are no examples of using the `distribute-list`, `offset-list`, or `distance` statements with the OSPF routing protocol. In general, these commands are intended for distance vector routing protocols such as RIP, IGRP, and EIGRP and not for Shortest Path First protocols such as OSPF. You can use `distribute-list` statements to filter routes between OSPF areas (on Area Border Routers, or ABRs), between different OSPF autonomous systems (on Autonomous System Border Routers, or ASBRs), or when redistributing routes between OSPF and other routing protocols. Using the `distribute-list` statement within an OSPF area will not work, and the other policy statements should not be used. Instead, use the access list alternatives described at the end of the chapter.

Route preferences through administrative distance

So far, `offset-list` and `distribute-list` statements have allowed us to implement all of the policies that we have proposed so far. Let's see how these commands fare with the network shown in Figure 4-16.

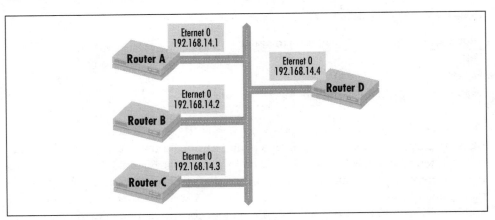

Figure 4-16. Preferring routes from a particular router

In this network, the paths through Router A are more reliable than the routes through Router B or C. The network administrator for this network knows that this is the situation, so despite the fact that some routes from Routers B and C have better metrics, he wants the following policy on Router D:

> Use routes through Router A unless Router A is down
>
> If Router A is down, use routes through Router B
>
> If Router A and B are down, use routes through Router C

Can we use `distribute-list` statements to implement this? We cannot, since there is no way to prefer route updates from a single router among many from the same interface with `distribute-list`. Can we use `offset-list` to implement this policy? Again, `offset-list` statements can only build policy sets of routes mentioned in routing updates. To implement this policy, we need a way to build a policy set that is not based on the network numbers in routing updates, but on some other feature of a route update, in this case the next hop or source of the routing update.

This leads us to a whole new category of policy tools that I have not yet covered: controlling routes based on characteristics of routes. All of the previous policies that we have looked at built policy sets based on the destination networks. With this set of tools, we will build policy sets based on characteristics of routes.

So how do we implement the policy preferring traffic through Router A? First, we need a way to prefer routes based on their source of routing updates. To do that, we use the concept of *administrative distance*. In Cisco routers, all routing updates have an additional metric assigned to them called administrative distance. Each routing source has a default administrative distance, as shown in Table 4-2.

Table 4-2. Default administrative distance for routing protocols

Routing protocol	Default distance
Connected Interface	0
Static Route	1
EIGRP Summary	5
EIGRP Internal	90
IGRP	100
OSPF	110
RIP	120
EIGRP External	170
Unknown	255

When a router gets routing information about a route from different sources, the router uses the routing information from the source with the lowest administrative distance. This means that static routes take precedence over EIGRP routes if a route has been statically routed and also learned from EIGRP. Another way to think of administrative distance is to consider it another metric assigned to route updates. This metric takes priority over any other metric that the route updates may have. Like other metrics, the lowest value is preferred. An administrative distance of 255, the maximum distance possible, means that a route is unreachable.

How do we use administrative distance to prefer routes from a particular routing source? The **distance** directive for routing protocols can change the administrative distance for particular routing updates. Here is how we would use distance to implement the policy defined previously:

```
router rip
network 192.168.14.0
distance 121 192.168.14.2 0.0.0.0
distance 122 192.168.14.3 0.0.0.0
```

The first number after the **distance** keyword is the new administrative distance for the IP address and mask that follow. The IP address and mask used in the **distance** statements have the same format and behavior as the IP address mask used in access lists. The first **distance** directive in this example sets all routing updates from 192.168.14.2 (Router B) to an administrative distance of 121. The second **distance** directive sets all routing updates from 192.168.14.3 (Router C) to an administrative distance of 122. Since RIP protocol updates have a default administrative distance of 120, all routes from Router A will have a lower administrative distance of 120. Thus Router D will prefer routes from Router A for any route heard from each of Routers A, B, and C. If Router A does not send out a route update for a particular network but Router B does, then Router D will use the routes from Router B unless it hears a routing update from another source with a lower administrative distance.

The **distance** directive allows tremendous flexibility in implementing routing preferences. Let's implement a variation of the policy that we defined earlier:

Use routes through Router A unless Router A is down

If Router A is down, use routes through Router B or Router C

This policy differs from the former in that there is no preference between routes through B or C. We implement this policy as follows:

```
router rip
network 192.168.14.0
distance 121 192.168.14.2 0.0.0.1
```

Since route updates from Router A have the RIP default administrative distance of 120, they are preferred first. If Router A is down, both Router B and C's updates have distance 121, so that Router D uses the route from the two routers that has the best metrics.

Let's implement the following policy on Router D with `distance`:

> Use routes through Router A unless Router A is down
>
> If Router A is down, use routes through Router B
>
> Never use routes through Router C

We can implement this with the following configuration:

```
router rip
network 192.168.14.0
distance 121 192.168.14.2 0.0.0.0
distance 255 192.168.14.3 0.0.0.0
```

As in the previous example, route updates from Router A get the default RIP distance of 120. Route updates from Router B get a distance of 121, making them less preferred than the route updates from A. Route updates from Router C receive the distance of 255. Routes with an administrative distance of 255 are considered unreachable and are thus ignored.

Here is another way to implement the policy:

```
router rip
network 192.168.14.0
distance 255
distance 120 192.168.14.1 0.0.0.0
distance 121 192.168.14.2 0.0.0.0
```

The first `distance` statement sets the default administrative distance for RIP to 255. That means that all routing updates from routers that do not have an explicitly set administrative distance are ignored. The next `distance` statement sets the administrative distance of Router A's routes to 120 while the final `distance` statement sets Router B's routes to a distance of 121. This configuration works because Router A has the lowest administrative distance, followed by Router B. All other routing updates are considered unreachable.

Using `distance 255` in this manner has a number of tradeoffs that you need to consider. By ignoring all updates without explicitly set distances, the router will also ignore updates from a router that is put on the network without authorization or notification to the network administrators. This can be a good thing, since a network administrator will not have to worry about some rogue router being put on the network and suddenly accepting traffic. It can also be an annoyance, though, as the network administrator needs to explicitly define a distance for every subnet or router that sends routing updates.

So far, I've set all routing updates from a source to have the same administrative distance. You can also set specific routes from a source to have specific administrative distances. In Figure 4-17, network 192.168.18.0/16 contains servers dedicated to an application critical to users on networks 10.0.0.0/8 and 172.28.0.0/16.

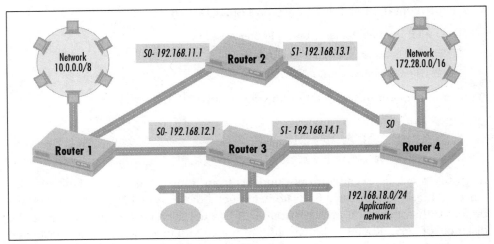

Figure 4-17. Dedicating bandwidth to an application

The application is so critical that the path leading to network 192.168.18.0/24, from Router 1 via Router 3 to Router 4, should be dedicated to traffic to and from 192. 168.18.0/24 in order to maximize the application's performance. Transit traffic between networks 10.0.0.0/8 and 172.28.0.0/16 should not slow down the application. The only time that traffic between these networks should use the dedicated bandwidth is if another path between the networks through Router 2 is unavailable. Let's summarize the policy that we need to implement:

> The connections to Router 3 should only see traffic to and from network 192.168. 18.0 unless the path through Router 2 is unavailable

We implement this policy by making the routes for 192.168.18.0/24 from Router 3 have a lower administrative distance than any other routes that it advertises. On Router 1, we use the following configuration fragment:

```
access-list 1 permit 192.168.18.0
access-list 2 permit any
router rip
 network 192.168.11.0
 network 192.168.12.0
 distance 119 192.168.12.1 1
 distance 121 192.168.12.1 2
```

Access list 1 creates a policy set with the application server's network, 192.168.18. 0/24. The first **distance** statement sets the routes in the policy set defined by access list 1 (the server network) that are advertised from Router 3 to an administrative distance of 119. The second **distance** statement sets all other routes from Router 3 to an administrative distance of 121. Route advertisements for the networks other than the application network are preferred through Router 2. Route advertisements for the application server network have a distance set lower than the default. If a route to 192.168.18.0/24 is heard from another router, the route via Router 3 is the preferred route unless the direct link to Router 3 is down.

The configuration on Router 4 is very similar:

```
access-list 1 permit 192.168.18.0
access-list 2 permit any
router rip
 network 192.168.13.0
 network 192.168.14.0
 distance 119 192.168.14.1 1
 distance 121 192.168.14.1 2
```

The IP address for the serial link to Router 3 and the connected networks are different, but the use of `distance` is the same.

You may have noticed that we could have implemented the routing policy by using `offset-list` statements instead of `distance`. We could have used the following on Router 3:

```
access-list 1 deny 192.168.18.0
access-list 1 permit any
router rip
network 192.168.12.0
network 192.168.14.0
network 192.168.18.0
offset-list 1 out Serial 0 2
offset-list 1 out Serial 1 2
```

This configuration works because we add a metric bias to everything but the application server network to our route advertisements, making advertisements for those routes look better through paths other than through Router 3.

Since I've shown two different ways to implement this policy, you may be wondering when you should use `offset-list` and when to use `distance`. To know which technique is most appropriate, you need to know about the strengths and weaknesses of each technique. I have talked about the limitations of `offset-list` statements already, so let's talk about the tradeoffs of using the `distance` statement. As you may have already noticed, `distance` works only on incoming route advertisements. You cannot send another router the distance you want them to use when considering routes. If you want to influence the route preferences of routers to which you send updates, you need to use `offset-list` statements.

One important characteristic about administrative distance is that it overrides any other metric values that a route update may have. Let's say that in our previous example we were using EIGRP instead of RIP. Remember that routing protocols such as EIGRP take into consideration factors like bandwidth and network loading to calculate routing metrics. If you use the `offset-list` approach to implement policy, a change in network traffic could change routing metrics so drastically that your policy could become undone. You could also set bias values so high that the networks you advertise are advertised as unreachable. Manipulating administrative distance, in contrast, works no matter the value of routing metrics, instead working by affecting the order in which you consider route updates for inclusion into the routing table.

Alternatives to access lists

As I have mentioned, the CPU costs imposed by access lists can be significant. In addition, access lists take time to administer. Some alternatives to access lists can reduce CPU costs, while others simply limit the number of access lists you need to manage. I cover these alternatives in this section.

Static routing

One common technique for replacing access lists is to use static routes. You can set route preferences on routers that you administer by explicitly configuring routes. Since static routes by default have a more preferable administrative distance than any dynamic routing protocol, configuring a static route to a network can cause a router to ignore any dynamic routing protocol's routing update to that network.

The simplest way to eliminate access lists for routing policies is to completely remove the dynamic routing protocols and use static routes everywhere. This may be possible in simple networks like the one shown in Figure 4-2. You can configure static routes on the central router and define fixed routes to all of the networks in a central location. Static routes explicitly define routing policies, so you do not need to use access lists to filter routing updates.

As a network becomes more complex, a purely static routed network might become difficult to manage. Still, to reduce the use of access lists a combination of dynamic and static routes is possible. With stub networks, for example, connections between the stub networks and the transit or default network can be static routed, eliminating the need for dynamic routing protocols and routing access lists. Let's revisit Figure 4-9 and see how we can use static routes instead of access lists. Recall that a key issue in this network was making sure the site networks did not advertise a network they did not own. To see how this occurs with static routes, let's say that Router 1's serial interface uses IP address 192.168.12.1 and Router 3's serial interface has IP address 192.168.12.2. Router 4's serial interface to Site E has IP address 192.168.13.1, and Router 6's serial interface has IP address 192.168.13.2. Router 1 would use the following configuration to define its routing:

```
default-network 172.28.0.0 192.168.12.2
ip route 172.28.0.0 255.255.0.0
router rip
network 19.0.0.0
redistribute static
```

Since 172.28.0.0/16 is the central transit network for this intranet, we define it as the default network and set up a default route to Router 3. We then redistribute our default network within Site D. We define network 19.0.0.0 in the routing statement, but not network 192.168.12.0/24. This causes the RIP routing process to send and listen to RIP routing updates only on interfaces that are on network 19.0. 0.0. Therefore, Router 1 does not send routing updates out of its serial link to Router 3 or listen to any updates on that interface. This configuration saves considerable CPU resources on the router, since there are fewer router updates to process, and no route filtering to be done.

Router 3 would use the following configuration:

```
ip route 19.0.0.0 255.0.0.0 192.168.12.1
router rip
network 172.28.0.0
redistribute static
```

The route to network 19.0.0.0 is hardcoded into the router's configuration, so no route update can change it. As with Router 1, there is no **network 192.168.12.0** statement. This means that Router 3 does not send updates out of its serial interface to Site D or listen to any updates from it. Our policy to maintain network robustness is enforced by the static routes and careful redistribution, instead of an access list and a **distribute-list** statement.

Continuing with our example, Router 6 has a configuration very similar to Router 1:

```
default-network 172.28.0.0
ip route 172.28.0.0 255.255.0.0 192.168.13.1
router rip
network 10.0.0.0
redistribute static
```

while Router 4 is configured like Router 3, with a static route replacing the access list and **distribute-list** statement:

```
ip route 10.0.0.0 255.0.0.0 192.168.13.2
router rip
network 172.28.0.0
redistribute static
```

Implementing route preference with static routes

We can also use static routes to implement routing preferences through route elimination. In the example associated with Figure 4-14, we used **distribute-list** statements and an access list to force traffic between network 10.0.0.0/8 and 172. 20.0.0/16 over an encrypted path. If the serial interface on Router 2 connecting to Router 3 uses IP address 192.168.10.2, then the following static route on Router 3 will force traffic to network 10.0.0.0/8 over the encrypted network path:

```
ip route 10.0.0.0 255.0.0.0 192.168.10.2
```

We would also have to put in a similar static route from Router 1 to Router 2 for the traffic from network 10.0.0.0/8 to use the encrypted path. Note that this use of static routes to implement a routing policy only works if we have administrative control or influence over Router 1 and Router 3. If we can't have Router 1 configured with a static route, we'll have to use `distribute-list` statements as we did originally.

Floating static routes

You can change the administrative distance of a static route to create what is called a *floating* static route. Floating static routes can be used to define a backup route and thus to implement routing preferences. Let's revisit Figure 4-14. In this figure, we prefer that traffic between network 10.0.0.0/8 and 172.20.0.0/16 go through the larger bandwidth path. Let's say that the 56-Kb serial line between networks 10.0.0.0/8 and 172.20.0.0/16 has IP addresses 192.168.15.2 at the network 10.0.0.0/8 side and 192.168.15.3 at Router 2. The IP address of serial 1 on Router 2 is 192.168.16.3, and the IP address of the serial interface on Router 1 leading to Router 2 is 192.168.11.2. We can define the following static route and router configuration on Router 2:

```
ip route 172.20.0.0 255.255.0.0 192.168.15.2 121
router rip
network 192.168.16.0
```

The static route is set to have an administrative distance of 121. Only network 192.168.16.0 is defined to send and receive RIP routing updates. The result is that Router 2 will hear a route to network 10.0.0.0/8 via RIP only through the higher bandwidth path. Since we set administrative distance of the static route to be higher than that of default RIP updates, the RIP update takes precedence. If the 1.544-Mb line goes down, then the static route over the smaller bandwidth path is used. To take care of traffic in the other direction, from network 10.0.0.0/8 to network 172.28.0.0/16, a similar setup needs to be done on the router connecting network 10.0.0.0/8 to Router 1.

Compared to our earlier policy implementation, the floating static route is much simpler. So why would we use the first implementation? Again, the issue is administrative control. The first implementation works if the network administrator of Router 2 does not have administrative control over network 10.0.0.0/8 routers. The floating static route technique works only if a floating static route is set up at network 10.0.0.0/8.

Static routes to the null device

Another simple way to deny routing updates from a given network is to route the network to the null interface. For example, if we wanted to deny all routing updates to network 192.168.30.0/24, we could set up the following static route:

```
ip route 192.168.30.0 255.255.255.0 Null0
```

Using this technique can conserve router resources since the router no longer needs to use access lists to filter route updates containing this network.

You have to be careful about redistributing the static route for a network routed to `Null0`. You can easily advertise a route that will cause all of the traffic to a network to be dropped. For if we redistributed the previous static route into another routing protocol, all packets destined for network 192.168.30.0/24 could get sent to a router that would simply drop them.

Denying all route updates in or out of an interface

Denying all routing updates through an interface is such a common operation that there are Cisco configuration commands designed to provide these functions.

Often you may not want to send routing updates out of an interface. This may be because there are no systems that need to listen to your routing broadcasts, or you may not want routers on that interface to send traffic through. Whatever the reason, you can use the `passive-interface` command to stop sending routing updates out of a specific interface. Let's look once again at the network in Figure 4-10. In this network, we don't need to broadcast routing updates on the host segments. In the original policy implementation, I created a policy set with nothing in it and used that policy set to stop route advertisements. `passive-interface` can have the same effect:

```
access-list 1 deny any
access-list 2 permit 192.168.29.0
access-list 2 permit 192.168.30.0 0.0.1.0
!
router eigrp 10
 network 192.168.20.0
 network 192.168.29.0
 network 192.168.30.0
 network 192.168.31.0
! no routes to the host segments
 passive-interface Ethernet 1/0
 passive-interface Ethernet 1/1
 passive-interface Ethernet 1/2
! no routes from the host segments
 distribute-list 1 in Ethernet 1/0
 distribute-list 1 in Ethernet 1/1
 distribute-list 1 in Ethernet 1/2
! advertise only connected routes
 distribute-list 2 out fast 0/0
```

The `passive-interface` command saves significant CPU resources when compared with the way I previously implemented this policy. Instead of examining all of the routes it knows about and then not sending any of them out, the router simply doesn't try to send any routes out of the three Ethernet interfaces at all.

Using distance to ignore updates

In this example, we also do not want to receive any updates from the host segments. A more elegant way to do that is to use the `distance` statement. If we set the administrative distance of any routing update from the host segments to 255, then any routing update from those segments is ignored. The complete configuration then becomes:

```
access-list 2 permit 192.168.29.0
access-list 2 permit 192.168.30.0 0.0.1.0
!
router eigrp 10
network 192.168.20.0
network 192.168.29.0
network 192.168.30.0
network 192.168.31.0
! no routes to the host segments
passive-interface Ethernet 1/0
passive-interface Ethernet 1/1
passive-interface Ethernet 1/2
! no routes from the host segments
distance 192.168.29.0 0.0.0.0 255
distance 192.168.30.0 0.0.0.1 255
! advertise only connected routes
distribute-list 2 out fast 0/0
```

Using `distance` doesn't save as much CPU as the previous change. If there are route updates from the host segments, the router still must look at them in order to assign the administrative distance of 255. It does simplify and reduce the size of the configuration, however, which can be a significant improvement in some situations.

Omitting network statements

Notice that we don't want to send or receive routing updates from the host segments. For segments like these, there is one more access list alternative that is more elegant and can save even more router CPU cycles. Recall that in a routing process definition, the `network` statement is used to indicate which interfaces will send and receive routing updates. Since we don't want any routing update activity on the host segments, we can omit the network statements of host segments:

```
access-list 2 permit 192.168.29.0
access-list 2 permit 192.168.30.0 0.0.1.0
router eigrp 10
network 192.168.20.0
! advertise only connected routes
distribute-list 2 out fast 0/0
```

Omitting the `network` statements saves the router a lot of processing because the interfaces for the host segments are not involved in routing activity at all.

In this chapter:
- *Router resource access control lists*
- *Packet-filtering access control lists*
- *Route-filtering access control lists*

5

Debugging Access Lists

Once you've formatted access lists and used them to implement policies, how do you know if your access lists are correct? How can you find problems with them? We'll look at these questions in this chapter, first verifying that your access lists are working correctly in the areas of router resource control, packet filtering, and route filtering. More generally, I will talk about how access lists can go wrong and what are the typical failure modes of access lists. Finally, we'll look at some tips and tricks for debugging access lists in detail.

Router resource access control lists

In this section, I discuss how to debug router resource access lists. The first part describes how to check them for correctness since it doesn't make sense to debug a list that is configured properly. The second part discusses what generally happens when access lists go wrong, and the last part goes over specifically how to debug router resource access lists.

Checking for correctness

In Chapter 3 we configured the router to control resources such as Telnet and time services. The approach to verifying if these access lists function correctly is very basic: test if access works correctly for those who are permitted, and test if access does not work for those who are not permitted. Let's look at one of our early examples of router resource policies and look at how we can test it. In the first example in Chapter 2, we had a policy like the following:

> Only the hosts at IP addresses 192.168.30.1 and 192.168.33.5 may telnet into the router

The access list that defines the policy set for this policy is:

```
access-list 1 permit 192.168.30.1
access-list 1 permit 192.168.33.5
```

We use the policy set as follows:

```
line vty 0 4
 access-class 1 in
```

In order to verify that the access list actually implements the policy, we need to check that what we defined in the policy set matches what is in the policy definition. There are two ways to do this. The first is by inspection: we manually check whether the access list matches our policy. While this method can work for small access lists, it becomes much more difficult as access lists grow in size and really isn't a particularly reliable way to verify that an access list is correct. The second way is to test whether access lists actually function as desired. In this instance, we would attempt to telnet to the router from the hosts at 192.168.30.1 and 192.168. 33.5. If we succeed in getting a prompt from the router, we know that the access list is allowing the correct host to connect to the router.

We should also make sure that forbidden hosts do not have access. If for some reason we forgot to apply an access list (not putting in the **access-class** statement, for example), the default policy set permits everything, giving us the same results as the test we did earlier. When we telnet to the router from the host at 192.168.3.59, the router should refuse the connection and not provide a login prompt. In general, the following algorithm is useful for verifying a policy against the access lists you implemented:

> Make sure what hosts that are permitted have access to the resource
>
> Make sure that the hosts that are not permitted do not have access to the resource

You will not always be able to completely test all cases (as access lists grow, you will not be able to test every entry), but being reasonably sure that the above two conditions are true is how to verify correctness.

Manual tests of masks

Testing for both what is permitted and what is denied is particularly useful when you use masks in a policy. Let's look at the following policy and its implementation:

> Only the hosts at IP addresses 192.168.30.4 through 192.168.30.7 and IP address 192.168.33.5 may telnet into the router

We define the appropriate policy set and apply it as follows:

```
access-list 1 permit 192.168.30.4 0.0.0.3
access-list 1 permit 192.168.33.5
```

```
! line definition
line vty 0 4
access-class 1 in
```

Notice that the first access list entry has a mask, as we covered in Chapter 2. When you use a mask like this, in addition to testing that the hosts in the mask range have access to the resource being controlled, make sure that the hosts just outside of the mask range (hosts at IP addresses 192.168.30.3 and 192.168.30.8) do not. What happens if you specify a mask that is too large, as in the following list?

```
access-list 1 permit 192.168.30.4 0.0.0.7
access-list 1 permit 192.168.33.5
```

Testing only the permitted hosts will miss the fact that you also included hosts 192.168.30.1, 192.168.30.2, and 192.168.30.3 in the policy set. Testing the hosts just outside the range permitted by the mask catches this problem.

When access lists don't work

I have talked about making sure that access lists are functioning properly by implementing the policies that you intend. But what happens if your access lists do not function as expected? This section describes how an access list can do other than what you intend and how you can use the various tools available on a Cisco router to find where you made a mistake. I will first go over ways that access lists can go wrong. After that, I will cover how to debug router resource access lists, extended access lists, and router filtering access lists.

There are typically a number of ways access lists can go wrong. First, they can be applied incorrectly, meaning that you have either applied the wrong access list to a router resource, interface, or distribute list; applied the correct access list but with the wrong directionality (inbound instead of outbound or the reverse); or forgotten to apply one altogether. This should be the first thing you check.

If you are applying an access list correctly, and your policy is still not being implemented properly, then one of two things is happening. Either something you want to include into a policy set was excluded, or something you want excluded from a policy set was included. In the first case, you need to check whether some statement in the access list is excluding the IP addresses or packet types that you want in the policy set. (If you are certain that nothing is excluding the items desired, then the only other explanation is that you have forgotten to include it.) In the second case, you have included something in your policy set that you do not want, so to fix your access list, you need to find the permissive entry. These are the fundamental problems that can occur, and when I talk about debugging specific kinds of access lists in the following sections, I go over how to find bad or missing access list entries.

There is one final category of access list problems that you may encounter. If you are implementing security policies and routing policies, you have to be careful about their interaction. For instance, if an application does not work through an extended access list, it doesn't always mean there's a problem with the access lists; it could be a communication problem between the two systems you are routing. If you encounter what seems to be a routing problem with routing, there could be packet filtering that is disrupting route advertisements. I will also talk about this category of problems in later sections on debugging.

Debugging router resource access lists

If you find that your router resource access lists are not working, typically one of two things is happening. Either something that needs access to a router resource does not have access, or something that should not have access to the resource does. I'll go over each case and what to look for when trying to find what the problem is.

If a host or router that should have access cannot access a resource on a router you control, the first thing to check is whether there is network connectivity between the host in question and the router. The easiest way to do this is to use the *ping* command. The format of ping is the command *ping* followed by the name or IP address of the host you want to check on. Let's say that we want to check on connectivity to a host at 10.1.1.2, and the route to 10.1.1.2 goes through an Ethernet interface with IP address 192.168.3.2. We would use the following command, which can be executed from user EXEC mode or privileged EXEC mode:

```
ping 10.1.1.2
```

If there is a functioning route to IP address 10.1.1.2 and a route from the host 10.1.1.2 back to the router interface with IP address 192.168.3.2, we would see output like this:

```
Type escape sequence to abort.
Sending 5, 100-byte ICMP Echos to 10.1.1.2, timeout is 2 seconds:
!!!!!
Success rate is 100 percent (5/5), round-trip min/avg/max = 1/2/4 ms
```

If either the transmit and return path between 10.1.1.2 and 192.168.3.2 is unavailable, the ping will not be successful:

```
Router1# ping 10.1.1.2

Type escape sequence to abort.
Sending 5, 100-byte ICMP Echos to 10.1.1.2, timeout is 2 seconds:
.....
Success rate is 0 percent (0/5)
```

If the ping attempt is not successful, there is either a route missing at the target host for the router, a route missing at the router for the host, or some other packet filter along the path getting in the way. Let's put off a discussion of packet filtering extended access lists until the next section and assume that the problem is with a missing route. Check the routing on the host or the router. If the route is missing, and there is no default route, then you need to make sure that the route is there and again check if the resource access works. If the route is there, it implies that the problem may be with a packet filter along the way. I will talk about finding problematic packet filters in later sections.

If the ping attempt is successful, the problem is with your access list. You either excluded some IP addresses from your policy set or forgot to include an appropriate entry.

Looking at an example will illustrate this better. Let's say we have the following policy for a router:

> All of the hosts with IP addresses 192.168.32.32 through 192.168.32.63 except 192.168.32.40 through 192.168.32.43 can have SNMP read access

and implement it as follows:

```
access-list 1 deny 192.168.40.0 0.0.0.7
access-list 1 permit 192.168.32.0 0.0.0.31
snmp community string public ro 1
```

We notice that host 192.168.32.44 does not have SNMP access. We can ping 192.168.32.44 from the router, so routing is not an issue. On examination, we see that the initial deny mask is too large. Access list 1 should be defined as:

```
access-list 1 deny 192.168.40.0 0.0.0.3
access-list 1 permit 192.168.32.0 0.0.0.31
```

The other way that router resource access lists can go wrong is if something that should not have permission does have permission. This means that somehow you have inadvertently allowed something in a policy set you shouldn't have, and again a previous example illustrates this well. Recall that we have a policy for a router as follows:

> Only the hosts at IP addresses 192.168.30.4 through 192.168.30.7 and IP address 192.168.33.5 may telnet into the router

We define the appropriate policy set and apply it as follows:

```
access-list 1 permit 192.168.30.4 0.0.0.7
access-list 1 permit 192.168.33.5
! line definition
line vty 0 4
access-class 1 in
```

After testing, we notice that host 192.168.30.8 has Telnet access to the router. We made the mask on the first entry of access list 1 too large. Access list 1 should be:

```
access-list 1 permit 192.168.30.4 0.0.0.3
access-list 1 permit 192.168.33.5
```

Packet-filtering access control lists

Here I talk about debugging the packet filters that you implement with access control lists. Like the previous section, I first talk about how to verify that your access lists are correct, followed by a section about how to find the problems in the access lists that you find to be wrong.

Checking for correctness

One of the first things you want to do is make sure that your access lists are applied to the interfaces you intended. You or another network administrator may have removed access lists or applied other access lists in order to debug problems or temporarily enable certain functionality for a variety of reasons, such as host installations or debugging. One way to do that is to show the running configuration with the *show running-confg* command. If you have a large configuration, this command may take a while, and it is easy to miss the interface you want to look at when many of them are scrolling by.

Using show ip interface to display applied access lists

A better way is to use the *show ip interface* command. This command yields output that looks like the following:

```
Serial 0 is up, line protocol is up
  Internet address is 192.168.1.2/24
  Broadcast address is 192.168.1.255
  Address determined by non-volatile memory
  MTU is 1500 bytes
  Helper address is not set
  Directed broadcast forwarding is enabled
  Outbound access list is 102
  Inbound access list is 101
  Proxy ARP is enabled
  Security level is default
  Split horizon is enabled
  ICMP redirects are always sent
  ICMP unreachables are always sent
  ICMP mask replies are never sent
  IP fast switching is enabled
  IP fast switching on the same interface is enabled
  IP Optimum switching is disabled IP
  Flow switching is enabled IP
  CEF switching is enabled IP
```

```
Distributed switching is enabled
IP LES Flow switching turbo vector IP
Flow CEF switching turbo vector
IP multicast fast switching is disabled
IP multicast distributed fast switching is disabled
Router Discovery is disabled
IP output packet accounting is enabled
IP access violation accounting is disabled
TCP/IP header compression is disabled
Probe proxy name replies are disabled
Gateway Discovery is disabled
Policy routing is disabled
Web Cache Redirect is disabled
BGP Policy Mapping is enabled (source ip-prec-map)
```

The *show ip interface* command displays what IP configurations are applied relative to an interface. On this serial interface, we can see that it has an `Inbound access list` of 101 and an `Outbound access list` of 102. Further down the listing, we can see that `IP output packet accounting` is enabled, while `IP access violation accounting` is disabled. Though I'll talk about these last two features later, you can see that this command shows the access lists applied to a particular interface, allowing you to verify that you used access lists correctly.

The *show ip interface* command followed by an interface shows the IP configuration for just that interface. Without the interface specification, the command shows the IP configuration for all interfaces.

Testing the functionality of packet filters

Once you know that your access lists are properly applied, the most direct way of checking packet filtering access lists is the same method as for router resource access lists: test if what you permit is allowed and what is denied is not allowed through your router. Let's look at some of the extended access lists to see how we can verify access list correctness. Recall our first example of extended access lists, which implemented the following policy:

> HTTP and SSL packets only to the host at 192.168.35.1

We created a policy using the following access list:

```
access-list 101 permit any host 192.168.35.1 eq http
access-list 101 permit any host 192.168.35.1 eq 443
```

and applied it with:

```
interface ethernet 0
access-group 101 out
```

The host with IP address 192.168.35.1 lies on Ethernet 0.

How do you verify that the access list fulfills the policy? As with verifying access lists for router resource restriction, you can manually check if the applications that use these protocols are working. Since the default access list permits everything (recall that an access list that is applied but has no entries permits everything), you also need to check that blocked applications do not work. For this example, you might start the web server on host 192.168.35.1, open a web browser on a host on a different segment, and then see if you can access the web server and do SSL transactions. If web access and SSL transactions work, you then check to see if other applications do not work. An easy way to test this is to make sure that a Telnet connection attempt to the host times out. Telnet is particularly convenient because Telnet clients are easily available. You would type the following on the test host:

```
telnet 192.168.35.1
```

If the access list functions correctly, the connection attempt should time out. If you do manage to connect or receive a connection refused message (meaning that the web server does not run Telnet service on the standard Telnet port), the access list is not functioning as intended.

TCP port probing using Telnet

As a network administrator, you will not always have the luxury of testing the applications that you permit or deny through a router. In that case, there are a number of ways to check that your access lists are working correctly. These methods are not as reliable as actually testing the applications—they cannot show that your access list is absolutely right—but they can let you know if you did something wrong. As an example of this, let's look at how we can verify the correctness of our current example if we don't have access to a web browser. The network is shown in Figure 5-1.

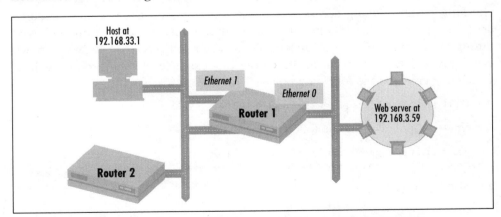

Figure 5-1. Checking extended access list correctness without application access

After implementing access list 101 on Ethernet 0 of Router 1, we need to verify that the list functions correctly—meaning it implements our policy, assuming host

192.168.33.1 lacks a web browser and we only have access to Router 2, which also lacks a web browser. How can we verify correctness in either scenario?

One simple technique you can use is *port probing*. The *telnet* command makes it easy to probe if TCP-based services are accessible. From either the host at 192.168. 33.1 or Router 2, we can see which ports on the web server are accessible through Router 1. If the access list is working correctly, when we execute the following commands on either the host or the router:

```
telnet 192.168.35.1 80
telnet 192.168.35.1 443
```

we should get a connection setup confirmation or a connection refused message.

The first command attempts to connect to the web server's HTTP port. The second command attempts to connect to the web server's SSL port. Since access list 101 allows any host to access these two ports on the web server, connecting to either port should evoke a response from the web server. If the connection attempt times out, and we know that the web server is operational, then our access list must be incorrect. As in previous examples, we also need to check whether the access list is blocking other protocols with:

```
telnet 192.168.35.1
```

The result of this particular *telnet* command should be a timeout; in other words, connections should not be achieved or refused.

You can specify which interface you want to telnet from a router using the global configuration command `ip telnet source-interface` followed by an interface. This command is useful when you want to test the path through a particular interface of a router.

Using *telnet* to probe ports is convenient. You can use any host or router to run tests like this. A network administrator implementing access lists is much more likely to have access to a router than to a host running the permitted application, since the administrator often has access only to network equipment while hosts are commonly run by other organizations. The Telnet technique does have its limitations. It can be time-consuming to check large numbers of ports.

Only TCP ports can be probed in this manner. To check both UDP and TCP port availability, port scanning software is available. These scanning packages check every UDP and TCP port that is accessible on a network that you can define. While automated and much more thorough than manual port checks, this software typically can only be run from a host and is generally not available on routers.

Access list entry accounting

Another way to verify if your access lists are correct is to see which access list entries are being used. When an application sends traffic through a router and that traffic gets filtered through an access list, then the Cisco router doing the packet filtering logs which entries of the access list are used. The *show access-list* command not only shows the entries an access list has, but also how many times a particular access list entry has been used. For our simple example, the command *show access-list 101* should yield something like this:

```
access-list 101
      permit any host 192.168.35.1 eq www (10 matches)
      permit any host 192.168.35.1 eq 443 (1 match)
```

An access list entry that functions properly should generate matches when users use the application that the entry tries to control. If there is successful www (web) access to the web server at 192.168.35.1, then the entry allowing web access to the server should have matches. If there are no matches when application traffic is generated, then there is something wrong with the access list.

This method is not sufficient to prove that all of a router's access lists are correct. For example, if we have an access list blocking traffic from the web server to certain clients (on Ethernet 1 in this case) but not others, we could have www matches to the web server on access list entries, but our policy could still not be implemented correctly. Though not a sufficient condition for verifying correctness, access list entry matches are a necessary condition for correctness and can be a useful indicator of problems.

IP accounting

The IP accounting facility is another way to check if extended access lists are correct. IP accounting lets you keep track of the source and destination IP addresses of transit packets (packets that go out of an interface and come in through an interface, possibly the same interface). It also allows you to track the source and destination IP addresses of packets that violate access lists—packets that are not accepted into the policy set of packets allowed through an interface. There are two ways you can use this capability. Transit packet IP accounting shows you what packets have successfully made it through an access list on a given interface, while access violation IP accounting tracks the packets that have been denied.

Let's turn on IP accounting for our web server example and see how we can use it. These tools are enabled with the following configuration fragment:

```
interface ethernet 0
 ip accounting output-packets
 ip accounting access-violations
interface ethernet 1
 ip accounting output-packets
 ip accounting access-violations
```

The `ip accounting` interface statement without a keyword turns on IP accounting for transit packets. Like outgoing access lists, IP accounting does not capture packets generated from the router, such as NTP queries or Telnet sessions originated from the router, so don't expect those types of traffic to be recorded by IP accounting. Once we have configured IP accounting for output packets and access violations, we need to look at the contents of the accounting database. We do this with the *show ip accounting* command. For our web server example, this yields:

```
Source           Destination        Packets        Bytes
192.168.31.2     192.168.35.1          9           13052
192.168.35.1     192.168.31.2         10          957200
192.168.35.1     192.168.70.2          6            8572
192.168.70.2     192.168.35.1          8            1303

Accounting data age is 10
```

Here you can see what traffic is going through the router, in particular, traffic going to and from the web server. Packets with a destination of 192.168.35.1 (the web server IP address) have made it through the access lists. Return traffic (with a source IP address of the web server) has also been recorded. Each accounting table entry shows the number of packets and bytes sent from one source IP address to a destination IP address. The final line tells you how many minutes have passed since the accounting table has been turned on or cleared. If you see traffic to and from some other host (perhaps 192.168.35.2), then you know you have a problem with your access lists.

To see if your access lists are rejecting what they should accept, use the *show ip accounting access-violations* command. For our example, it should yield this:

```
Source            Destination        Packets        Bytes ACL
192.168.75.2      192.168.35.2          65          36943 101
192.168.30.1      192.168.35.3          24          16115 101
192.168.152.26    192.168.35.1           8            818 101

Accounting data age is 3
```

You can see that attempts to reach host 192.168.35.2 fail because access to this host is not permitted. This is correct and functioning as we intended. What about the last line? Didn't we allow access to host 192.168.35.1? We did, but only for web and SSL, and we verified earlier that web and SSL traffic could get through. If someone tried to connect to 192.168.35.1 with a protocol other than SSL or HTTP, then this would also show up as an access violation.

Debugging extended access lists

As with router resource access lists, extended access lists used for packet filtering have two failure modes: some application or utility that should be permitted is denied or something that should be denied is permitted. For the first case, as with

Managing the IP accounting database

One database is used for storing both transit accounting and access list violation information. This single database is limited in size, and accounting information is lost when the database is full and no new entries can be entered. You can see when the database is full if you see a message like:

```
Accounting threshold exceeded for 13475 packets violating access list(s)
```

at the end of *show ip accounting* output. There are several ways to deal with this. To make the table bigger, you can use the `ip accounting-threshold` configuration directive, followed by the size of the database you want. The default size is 512 entries. Keep in mind, though, that the accounting table takes up router memory. If memory becomes an issue, you may not be able to increase the size of the accounting table as much as you may like.

While both the access list violation information and the transit information are stored in the same database, you can define how many entries are dedicated to each. The directive `ip accounting transits`, followed by the number of entries you want, lets you set the number of entries in the accounting table that are dedicated to storing IP packet transit info.

You can limit what entries go into the IP accounting table using the `ip accounting-list` statement followed by an IP address and an optional mask. For example, the following configuration commands:

```
ip accounting-list 192.168.30.1
ip accounting-list 10.0.0.0 0.255.255.255
```

allow only packets originating from or destined for host 192.168.30.1 or network 10.0.0.0/8 into the IP accounting database. Keep in mind, however, that this can be yet another access list that you may need to debug! Finally, another way to deal with a lot of accounting information is to periodically clear the database. The command *clear ip accounting* can be used to empty the IP accounting table. You also may want to use this command after making access list changes.

Keep in mind that when using IP accounting, as with access list entry accounting, correct behavior as seen from this tool is a necessary but not sufficient condition of correct implementation. IP accounting does not provide any information about ports or protocols used, so the packets you see in the database may not be the ones you expect.

router resource access lists, you need to verify routing in order to find the problem. However, using *ping* may or may not work this time because of the packet filters you are setting up. In any case, you have to ensure that the end points of an application, the client and server, have routes to each other. If you have verified the routing, and your application still does not work, you have to find where and how you inadvertently excluded packets from your target policy, which I'll describe shortly.

One common way to break applications with extended access lists is not to take into account packet flow in both directions: from client to server and from server to client. As an example, let's say we are trying to permit FTP from everywhere to an FTP server host set up as in Figure 5-2.

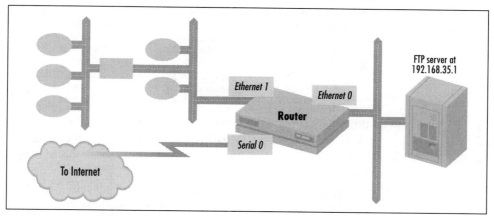

Figure 5-2. An FTP server

Since ports 20 and 21 are used on the server, let's set up our router as follows:

```
access-list 101 permit tcp any host 192.168.35.1 range 20 21
access-list 102 permit tcp host 192.168.35.1 any established
interface ethernet 0
access-group 101 out
access-group 102 in
```

FTP will not work with this configuration. Why? While FTP servers do use ports 20 and 21 during an FTP transfer, the data connection is usually initiated from the FTP server with port 20 as a source port. Since only packets from already established connections are permitted from the FTP servers, clients can set FTP control sessions but can't do any data transfers. The following access lists take into account the packet flow of FTP:

```
access-list 101 permit tcp any host 192.168.35.1 range 20 21
access-list 102 permit tcp host 192.168.35.1 range 20 21 any gt 1023
```

In addition to not setting up connections in the direction you think (as in the previous example), there are other common instances in which applications do not behave the way that you think they will. In particular, the application may demand different source or destination ports than those you anticipated in your access lists. One way to check on actual port usage is to watch how an application actually behaves with the *netstat* command, available on most Unix and Windows systems. *netstat* prints TCP connection information, including the port numbers used for the TCP connections currently running on the box. For example, if you want to examine the port behavior of the Simple Mail Transport Protocol (SMTP), you could run *netstat* on a mail server. On a host called `host1`, *netstat* would yield something like this:

```
Active Internet connections
Proto Recv-Q Send-Q  Local Address       Foreign Address     (state)
tcp       0      0   host1.smtp          host2.1042          ESTABLISHED
tcp       0      0   host1.smtp          host3.4374          ESTABLISHED
tcp       0      0   host1.smtp          host4.1301          ESTABLISHED
tcp       0      0   host1.1252          host4.smtp          SYN_SENT
tcp       0      0   host1.smtp          host5.1249          ESTABLISHED
tcp       0      0   host1.1260          host4.smtp          ESTABLISHED
tcp       0      0   host1.smtp          host6.37688         ESTABLISHED
tcp       0      0   host1.1242          host7.smtp          SYN_SENT
```

The first column is the protocol. (In this excerpt, only the TCP connections are shown.) The next two columns show how many bytes of data have been queued for the connection either from the other host or to it. The next column contains the hostname of the local host, followed by the port number of that connection. If the port is assigned to a known protocol, the protocol is displayed. The next column contains the name of the host on the far end of the connection, followed by port number or protocol if the port is known. The final column describes the state of the connection; `ESTABLISHED` means the TCP has been set up and is ready to accept data across it. In this example, we see the state `SYN_SENT`. This means that the host is trying to set up a connection to the far host; it has sent a SYN packet to set up the connection, but it has not yet received an acknowledgement. A complete table of the possible values of the connection state and their meaning is in Table 5-1.

Table 5-1. Netstat TCP connection states and their relevance to packet filters

Connection state	Meaning
SYN_SENT	System that initiates a TCP connection has sent SYN packet but has not received an acknowledgment. If a connection persists in this state, it means that either the remote host is down or that a packet filter is blocking the path to the remote end.
SYN_RECV	System has received a SYN packet for TCP setup and has sent an acknowledgment, but has not received a confirmation from the initiating system. If a connection persists in this state, it means that the remote system initiating the connection has gone down, or a packet filter is blocking return packets.
ESTABLISHED	TCP connection has been established. A packet filter is not blocking this connection.

Table 5-1. Netstat TCP connection states and their relevance to packet filters (continued)

Connection state	Meaning
FIN_WAIT1	Socket is closed, and connection is shutting down. Since this is part of the connection shutdown procedure, this means that packet filter did not block this connection.
FIN_WAIT2	Connection is shut down, and socket is waiting for shutdown from remote end. Since this is part of the connection shutdown procedure, this means that packet filter did not block the setup of this connection.
LAST_ACK	The remote end shut down, the socket is closed, and the host is waiting for acknowledgement. Since this is part of the connection shutdown procedure, this means that packet filter did not block the setup of this connection.
CLOSE_WAIT	System has received a FIN packet to terminate the connection. Since this is part of the connection shutdown procedure, this means that packet filter did not block the setup of this connection.
TIME_WAIT	TCP connection has closed, but the system waits for an interval before releasing the local port used. Since this is part of the connection shutdown procedure, this means that packet filter did not block the setup of this connection.

We wanted to be sure of SMTP's port behavior. The *netstat* output shows that SMTP goes from a high port (greater than 1023) on the system initiating the SMTP connection to a low port (less than or equal to 1023) on the SMTP port of the system it connects to. If a host must send and receive mail, you must permit access to the SMTP port going out and let systems connect to its SMTP port.

It is not always possible to get access to every host when debugging extended access lists. But if you can, running *netstat* and using the connection state information can be very helpful in tracking why a TCP-based application may not be running. On the application server, if you see that SYN packets have arrived and are acknowledged (the SYN_RECEIVED state), but no connections are in the ESTABLISHED state, then the application is not working because response packets cannot return to the client. From the client host, if you see that the connections to the application server are always in SYN_SENT mode, that means that either return packets are not coming back or SYN packets are not getting to the server.

Let's look at an example of how *netstat* can be used in this fashion. Recall from the last example that bad access lists prevented FTP services; *netstat* could have been used to find the problem, yielding the following output:

```
Active Internet connections
Proto Recv-Q Send-Q  Local Address      Foreign Address          (state)
tcp        0      0  server.ftp         client.1042           ESTABLISHED
tcp        0      0  server.ftpdata     client.1043           SYN_SENT
```

The FTP control connection is established, but the attempted TCP connection from the server to the client is not succeeding because it is stuck in the SYN_SENT state. This points toward the problem with setting up the data connection we identified.

Access list entry accounting

> Access list entry accounting doesn't work with certain switching modes. Test this feature with your version of the IOS and the switch mode you want to use before you decide to rely on it for debugging.

There are a number of facilities on Cisco routers that allow you to gather more information to find where you may have allowed too much or too little into your packet filtering policy set. The first is one I discussed when talking about verifying correctness: access list entry accounting. Since Cisco routers count the number of times that extended access lists entries are used, you can use this feature to see why an access list may not be working. Consider a policy that says:

Disallow all FTP, Telnet, and SSH access to a host but allow SMTP access

The SSH protocol typically uses port 22, which means the forbidden ports are adjacent. Let's say we yielded to temptation and implemented an outgoing access list to the host with the following:

```
access-list 101 deny tcp any host 192.168.35.1 range 20 25
access-list 101 permit tcp any host 192.168.35.1 eq SMTP
interface ethernet 0
 access-group 101 out
```

However, after access list 101 is implemented, we find that SMTP to the host does not work. Access list accounting can help us find the problem. The command *show access-list 101* yields something like this:

```
access-list 101
        deny tcp any host 192.168.35.1 range 20 25 (100 matches)
        permit tcp any host 192.168.35.1 eq smtp
```

The entry permitting SMTP has no matches, but the entry denying the range has many matches. This indicates that the first entry is matching all of the SMTP packets, so we know our problem is that the range of TCP ports is too large on our first entry. Access list 1 should be:

```
access-list 101 deny tcp any host 192.168.35.1 range 20 23
access-list 101 permit tcp any host 192.168.35.1 eq smtp
```

Access list accounting can show which entries are executed and which are not, indicating where an overly permissive or restrictive entry may lie.

Sometimes when using access list accounting, you may want to reset all of the matches to 0. This can be useful, particularly when the counts become very high and it gets hard to remember if the counts changed. The command *clear access list counters* resets all of the match counts on all access lists to 0. When followed by an access list number or name, it clears only that particular access list.

IP accounting

Another facility useful for debugging is IP accounting. Looking at the access violation database can help you figure out exactly what is getting rejected and where in an access list this might be happening. It is particularly useful when there is a problem with IP address masking. In our FTP server example, let's add Telnet access to the FTP server from hosts 192.168.30.4 and 192.168.30.5. Let's say we implemented access lists as follows:

```
access-list 101 permit tcp any host 192.168.35.1 range 20 21
access-list 101 permit tcp host 192.168.30.5 host 192.168.35.1 eq telnet
access-list 102 permit tcp host 192.168.35.1 any established
access-list 102 permit tcp host 192.168.35.1 eq 20 any gt 1023
!
interface Ethernet0
 access-group 101 out
 access-group 102 in
```

Telnet to the FTP server doesn't work from 192.168.30.4 but does from 192.168.30. 5. To debug the problem, we can turn on IP accounting for access list violations:

```
interface Ethernet 0
ip accounting access-violation
```

After trying to telnet, the output of *show ip accounting access-violation* is:

Source	Destination	Packets	Bytes	ACL
192.168.30.4	192.168.35.1	5	4343	101

This output shows that something is blocking 192.168.30.4 but not 192.168.30.5. A look at access list 101 shows that 192.168.30.4 is not in any entry or included in any mask, so there must be a problem in the entry allowing Telnet. Sure enough, the entry does not include 192.168.30.4. The correct access lists are:

```
access-list 101 permit tcp any host 192.168.35.1 range 20 21
access-list 101 permit tcp 192.168.30.4 0.0.0.1 host 192.168.35.1 eq telnet
access-list 102 permit tcp host 192.168.35.1 any established
access-list 102 permit tcp host 192.168.35.1 eq 20 any gt 1023
```

This example shows us how to find why packets that should be permitted are denied. The access violation database is also helpful in the opposite case, finding out why something is being permitted instead of denied. Let's say we implemented the previous Telnet policy with the following:

```
access-list 101 permit tcp any host 192.168.35.1 range 20 21
access-list 101 permit tcp 192.168.30.4 0.0.0.3 host 192.168.35.1 eq telnet
access-list 102 permit tcp host 192.168.35.1 any established
access-list 102 permit tcp host 192.168.35.1 eq 20 any gt 1023
```

To turn on transit packet accounting, we use the *ip accounting* command:

```
interface Ethernet0
 ip accounting output-packets
interface Ethernet1
 ip accounting output-packets
```

IP accounting is turned on for both interfaces so we can capture the traffic to and from the FTP server. The output of *show ip accounting* might look like this:

Source	Destination	Packets	Bytes
192.168.30.4	192.168.35.1	9	9052
192.168.30.5	192.168.35.1	8	8304
192.168.30.7	192.168.35.1	6	6572
192.168.35.1	192.168.30.4	10	12200
192.168.35.1	192.168.30.5	9	11206
192.168.35.1	192.168.30.7	8	10208

In addition to 192.168.30.4 and 192.168.30.5, host 192.168.30.7 has access. Since it is not much farther from the hosts we intended, the implication is that there is a bad mask. Indeed, that is the problem: the mask for access list 101's Telnet entry is too inclusive.

 Like access list entry accounting, IP accounting doesn't work with certain switching modes. With some versions of the IOS on certain hardware platforms, turning on IP accounting can even disable packet forwarding! Test before using this feature.

Access list entry logging

The last debugging technique we'll discuss uses the router's logging capability. An extended access entry that ends in the keyword **log** sends information about the packet that matched the entry to the router's log. Recall the example in which we denied a number of TCP-based services to a host but allowed SMTP to it. Our original configuration had a problem with the first entry. To find the problem, we could enable logging with the following configuration:

```
access-list 101 deny tcp any host 192.168.35.1 range 20 25 log
access-list 101 permit tcp any host 192.168.35.1 eq SMTP
logging buffered
interface ethernet 0
access-group 101 out
```

The first line of access list 101 contains the keyword `log` at the end. This means that the information on each packet that matches this line is sent to the router's log. The configuration entry `logging buffered` instructs the router to send the output to the router's logging buffer. An alternative here is to substitute `buffered` with the IP address of a host that will receive the logging output through the syslog protocol. For example, the global configuration command `logging 192. 168.33.2` sends logging information to host 192.168.33.2 via syslog. The host receives syslog information at the `debug` information level.

When SMTP traffic goes through the router, it matches the first line of access list 101, and detailed information about the packets is sent to the router's log. The command *show logging* prints the router's log, in this case producing the following:

```
%SEC-6-IPACCESSLOGP: list 101 denied tcp 172.28.178.207 (1129) -> 192.168.35.
1(25), 1 packet
%SEC-6-IPACCESSLOGP: list 101 denied tcp 172.28.178.207 (1130) -> 192.168.35.
1(25), 1 packets
```

Logging output shows the source IP address, source port, destination IP address, and destination port for each packet. In this case, the output shows that SMTP traffic is getting blocked and immediately lets you know where the problem entry is.

You can systematically move the location of the logging entry from the start of an access list to the end to find where a given packet matches. If you are looking to see why packets are denied and no entry in a list generates a log output, then you are not permitting anywhere the packets you are testing (hitting the implicit deny).

A few notes about using the logging facility are important. If you use the router's logging buffer to store log output, it can fill up. You can clear it by issuing the command *no logging buffered* to turn logging off and then on again. Also, logging many events puts a load on the router that you need to monitor. If you are logging via syslog to a remote host, realize that the syslog input also puts a load on the host. If many logged events are coming in very quickly, there is the potential for the remote host doing syslog to lose events. Still, when used carefully, the logging facility can be a powerful tool for finding problems with extended access lists.

Route-filtering access control lists

As in previous sections, I start with a discussion of verifying route-filtering access control lists for correctness and then talk about debugging.

Checking for correctness

When checking the correctness of route filtering access control lists, you cannot rely on the technique we used previously (making sure that applications run correctly). Applications can run correctly even when taking a route that does not match the policy you are trying to implement. To make sure that route filtering access lists are correct, you need to use various diagnostic tools implemented in routers and hosts. The first tool is an examination of the routing table. The command *show ip route* displays a Cisco router's routing table. For routing policies that affect incoming routing updates, the *show ip route* command can verify that your routing policy implementation is correct.

Let's look at one of our previous routing policy implementations to see how we can use *show ip route* to verify an implementation's correctness. The first example in Chapter 4 deals with the network shown in Figure 5-3.

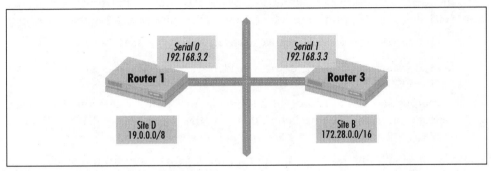

Figure 5-3. Restricting routes sent and received

Router 3, located in Site B, seeks to restrict the routes it receives from Site D. Since Site D uses only network 19.0.0.0/8 and does not transit any traffic from any other sites, Site B should hear about network 19.0.0.0/8 only in the routing updates it gets from Router 1. We implement the policy with the following:

```
access-list 1 permit 19.0.0.0
router eigrp 1000
network 192.168.3.0
distribute-list 1 in serial 1
```

How can we use *show ip route* to verify that this is correct? We have to make sure that network 19.0.0.0/8 is the only network learned from Router 1. Here is the relevant output from executing *show ip route* on Router 3:

```
Codes: C - connected, S - static, I - IGRP, R - RIP, M - mobile, B - BGP
       D - EIGRP, EX - EIGRP external, O - OSPF, IA - OSPF inter area
       N1 - OSPF NSSA external type 1, N2 - OSPF NSSA external type 2
       E1 - OSPF external type 1, E2 - OSPF external type 2, E - EGP
       i - IS-IS, L1 - IS-IS level-1, L2 - IS-IS level-2, * - candidate default
       U - per-user static route, o - ODR

Gateway of last resort is 172.28.1.5 to network 172.28.0.0
D EX 19.0.0.0/8 [170/2202624] via 192.168.3.2, 3w5d, Serial1
D EX 10.0.0.0/8 [170/2239232] via 172.28.1.5, 3w5d, FastEthernet0/0
D EX 192.168.4.0/24 [100/2174464] via 172.28.1.5, 3w5d, FastEthernet0/0
```

```
D EX 198.175.107.0/24 [100/2239232] via 143.183.152.251, 3w5d, FastEthernet1/0
C    192.168.1.0/24 is directly connected, Serial1
172.28.0.0/16 is variably subnetted, 226 subnets, 4 masks
C       172.28.1.0/26 is directly connected, FastEthernet1/0
```

The first part of this output explains the different codes used in the routing table output. For example, the code in front of a route describes how the route was learned. The first line of the entry with network 19.0.0.0/8 begins with a D, meaning that a route has been learned via EIGRP. Table 5-2 contains a summary of possible codes and what they mean. The next part of the output describes default routing—where the router sends packets to networks not in its routing table. I'll describe this in detail later.

Table 5-2. Routing protocols and their meanings

Route code	Meaning
C	Network is directly connected to the router
S	Route was statically configured
I	Route was learned via IGRP
R	Route was learned via RIP
M	Route was learned by the mobile IP protocol
B	Route was learned by BGP
D	Route was learned by EIGRP
EX	Route is an EIGRP external route
O	Route was learned by OSPF
N1	Route is an OSPF NSSA external route type 1
N2	Route is an OSPF NSSA external route type 2
E1	Route is an OSPF external route type 1
E2	Route is an OSPF external route type 2
E	Route was learned by EGP
i	IS-IS
L1	IS-IS level-1
L2	IS-IS level-2
*	Route is a candidate default route
U	Route is a per-user static route
o	Route is an on demand route

The last part is a series of lines that list the contents of the routing table. Each line describes the path to each distinct network in the routing table, and each is composed of a number of distinct parts. The routing protocol used to learn the path to that network appears before the network number. The next part of each line, within the brackets, is the administrative distance and the routing protocol metric.

In this example, you can see that the networks 19.0.0.0/8 and 10.0.0.0/8 have an external EIGRP administrative distance of 170. If a network is directly connected to the router, then the administrative distance/metrics section is omitted (connected networks have an administrative distance of 0). Next is the next hop, where the router forwards packets bound for that network. You can see that packets bound for network 19.0.0.0/8 should be forwarded to 192.168.3.2. Packets for network 10.0.0.0/8 should be forwarded to the router with IP address 172.28.1.5. Directly connected networks list the interface that the networks are connected to instead of an IP address. After the next hop is a string indicating how long the router has known the route. Routing protocols such as IGRP and RIP broadcast their routes only periodically, so this number is usually pretty low. EIGRP and BGP, routing protocols that send out routing updates only when network topologies change, have large values here, possibly days or weeks. Static routes and connected routes do not list the time since these routes are not learned dynamically. The last part of the routing table entry description is additional route information. Some routing protocols list what router interface the packets for the network will take. For example, packets bound for network 19.0.0.0/8 will travel out through interface serial 1.

How we can use this input to check on our policy implementation? First, let's look at the routing information for network 19.0.0.0/8. Our policy requires that this is the only route learned from Site D. In looking at the *show ip route* output, note that the only route learned via EIGRP from Site D's Router 1 is 19.0.0.0/8, and the next hop for the network is 192.168.3.2, the serial interface of Router 1. It seems that our implementation is correct. Is it really? If Router 1 advertised only the route 19.0.0.0/8, the output would be the same whether or not access list 1 was defined and applied with a `distribute-list` command. To be more certain, you need to make sure that the access lists are really used, with the *show ip interface* command or by checking the router's configuration.

Limiting routing output

The command *show ip route* can produce a lot of output, depending on the size of the router's routing table. There are a number of command qualifiers that can limit the output to what a network administrator finds useful. For instance, *show ip route* followed by a network number provides detailed routing information for that network. For example, typing:

```
show ip route 19.0.0.0
```

produces output like this:

```
Routing entry for 19.0.0.0/8
  Known via "eigrp 1000", distance 170, metric 2202624, type external
  Redistributing via eigrp 1000
  Last update from 192.168.3.2 on Serial0, 3w5d ago
  Routing Descriptor Blocks:
```

```
* 192.168.3.2, from 192.168.3.2, 3w5d ago, via Serial1
    Route metric is 2202624, traffic share count is 1
    Total delay is 22470 microseconds, minimum bandwidth is 1544 Kbit
    Reliability 1/255, minimum MTU 1500 bytes
    Loading 255/255, Hops 6
```

As you can see, detailed routing information about the network 19.0.0.0 route table entry is displayed. Information about how the route is redistributed and the components that make up the route metrics (such as delay, bandwidth, reliability, and loading) is also included.

Filtering router output

Commands such as *show access-list* or *show ip route* can generate so much output that they can be difficult to use for debugging. Versions of the Cisco IOS starting 12.0(1) T allow an administrator to include or exclude the output containing a specific string. The output modifier "|", when followed by the keywords inc, exc, or begin, plus a string, can be used to modify the output. For example, the command *show ip route | inc 172.28* displays all the lines of *show ip route* that contain the string 172.28. If we use the command *show ip route | exc 172.28*, the lines that do not have 172.28 are be shown, while *show ip route | inc begin 172.28* shows the lines that begin with 172.28. *show ip access-list | inc match* shows all of the access list entries that have a match. Other uses for these output modifiers include displaying the routes to all the subnets of a particular network, showing all of the access list entries that affect traffic to a specific destination, and displaying data in the IP accounting database that pertains to a specific IP address.

We can also display only the routes learned by a specific routing protocol. For example, the following command:

```
show ip route eigrp
```

shows all of the routes learned by EIGRP:

```
D EX 19.0.0.0/8 [170/2202624] via 192.168.3.2, 3w5d, Serial1
D EX 10.0.0.0/8 [170/2239232] via 172.28.1.5, 3w5d, FastEthernet0/0
D EX 192.168.4.0/24 [100/2174464] via 172.28.1.5, 3w5d, FastEthernet0/0
```

Typing the following:

```
show ip route connected
```

produces:

```
C    192.168.1.0/24 is directly connected, Serial0
172.28.0.0/16 is variably subnetted, 226 subnets, 4 masks
C       172.28.1.0/26 is directly connected, FastEthernet0/0
```

Default gateway information and an explanation of routing codes are not displayed when the routing protocol is added.

In Chapter 4, I showed how you could use the default route to limit the number of routes that need to be accepted. In our example (see Figure 4-12), we limited incoming routes to default network 172.28.0.0 with an access list and `distribute-list` on Router 1:

```
default-network 172.28.0.0
access-list 1 permit 172.28.0.0
router eigrp 1000
network 192.168.3.0
distribute-list 1 in serial 0
```

In this case, the default network information is very useful for verifying the correctness of the policy implementation. A correct implementation of the policy yields *show ip route* output such as the following:

```
Codes: C - connected, S - static, I - IGRP, R - RIP, M - mobile, B - BGP
       D - EIGRP, EX - EIGRP external, O - OSPF, IA - OSPF inter area
       N1 - OSPF NSSA external type 1, N2 - OSPF NSSA external type 2
       E1 - OSPF external type 1, E2 - OSPF external type 2, E - EGP
       i - IS-IS, L1 - IS-IS level-1, L2 - IS-IS level-2, * - candidate default
       U - per-user static route, o - ODR

Gateway of last resort is 192.168.3.3 to network 172.28.0.0
D*EX 172.28.0.0/16 [170/2202624] via 192.168.3.3, 3w5d, Serial0
C    192.168.3.0/24 is directly connected, Serial0
19.0.0.0/8 is variably subnetted, 200 subnets, 2 masks
C       19.1.1.0/24 is directly connected, FastEthernet0/0
```

The default network 172.28.0.0/16 has been learned from Router 3's 192.168.3.3 interface. We can see that it is properly handled because it's the only network learned from Router 3. It is listed as the default network in the default routing information section, and we can also see that it is the default network because its routing table entry has been flagged with an asterisk. With this information, we can conclude that the policy implementation is correct.

Verifying the correctness of access lists in outbound distribute-list statements

So far, we have only looked at verifying the correctness of access lists referenced by inbound `distribute-list` statements. How would you check for the correctness of access lists used in outbound `distribute-list` statements? One way is to look at the routing table of a router receiving the filtered routes. In Chapter 4, I showed an example of Site D filtering the routes it distributes in order to prevent any routing problems within Site D from spreading to other sites. Only network 19.0.0.0/8 should be advertised from Site D, so I configured the following on Router 1:

```
access-list 2 permit 19.0.0.0
router eigrp 1000
```

```
network 192.168.3.0
distribute-list 2 out serial 0
```

How would you verify that this configuration implements our policy? Looking at Router 1's routing table does no good since it doesn't listen to its own updates. The routing table we need to look at is on Router 3. If we disable the inbound `distribute-list` on serial 1 of Router 3, we can look at its routing table to see if 19.0.0.0 is the only route sent from Router 1. For verifying policies using outbound `distribute-lists`, examining the routing tables of the routers receiving the route updates is a good technique. Another method is to use the *debug* facility and watch routing updates sent from the router to make sure the proper routes are being advertised. I'll talk about using *debug* later in this chapter.

Verifying that hosts receive correct routing information

This technique also applies to hosts receiving routing updates. If you are filtering routes sent to hosts, checking the hosts routing table enables you to see if your policy implementation is correct. To look at a host's routing table, do the following command:

netstat -rn

To demonstrate this command, let's say we advertise routes via RIP to the hosts on segment 172.28.1.0/24.

For a host on that segment, *netstat* would produce output like the following:

```
Routing tables

Internet:
Destination        Gateway          Flags     Refs       Use  Interface
default            172.28.1.5       UGS         0   1519419  de0
10                 172.28.1.5       UG          0       429  de0
192.168.3.0        172.28.1.5       UG          0         5  de0
192.168.4.0        172.28.1.6       UG          0        12  de0
19                 172.28.1.6       UG          0    123543  de0
172.28.1.0         172.28.1.10      UG          0      2386  de0
```

The first column lists networks or hosts, and the second column shows the next hop or gateway to reach the host or network from the first column. Thus the route to network 10.0.0.0/8 goes through the router at 172.28.1.5, and the route for 19.0.0.0/8 goes out through the router at 172.28.1.6. Traffic to subnet 172.28.1.0 is local, so the gateway is listed as the host's own IP address, 172.28.1.10. The third column contains various flags associated with the route. This column is important. When only the UG flag is listed, it means that the host has learned routes from routing protocols. The presence of a capital "S" means that the route has been statically assigned. Like static routes on routers, static routes on hosts are not learned dynamically.

Traceroute

The technique of looking at adjacent routing tables has limitations. Although a particular route for a network may not be present in a routing table, that does not necessarily mean it is not being advertised. A route with a better metric may be advertised from elsewhere, and only when that second route goes away does the first route appear. Applying this potential trap to our situation, let's say that for some reason, Router 1 also advertises network 10.0.0.0/8, and Router 3 hears this advertisement. If Router 3 hears an advertisement with a better metric for network 10.0.0.0/8, the route to 10.0.0.0/8 through Router 1 does not appear in the routing table. Only when the second advertisement goes away for some reason is the bad advertisement noticed. In general, the technique of looking at routing tables is a necessary but not sufficient condition for correctness.

Another limitation of this technique is that we've been assuming we have access to neighboring routers. In situations where routers under your control border routers under someone else's administrative control, this can often be a problem since the other network administrators may be unwilling or unable to grant you SNMP read access, Telnet access, or the passwords to these routers. In that case, you have to resort to other tools like `traceroute`, which shows the path of a packet to its destination. Traceroutes are initiated with the *trace* command, followed by the hostname or IP address of the host or router to which you want the path to go. Recall that the example network we've been working with is part of a larger network, shown in Figure 5-4.

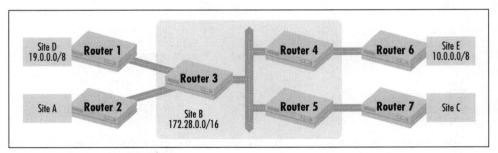

Figure 5-4. A corporate network

Let's say that an interface of Router 6 has an IP address of 10.1.1.2 and that the Router 1 interface going to Site B has an IP address of 192.168.3.2. If we wanted to traceroute from Router 1 to Router 6, we issue the following command:

```
trace 10.1.1.2
```

which produces the following output:

```
Type escape sequence to abort.
Tracing the route to router6-e0.somecompany.com (10.1.1.2)
```

```
1 router3-s1.somecompany.com (192.168.3.3) 4 msec 3 msec 2 msec
2 router4-e0.somecompany.com (172.28.1.6) 4 msec 6 msec 5 msec
3 router6-s0.somecompany.com (192.168.4.2) 20 msec * 16 msec
```

The first hop from Router 1 is to Router 3, at IP address 192.168.3.3. The next hop goes to an interface of Router 4, at IP address 172.28.1.6. The final hop is to the serial 0 interface of destination Router 6, at 192.168.4.2. The three items listed after the IP address of each hop describe the time taken for each traceroute probe packet to get a response. If no response is reached, an asterisk is printed.

Running traceroute on hosts

Most Unix and Windows systems either have the *traceroute* command or can run it. From Unix systems with traceroute, use the *traceroute* command followed by the host name or IP address. On Windows 95, 98, or NT, use the command *tracert* followed by the hostname or IP address. If you *tracert* from host 172.28.1.11 to 10.1.1.2, you should see output like the following:

```
Tracing route to router6-e0.somecompany.com [10.1.1.2]
over a maximum of 30 hops:

 1    1 ms      0 ms      0 ms  router4-e0.somecompany.com [172.28.1.6]
 2   18 ms     19 ms     17 ms  router6-s0.somecompany.com [172.28.1.6]
```

This version of traceroute differs in that the response times are listed before the hostname. This version also uses ICMP from probe packets instead of UDP.

Traceroute is useful for verifying a number of routing policy implementations. For outbound `distribute-list` and outbound `offset-list` statements, doing a traceroute from a remote network to an IP address in a network you are advertising can show you if the policy you are implementing for the network is working properly. You can see whether the packets to a network are taking the path your policy dictates. If you don't have access to a host or a router in a remote network to do a traceroute back to the network, you can have someone in another organization do the traceroute for you. On the Internet, there are a number of publicly available traceroute servers that allow you to traceroute back to your own network or to other networks. For an inbound `distribute-list` or `offset-list`, doing a traceroute to a network you have a policy about can show you whether the next hop is appropriate.

Let's see how we can use traceroute to verify the correctness of some of our policies. Recall that we defined a policy that limits networks advertised out of Site D (on Router 1) to network 19.0.0.0/8 and a policy that limits routes received from

Site D (on Router 3). The network administrators of Site D could ask someone at another site, such as Site B or Site E, to do a traceroute to a host in network 19.0. 0.0/8. If the traceroute goes through Router 1, then Site D knows that Router 1's route filters have not accidentally filtered out its network 19.0.0.0/8 advertisements and that Router 3 has also properly filtered incoming advertisements.

When you execute the command *trace* with no arguments from enable mode, you have access to a number of useful options. In particular, you can choose the source IP address of the traceroute probes. Since traceroute responses are sent back to the source address (see the upcoming sidebar "Traceroute: how it functions and how to filter it"), you can use this option to determine if a destination has a route back to the network the source address belongs to. The source address must be an interface of the router sending the traceroute. We can use this to see whether Site B can reach Site E's network 10.0.0.0/8 and whether Site E has a route back to Site B's network 19.0.0.0/8. We should use traceroute from Router 1 as follows:

```
Router1# trace
Protocol [ip]:
Target IP address: 10.1.1.2
Source address: 19.1.1.1
Numeric display [n]:
Timeout in seconds [3]:
Probe count [3]:
Minimum Time to Live [1]:
Maximum Time to Live [30]:
Port Number [33434]:
Loose, Strict, Record, Timestamp, Verbose[none]:
Type escape sequence to abort.
```

You can see the many options possible with traceroute. We can set the port number used, probe count, and a number of different options. In this example, we only use the option for setting a source address. We traceroute from interface IP address 19.1.1.1 on Site B to address 10.1.1.2 on Site E. If we see output like the following:

```
Tracing the route to router6-e0.somecompany.com (10.1.1.2)

  1 router3-s1.somecompany.com (192.168.3.3) 4 msec 3 msec 2 msec
  2 router4-e0.somecompany.com (172.28.1.6) 4 msec 6 msec 5 msec
  3 router6-s0.somecompany.com (192.168.4.2) 20 msec * 16 msec
```

we know that Site B can reach Site E and vice versa.

Debugging routing policies with access list accounting

One of the more difficult routing policy implementations to verify is route preference. Let's look at a policy we implemented in Chapter 4. As a reminder, Figure 5-5 shows a network where we prefer that traffic use one path and then another if the first is down.

Traceroute: How it functions and how to filter it

Traceroute is a very useful tool for debugging route filtering. It is easy to stop it from functioning with packet filters, however. Traceroute works by sending out a number of UDP or ICMP packets (the default is typically 3, although this can be set) with increasing Time To Live (TTL) parameters. To learn the first hop, the host or router doing traceroute sends out a packet with a TTL of 1. When this packet arrives at the first router hop, the TTL has expired, so the first hop router sends back an ICMP TTL Exceeded packet back to the sender. Thus the sender learns the identity of the first hop. The sender then sends out a packet with a TTL of 2. The packet expires at the second hop, so the second hop router sends an ICMP TTL Exceeded packet back to the sender. This process continues until the destination is reached.

From this description, you can see that the sender needs to send out UDP or ICMP (depending on the implementation) in order for traceroute to function. If the sender uses UDP, those ports must be permitted. Usually, the destination port used can be set, and the source port is usually above 1023. The sender must also be able to receive ICMP time-exceeded packets. In addition, since the packets with increasing TTL have a source address of the interface of the router or system used, be careful that the IP address of the particular interface used to send packets has permission to send out and receive those packets. For example, if we say that access list 101 is assigned to filter incoming packets to a router interface leading to a host at 192.168.35.1, that host will do traceroute, and that access list 102 is assigned to filter outgoing packets, then the following extended access list entries will allow traceroute from any host:

```
access-list 101 permit udp host 192.168.35.1 any
access-list 102 permit icmp any host 192.168.35.1 ttl-exceeded
```

This assumes we use UDP for the increasing TTL packets.

Letting out all UDP is very broad, and you may want to narrow the number of UDP ports allowed out. The default UDP port that traceroute starts with is 33434. Some traceroute implementations increase the destination port number with each set of probes, so the following two access list entries should work:

```
access-list 101 permit udp host 192.168.35.1 ge 33434
access-list 102 permit icmp any host 192.168.35.1 ttl-exceeded
```

This network uses RIP as its routing protocol. The preferred path between network 10.0.0.0/8 is through Router 1, but if that path is down, traffic should go the 56-Kb path. In this example, the only router that we control is Router 2. In Chapter 4, I implemented the policy as follows:

```
access-list 1 permit 10.0.0.0
access-list 2 permit 172.20.0.0
```

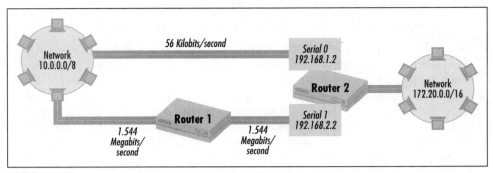

Figure 5-5. A network with a preferred routing scheme

```
!
router rip
 network 192.168.1.0
 network 192.168.2.0
 network 172.20.0.0
 offset-list 1 in 3 serial 0
 offset-list 2 out 3 serial 0
```

How can we test this implementation of routing preferences? If we can find a time when network downtime is tolerated, one way is to use the methods described previously to verify that there is the proper connectivity between the two networks. Once the preferred path is known to work, you can break the connectivity on the path through Router 1 and test if traffic uses the next preferred path.

Unfortunately for most network administrators, the opportunity to have some network downtime for testing is not readily available. In this example, we have access only over Router 2. How would we verify that we have implemented the proper policy? Fortunately for us, there are a number of facilities on Cisco routers that can help. Since we have access only to Router 2, we need to verify that our changes to routing advertisements are being properly acted upon. Traffic between networks 10.0.0.0/8 and 172.20.0.0/16 should be coming in and out of serial 1. Looking at our routing table verifies that traffic from network 172.20.0.0/16 to network 10.0.0.0/8 is going the right way. We need to verify that traffic goes from network 10.0.0.0/8 to network 172.20.0.0/16.

One way we can do this is with an incoming extended access list combined with access list accounting. We use an access list to monitor if traffic is coming into the interface with the following configuration commands:

```
access-list 101 permit ip 10.0.0.0 0.0.0.255 172.20.0.0 0.0.255.255
access-list 101 permit ip any any
!
int serial 1
 access-group 101 in
```

If traffic is coming into serial interface 1 from network 10.0.0.0/8 bound for net-work 172.20.0.0/16, the fact that the traffic has gone through is recorded by access list accounting. The command *show ip access-list 101* yields:

```
access-list 101
        permit ip 10.0.0.0 0.255.255.255 172.20.0.0 0.0.255.255 (100 matches)
        permit ip any any (10 matches)
```

You can see that traffic is coming in the way we intended. The access list does not interfere with traffic moving through the interface, as it lets all packets through but counts traffic going by. You could put a similar access list on serial interface 0 to verify that traffic from network 10.0.0.0/8 to network 172.20.0.0/8 is not going in through that interface.

Verifying routing protocol activity using debug

The previous access list technique lets us know if incoming traffic is okay, as it goes into the interface preferred by the policy. What about our implementation of backup routing? We need to make sure that our route advertisements are okay. To do that, we use the debug feature of the Cisco router, which allows us to see key events and data. To see debug output, we first need to issue the command *terminal monitor* if we are not using the router's system console port. This com-mand sends debug output to our terminal session. Debug output is also sent to the router's console by default.

To see the debug output, we have to turn on routing debug output. Since we are using RIP as a routing protocol, we use the command *debug ip rip*, which limits debugging output to only that concerning RIP. When we issue this command, we start to see output like this:

```
RIP: received update from 192.168.2.1 on Serial0
        network 10.0.0.0 in 1 hops
        network 192.168.3.0 in 1 hops
RIP: received update from 192.168.1.1 on Serial1
        network 10.0.0.0 in 2 hops
        network 192.168.3.0 in 1 hops
RIP: sending update to 192.168.2.255 via Serial0 (192.168.2.2)
        network 172.20.0.0, metric 4
        network 192.168.1.0, metric 1
        network 192.168.3.0 metric 2
RIP: sending update to 192.168.1.255 via Serial1 (192.168.1.2)
        subnet 172.20.0.0, metric 1
        network 192.168.2.0, metric 2
```

The debug output shows that Router 2 is sending the correct output out through serial interface 0. Network 172.20.0.0/16 is advertised with a metric of 4, demon-strating that the offset of 3 is being added to the route metric as intended. Advertise-ments of network 10.0.0.0/8 are coming in with a metric of 1 through serial interface 0 and with a metric of 2 through serial interface 1. Since you see the correct advertisements coming in, you are reasonably sure that your router can use the path out through serial 0 as a backup. The `offset-lists` take care of increasing the metric to make the path through Router 1 the preferred route. This can be verified by looking at the route table and seeing the route to network 10.0.0.0/8.

To turn off debugging, use the *undebug* command. In this case, you invoke it with *undebug ip rip*. You could also use *undebug all* to turn off all debugging. If you don't want to receive debug output while using a terminal, use the command *terminal no monitor*. It is a good idea to make sure that all debugging output is off when you invoke the *terminal no monitor* command.

There are two important caveats of the *debug* command. First, don't overdo it with debug information. Too much information can be impossible to process meaning-fully. A router with multiple interfaces sending and receiving periodic routing updates can scroll information so fast that you cannot see it unless you are recording your terminal session. Second, debug output is process-switched, so it places a burden on the router's main processor. Too much debug output can cripple a router and render it unusable.

Viewing routing topology

Using *debug* to see metric values works well for routing protocols such as RIP and IGRP that send out periodic updates of all of its routing information, but how would you verify routing preferences for a routing protocol such as EIGRP that only sends routing updates when conditions change? Recall that the routing table only contains the most preferred route, not any other routing information. Fortu-nately, these protocols typically have commands associated with them that display the topology learned by the routing protocol. For EIGRP, the command is *show ip eigrp topology*, so if you use EIGRP instead of RIP in the previous example, the *show ip eigrp topology* command produces output like this:

```
P 10.0.0.0 255.0.0.0, 2 successors, FD is 2236672
        via 192.168.2.1 (2236672/2234624), Serial1
        via 192.168.1.1 (2237184/2234624), Serial0
P 192.168.3.0 255.255.255.0, 2 successors, FD is 2236672
        via 192.168.2.1 (2236672/2234624), Serial1
        via 192.168.1.1 (2237184/2234624), Serial0
```

Unlike with the *show ip route* command, you can see the different paths to each network and the metrics (the first number within the parentheses) for each path. The path through Router 1 (via 192.168.2.1) is preferred, since it has a lower metric of 2236672. You can also see the backup paths over the 56-Kb link have a higher metric of 2237184. In this way, you verify that the preferred and the backup path advertisements are coming as intended. *show ip eigrp topology* has the limita-tion of being able to look only at incoming route updates, but it is still useful, as it gives you visibility into the route preferences. Other routing protocols such as OSPF have similar commands.

Debugging route-filtering access lists

Like router resource access lists and extended access lists, a route-filtering access list can go wrong in two ways: the access list denies a route that should be permitted, or it permits a route that should be denied. Just as router resource access lists and extended access lists can seem to fail because of routing problems, route filtering access lists can seem to fail because of other issues, such as packet filtering extended access lists. In this section, I discuss how to find problems with router filtering access lists. I also talk extensively about how factors other than actual route-filtering access list errors can make it look like there are problems.

In this section, I focus on the more complex debugging case in which a route you want is missing in a routing table. When a route is not present, there may be either no path or the wrong path to a given network. Let's look at the example shown in Figure 5-5. What if the routing table of Router 2 looked like the following?

```
C 172.20.0.0/16 is directly connected, Ethernet0
```

Network 10.0.0.0/8 is not in the routing table at all, so clearly something went wrong. What could have happened? Before concluding there is an access list error, you need to rule out several other possibilities. The connectivity to network 10.0.0.0/8 could be down. If the serial lines connecting to interfaces serial 0 and serial 1 are down, no routing information can be learned through them. In this case, the *show interface* command would show the following for these two interfaces:

```
Serial0 is down, line protocol is down
  Hardware is HD64570
  Description: To network 10 via 56Kbit path
  Internet address is 192.168.1.2/24
  MTU 1500 bytes, BW 56 Kbit, DLY 20000 usec, rely 255/255, load 1/255
  Last input 03:25:35, output 03:25:35, output hang never
  Last clearing of "show interface" counters never
  Queueing strategy: fifo
  Output queue 0/80, 0 drops; input queue 0/100, 0 drops
  5 minute input rate 0 bits/sec, 0 packets/sec
  5 minute output rate 0 bits/sec, 0 packets/sec
     3976767 packets input, 371394120 bytes, 0 no buffer
     Received 732003 broadcasts, 120 runts, 0 giants, 0 throttles
     1235 input errors, 2 CRC, 680 frame, 0 overrun, 0 ignored, 0 abort
     0 input packets with dribble condition detected
     3586981 packets output, 1378381771 bytes, 0 underruns
     2 output errors, 0 collisions, 615 interface resets
     0 babbles, 0 late collision, 0 deferred
     0 lost carrier, 0 no carrier
     0 output buffer failures, 0 output buffers swapped out
Serial1 is administratively down, line protocol is down
  Hardware is HD64570
  Description: To network 10 via T1 path
  Internet address is 192.168.2.2/24
  MTU 1500 bytes, BW 1544 Kbit, DLY 20000 usec, rely 255/255, load 1/255
  Encapsulation HDLC, loopback not set, keepalive set (10 sec)
```

```
Last input 03:26:05, output 03:26:05, output hang never
Last clearing of "show interface" counters never
Queueing strategy: fifo
Output queue 0/80, 0 drops; input queue 0/100, 0 drops
5 minute input rate 0 bits/sec, 0 packets/sec
5 minute output rate 0 bits/sec, 0 packets/sec
    89764824 packets input, 4874394145 bytes, 0 no buffer
    Received 752342 broadcasts, 75 runts, 0 giants, 0 throttles
    52 input errors, 1 CRC, 20 frame, 0 overrun, 0 ignored, 0 abort
    0 input packets with dribble condition detected
    53586321 packets output, 61278388290 bytes, 0 underruns
    6 output errors, 0 collisions, 2 interface resets
    0 babbles, 0 late collision, 0 deferred
    0 lost carrier, 0 no carrier
    0 output buffer failures, 0 output buffers swapped out
```

The *show interface* command generates a lot of output, but I'll mention only key parts that are relevant to debugging route-filtering access list problems. The first line of output for each interface is usually the most important. It tells you the interface name, whether it is up or down, and whether the line connected to the interface is down. Often, if the line protocol is down, the interface will be listed as down as well. In the previous example, both interfaces are down. Serial interface 1 is said to be **administratively down**. This means that the interface was manually shut down. The line beginning with **Description:** displays whatever the person who configured the router decided to mention about the interface. It is often useful for determining the function of the interface and what it connects to.

Below the description is the interface's IP address and mask. Underneath is an important line that describes key properties of the line connected to the interface. These properties, such as bandwidth (**BW**) and delay, are used by some routing protocols as part of metric calculations. In the example, this line shows which interface has the 56-Kb line and which has the 1.544-Mb line. Two lines below that line are times listing the last input and output. This line is useful for listing when an interface or the line connected to it goes down.

The *show interface* command output reveals that what at first appeared to be a routing problem was actually caused by interfaces being down. Another clue that the interfaces are down is that the directly connected networks, 192.168.1.0/24 and 192.168.2.0/24, are not listed in the route table. If the interfaces were up, then the two networks would have been listed in the routing table.

When the wrong route is present

Another possibility is that the wrong route might be present. The *show ip route* command yields the following:

```
C 172.20.0.0/16 is directly connected, Ethernet0
C 192.168.1.0/24 is directly connected, Serial0
R 10.0.0.0/8 [120/1] via 192.168.1.1, 0:29, Serial0
```

There is a route to 10.0.0.0/8, but it uses the backup path through serial 0 instead of the path through serial 1. What could have happened? In this case, it is possible that the line connected to interface serial 1 is down, and *show interface serial1* would show the following:

```
Serial1 is down, line protocol is down
```

Let's now say that serial interface 1 is down, so the route to network 10.0.0.0/8 uses serial interface 0. Network 192.168.2.0/24 is not in the route table. This is additional evidence of serial interface 1 being down.

What if 192.168.2.0/24 did appear in the route table yet the route was still wrong? We'd then see the following:

```
C 172.20.0.0/16 is directly connected, Ethernet0
C 192.168.1.0/24 is directly connected, Serial0
C 192.168.2.0/24 is directly connected, Serial1
R 10.0.0.0/8 [120/4] via 192.168.1.1, 0:29, Serial0
```

Here, both serial interfaces must be up, since the directly connected networks on both interfaces are listed in the route table. However, this does not necessarily mean there are problems with our access list. Notice that the metric for network 10.0.0.0/8 is 4, which is what it should be after we increase its value with the `offset-list` command. This implies that the routing information coming into the serial 0 interface is being handled correctly, so it could be that the router on the other side of the 1.544-Mb line is down. We can confirm this by doing a ping of router 1's 192.168.2.1 interface. If *ping* reveals that it is down, then this problem has prevented the preferred route from entering Router 2's routing table.

If *ping* reveals the interface at 192.168.2.1 is up, then there are a number of possibilities why the correct route is still not there. Router 1's connectivity to network 10 might be down. Also, Router 1's administrators may have accidentally turned off sending routes to Router 2, through the `passive-interface` statement. Strange as it may seem, that actually does happen occasionally and can be detected using the *debug* command. You would notice that Router 1 seems to send no routing updates even though it is up.

Stopping routing updates with extended access lists

Make sure that you don't cause problems yourself. One way that routing updates can be ignored is with an overzealous incoming packet filter. If Router 2 makes the following attempt at anti-spoofing:

```
access-list 101 deny ip 172.20.0.0 0.0.255.255 any
access-list 101 deny ip 192.168.2.0 0.0.0.255 any
access-list 101 permit ip any any
interface serial 1
access-group 101 in
```

then all incoming routing updates are suppressed. At other times you might forget static routes you have set previously. If *show ip route* produces the following:

```
C 172.20.0.0/16 is directly connected, Ethernet0
C 192.168.1.0/24 is directly connected, Serial0
C 192.168.2.0/24 is directly connected, Serial1
S 10.0.0.0/8 [1/1] via 192.168.1.1, Serial0
```

a static route excludes any routing advertisement of network 10.0.0.0 since static routes have a higher administrative distance then any dynamic routing protocol.

If all else fails

You may encounter a situation where your access lists don't work even though there is no obvious reason. It may seem that your access lists are being totally ignored, or that your access list stops all traffic through an interface despite clearly permitting certain types of traffic. When you encounter this type of error, there may be a problem with your particular IOS. After you have exhausted all other debugging possibilities, check the Cisco web site for bugs in your IOS (*http://www.cisco.com/support/bugtools*). There are IOS versions in which access lists do not function correctly. The Cisco Bug Navigator™ can point out the IOS versions that have problems and the ones that have fixed those problems. If you don't find your problem, open up a case with the Cisco Technical Assistance Center (TAC). They should be able to help. Note that both of these options require a support contract, which I strongly recommend if you depend on Cisco access lists for mission critical applications.

When access lists are used incorrectly

Sometimes, access lists are correct but not used correctly. If you implement the access lists like this:

```
access-list 1 permit 10.0.0.0
access-list 2 permit 172.20.0.0
router rip
network 192.168.1.0
network 192.168.2.0
offset-list 1 in 1 serial 0
offset-list 2 out 1 serial 0
```

show ip route reveals the following:

```
C 172.20.0.0/16 is directly connected, Ethernet0
C 192.168.1.0/24 is directly connected, Serial0
C 192.168.2.0/24 is directly connected, Serial1
R 192.168.3.0/24 [120/1] via 192.168.2.1, 00:23, Serial1
R 10.0.0.0/8 [120/2] via 192.168.1.1, 00:23, Serial0
  10.0.0.0/8 [120/2] via 192.168.2.1, 00:23, Serial1
```

Notice that there are two routes associated with network 10.0.0.0/8, one for each of two possible paths, and they both have the same route metric. This is an indication that the offset used in the `offset-list` line is not high enough. Since the metrics to both paths are the same, the router installs both routes.

When route-filtering access lists are wrong

I have shown how different problems can make you think there are access lists problems when there are not. Let's look at a situation where there actually are problems with the access lists themselves. If we implement our policy in the following way:

```
access-list 1 permit 19.0.0.0
access-list 2 permit 172.20.0.0
router rip
network 192.168.1.0
network 192.168.2.0
offset-list 1 in 3 serial 0
offset-list 2 out 3 serial 0
```

show ip route reveals the following:

```
C 172.20.0.0/16 is directly connected, Ethernet0
C 192.168.1.0/24 is directly connected, Serial0
C 192.168.2.0/24 is directly connected, Serial1
R 192.168.3.0/24 [120/1] via 192.168.2.1, 00:23, Serial1
R 10.0.0.0/8 [120/1] via 192.168.1.1, 00:23, Serial0
```

The path to network 10.0.0.0/8 goes through serial 0, yet its metric is only 1. It looks like access list 1 has not put network 10.0.0.0 into its policy set of routes that will have its route metrics increased. A look at access list 1 reveals that network 19.0.0.0/8 is in the only entry instead of network 10.0.0.0/8. Once corrected, the proper route should be installed in the routing table.

6

Route Maps

In this chapter:
- *Other access list types*
- *Generic route map format*
- *Interior routing protocols and policy routing*
- *BGP*
- *Debugging route maps and BGP*

For more advanced network policies, Cisco routers have a policy structure called *route maps*. Route maps combine policy set definition with policy application, using the access list formats discussed in previous chapters. In this chapter I talk about using route maps for intranet routing policies and for routing policies in the Internet. Along the way, I cover some new access list types, key BGP (Border Gateway Protocol, the routing protocol used on the Internet) concepts, and how to implement commonly used Internet routing policies, focusing on the needs of multihomed organizations, not ISPs.

Other access list types

For most configurations, standard and extended access lists are enough to specify which sets of IP addresses or networks you want to influence with a policy. When you want to set policies with BGP or manipulate sets of networks based on their prefix length (the number of bits in the network mask), these types of access lists fall short. BGP is an *Exterior Gateway Protocol* (EGP) routing protocol. EGPs are designed for sending routing updates between large administrative domains. As a result, BGP routes carry a lot of information. Unlike *Interior Gateway Protocols* (IGP) such as OSPF or EIGRP, BGP routing updates carry complete path information. The routing updates can also carry flags added by network administrators called *community attributes*. Both paths and communities are often the basis of Internet routing policies. In this section, I talk about three new types of access lists: the prefix lists, the AS-path list, and the community list. Understanding these types of access lists is a prerequisite to using route maps, particularly with BGP.

Prefix lists

When working with networks of different prefix lengths, there are a number of situations where using standard access lists don't work. Let's say that you wanted to set up an access list that includes network 172.28.0.0/16 but doesn't include 172.28.0.0/24. Although you might try the following access list:

```
access-list 1 permit 172.28.0.0 0.0.0.0.0
access-list 1 deny 172.28.0.0 0.0.0.0.255
```

172.28.0.0/24 will still be included in the policy set in the first entry.

In general, standard access lists are unwieldy (if at all workable) when you want to include and exclude networks based on prefix length into a policy set. Let's say you want to include network 192.168.32.0/19 and all possible prefixes that are a part of it, i.e., all prefix lengths of network 192.168.32.0/19 equal to or greater than 19. We would have to implement this by denying shorter length prefixes and including everything else:

```
access-list 2 deny 192.168.64.0 0.0.192.0
access-list 2 permit 192.168.32.0 0.0.31.255
```

The `prefix-list` access list makes policies much easier to express, and as shown in our first example, makes them possible. To create a policy of the network 172.28.0.0/16 and not 172.28.0.0/24, we would use the following:

```
ip prefix-list Class-B-Only seq 5 permit 172.28.0.0/16
ip prefix-list Class-B-Only seq 10 deny 172.28.0.0/24
```

Like standard and extended access lists, entries are matched in sequence. In the case of prefix lists, the sequence number determines the order of matching, starting with the entry with the lowest sequence number and then going to the next largest sequence number until all entries have been compared. Prefix lists also have an implicit deny all at the end of the list, so for this policy, we could just say:

```
ip prefix-list Class-B-Only seq 5 permit 172.28.0.0/16
```

For our second example, one entry is all we need:

```
ip prefix-list Slash19-and-longer seq 10 permit 192.168.32.0/19 ge 19
```

Let's look at the format of the prefix list. After the required literal **ip prefix-list**, it takes a name that can be composed of letters, numbers, and other characters such as dashes. After the name there is the optional literal **seq**, followed by a sequence number. This sequence number is used to sort the sequence in which prefixes are evaluated in the list. If you don't enter a sequence number, one is created for you, with an increasing sequence by 5 (adding 5 to the last sequence number). The use of sequence numbers also allows a network administrator to change a line in a prefix list without deleting the whole list and reentering it with the modifications. After the sequence number, there is either a **permit** or **deny** literal, followed by a CIDR network specification (the prefix and prefix length separated by a slash). The last parts are optional sections specifying conditions on the length of prefixes. If no conditions are included regarding prefix length, a route must exactly match the specified network, including the prefix length.

In general, the format of the prefix list can be expressed as:

```
ip prefix-list name [seq sequence-number] {permit|deny} prefix/prefix-length [ge
greater-equal-to-value] [le less-equal-to-value]
```

Prefix lists are easier to manipulate then standard access lists. Since they have sequence numbers, you can delete specific entries with the following configuration command when in **ip prefix-list** configuration mode:

```
no ip prefix-list prefix-list-name seq sequence-number
```

where **prefix-list-name** is the name of the prefix list and **sequence-number** is the sequence number of the entry you wish to delete. Omitting the **seq** keyword and sequence number deletes the entire prefix list. If you wish to insert an entry in the middle of a prefix list, you can create an entry number with a sequence number between the sequence numbers of the entries that are before and after the new entries.

You can turn off automatic sequencing with the command:

```
no ip prefix-list sequence-number
```

Otherwise, the router will add five to the last sequence number to generate the next sequence number.

Prefix lists are viewed with the *show ip prefix-list* command. Similar to the *show access-list* command, when this command is given without a prefix list argument, all prefix lists are shown, but with an argument of a prefix list name, only that specific prefix list is shown. *show ip prefix-list detail* provides more information, such as the number of times individual entries are accessed, while *show ip prefix-list summary* shows only a summary of prefix lists and does not show individual entries.

Here are some examples using a prefix list called **Net10-prefixes**. The command *show ip prefix-list Net10-prefixes* shows the following:

```
RouterX# show ip prefix-list Net-10-prefixes
ip prefix-list Net-10-prefixes:  4 entries
   seq 5 permit 10.204.23.0/24
   seq 10 permit 10.204.28.0/24
   seq 15 deny 10.204.0.0/16
   seq 20 permit 10.0.0.0/8
```

This prefix list allows the prefixes 10.204.23.0/24, 10.204.28.0/24, but no other prefixes of 10.204.0.0/16. All other prefixes of 10.0.0.0/8 are allowed. The command *show ip prefix-list detail* shows detailed information about the prefix list. In the following example, you can see the number of entries (count), the number of entries with range statements, the range of sequence numbers (sequences), and the number of times the list is used in policy settings (refcount) for all access lists, plus the last prefix list modified:

```
RouterX# show ip prefix-list detail
Prefix-list with the last deletion/insertion: Net10-prefixes:
ip prefix-list Net10-prefixes:
count 1, range entries: 0, sequences 5 - 20, refcount: 1
   seq 5 permit 10.204.23.0/24 (hit count: 3, refcount: 1)
   seq 10 permit 10.204.28.0/24 (hit count: 0, refcount: 1)
   seq 15 permit 10.204.0.0/16 (hit count: 0, refcount: 1)
   seq 20 permit 10.0.0.0/8 (hit count: 0, refcount: 1)
```

The *show ip prefix-list detail* command shows matches (hit count) for each entry. These entry counters can be cleared with *clear ip prefix-list* followed by a prefix list name.

The prefix list can be used in BGP routing processes in the same way as standard access lists in distribute-list statements. Let's say we wanted to accept only the class B 172.28.0.0/16 and no longer accept prefixes of 172.28.0.0/16 from a BGP neighbor at 198.168.35.1 and AS 65351. We would use the following configuration:

```
ip prefix-list ClassB-only-172-28 seq 10 permit 172.28.0.0/16
!
router bgp 65350
 neighbor 192.168.35.1 remote-as 65351
 neighbor 192.168.35 1 prefix-list ClassB-only-172-28 in
```

The neighbor statement says that the only routes that exactly match the prefix list ClassB-only-172-28 are accepted from BGP neighbor 192.168.35.1.

Another policy that we might implement with prefix lists is the following:

Send only prefixes of network 10.0.0.0/8 with length smaller than /20 to BGP neighbor 192.168.35.1

Policies like this can reduce the number of routes that the receiver of the routes needs to process. This policy can be expressed as:

```
ip prefix-list Class10-Routes-19 seq 10 permit 10.0.0.0/19 le 19
router bgp 65000
neighbor 192.168.35.1 remote-as 65001
neighbor 192.168.35.1 prefix-list Class10-Routes-19 out
```

AS-path access lists

A key BGP concept is the *autonomous system* (AS). It is difficult if not impossible to set useful policies in BGP without understanding how ASes function, so I'll spend some time on this subject before talking about building policy sets based on AS-path information. In BGP, routing updates contain AS-path information. Autonomous systems are collections of networks governed by an organization—a single administrative domain. Typically, BGP routing information on the Internet has the originating organization's AS number, the ISP's AS number, and any other AS number on the route to the end network.

Routing policies are often set based on AS-path information. That implies that in route map construction, there is a mechanism to match against an AS path. I have shown how a standard access list can be used to match based on network address. Cisco routers also have an analogous construct for building policy sets called an *AS-path access list*. To use AS-path access lists, you first need to know how AS paths are stored in routing tables. AS paths are stored as a series of AS numbers such as this:

```
3 2 1 5 4
3 2 1
1 2 3
```

As routing updates pass through different administrative domains, each forwarding AS adds itself in front of the AS path. For example, the AS path from AS 1 is directly connected to AS 2. If AS 2 propagates a route inside AS 1 through BGP to another AS, the AS path to that network in the routing update is:

```
2 1
```

An autonomous system has the option of adding additional hops. Using the previous example, AS 1 and AS 2 can add extra hops in front (this is often done to influence the choice of routes—more on this later). Thus routes out of AS 1 passing through AS 2 could look like:

```
2 2 1
2 1 1
2 1 1 1
```

or even:

```
2 2 1 1
```

AS numbers are expressed as 16-bit numbers and stored as 16-bit values in routing updates. Thus AS numbers in BGP range from 1 to 65535. Certain numbers within this range are reserved for exclusive use within organizations, just as the TCP/IP protocol suite allows a certain set of IP addresses to be used exclusively within an organization. Hosts within an organization's private IP space cannot talk over the Internet to another organization. Similarly, there is a private AS number space.

These AS numbers are dedicated for use within an autonomous system. AS paths circulated within the Internet between organizations cannot have AS hops in this space. AS numbers between 64512 and 65535 are considered private. They are typically used inside what is called a *BGP confederation*. A BGP confederation is a set of autonomous systems that talk to each other using BGP and private AS numbers, but when talking to AS outside of the confederation, hide their private AS numbers and paths and present a single public AS number. When private AS numbers are used inside of a BGP confederation, the private AS numbers are listed within parentheses. An AS path within a confederation might appear like this:

```
(65000 65001) 2 1
```

When a route with this path is distributed to a public AS, the part within parenthesis disappears:

```
2 1
```

AS paths are matched into policy sets with AS-path access list entries. Each entry has the following format:

```
as-path access-list name {permit|deny} {regular expression}
```

name can be a number or a name. These names and numbers can be the same as already configured standard or extended access lists since they are used and applied differently. *regular expression* is in the regular expression format commonly used in Unix and Perl—an expression that matches some set of one or more strings. Table 6-1 shows special characters used in Cisco regular expressions.

Table 6-1. Characters used in Cisco regular expressions

Special character	Meaning
.	Match individual character
*	Match any number of preceding expression
+	Match at least one of preceding expression
^	Beginning of line
$	End of line
(	Start including next expressions as one unit until a matching parenthesis is reached
)	Include previous expressions, starting with a (as a single unit
—	Beginning of line, end of line, left or right parentheses, left or right bracket, or whitespace

The character . matches any one individual character in a string. A * means match 0 or more of the preceding expression, while + means match 1 or more of the preceding expression. Thus, the expression 2.* matches the strings "2", "23", "244",

and "25555", but 2.+ does not match the string "2". A ^ means match at the start
of the line, while a $ means match at the end of the line. In addition, Cisco
defines an operator particular to Cisco routers, the underscore (_). The underscore matches the beginning of a line, the end of a line, left or right parentheses,
left or right bracket, or any whitespace. It is typically used for delimiting individual AS numbers in a path.

Table 6-2 lists some regular expressions commonly used within AS-path matching.

Table 6-2. Commonly used regular expressions for AS-path matching

Expression	Meaning
x+	1 or more occurrences of **x**
x*	0 or more occurrences of **x**
^x	Expression that starts with **x**
x$	Expression that ends with **x**
xy	**x** followed by **y**
(xy)	**x** followed by **y**, taken together as a unit

Here are some examples of how AS-path matching works. The following AS-path
access list only includes routes with an AS path of 1 in the policy set. This is typically used when building a policy set of all routes originating from a neighboring
AS.

```
as-path access-list 5 permit ^1$
```

The following AS-path access list:

```
as-path access-list 6 permit _2_.*$
```

matches any AS path with AS 2 inside of it. Any route that transits AS 2 is included
in the policy set. This particular regular expression is used when you are con-
cerned with routes that transit a particular AS.

The AS-path access list entry:

```
as-path access-list 7 permit (_3)+$
```

includes all routes that originate with 3 and includes any number of prepends of 3.
You would use an entry like this when you have a neighboring AS that may
choose to do AS-path prepending.

Like other access lists, chains of individual entries can be created. These are
matched in the sequence that they are entered, just like standard and extended
access lists. For example, the AS-path access list:

```
as-path access-list 1 deny ^1$
as-path access-list 1 permit _1_.*$
as-path access-list 1 permit _2_.*$
```

does the following:

- Denies all routes directly from and originating in AS 1
- Permits all routes that transit through AS 1
- Permits all routes that transit through AS 2

AS-path access lists are usable by themselves and not just as part of route maps. A network administrator can apply AS path access list filtering directly to incoming and outgoing routes without using route maps. Consider the following example:

```
as-path access-list 1 permit ^1$
as-path access-list 1 permit _2_.*$
as-path access-list 2 permit _2_3$
```

AS-path list 1 includes routes directly from AS 1 with no transit ASes and all routes transiting through AS 2. AS path list 2 includes all routes that originate from AS 3 that pass through 2.

In a BGP route process definition, we can use AS-path access lists to control which routes are accepted based on the AS path. Using the AS-path access lists described earlier, consider the following:

```
router bgp 4
neighbor 192.168.30.1 remote-as 5
neighbor 192.168.30.2 remote-as 6
neighbor 192.168.30.1 as-path 1 in
neighbor 192.168.31.2 as-path 2 out
```

This example shows a route process accepting all routes from AS 5 that meet the stipulation of AS-path list 1—routes transiting through AS 2 or bound for AS 1. Only routes originating from AS 3 and transiting through AS 2 are allowed to pass on to AS 6. Since no AS path access list is applied to the incoming routes from AS 6, all routes are accepted from AS 6. Similarly, since no AS path access list is applied to the outgoing routes to AS 5, all routes are distributed to AS 5.

How do you learn the AS path associated with a route and verify if your AS-path access lists are correct? How can you find problems in AS path access lists? The *show ip bgp* command can help you verify the correctness and find problems with AS path access lists. *Show ip bgp* generates a list of all of the routes learned by BGP from the router's BGP peers and the AS path associated with each possible path. Here is sample output:

```
Router1# show ip bgp
BGP table version is 28690299, local router ID is 192.168.128.129
Status codes: s suppressed, d damped, h history, * valid, > best, i - internal
Origin codes: i - IGP, e - EGP, ? - incomplete

   Network          Next Hop        Metric LocPrf Weight Path
*> 10.0.0.0/8       192.168.128.138                0 2 1 i
```

```
*                192.168.128.139              0 3 1 i
*> 10.5.5.4/30   192.168.128.138              0 2 5 i
*> 172.24.0.0/16 192.168.128.136              0 (65001) i
*                192.168.128.137              0 (65002 65001) i
*> 192.168.32.3  192.168.128.136              0 (65001) i
```

There are multiple paths for some networks in the previous BGP table excerpt. The path preferred by the router has a greater-than sign (>) in front of it. The network number and prefix length are in the first column, followed by the next hop in the second. Since no metric or local preference has been set, the defaults are not shown. The default weight value of 0 is shown, however.

If there are many networks learned by BGP, the output can be very long. For a router taking in full Internet routes, this could be tens of thousands of lines long. *show ip bgp* followed by a network produces BGP routing information pertaining to a single network. For example, *show ip bgp 12.13.84.0* might produce output like this:

```
router1# show ip bgp 12.13.84.0
BGP routing table entry for 12.13.84.0/24, version 28270198
Paths: (2 available, best #2)
   7806, (aggregated by 7806 12.13.84.3)
     192.168.128.137 (metric 10) from 192.168.128.137
       Origin IGP, localpref 100, valid, external
       Community: 7806:100
   7806, (aggregated by 7806 12.13.84.2)
     192.168.128.136 (metric 6) from 192.168.128.136
       Origin IGP, localpref 100, valid, external, best
       Community: 7806:100
```

This output shows two paths to network 12.13.84.0/24, one through the router at 192.168.128.136 and the other from the router at 192.168.128.137. Values of route attributes such as local preferences, metrics, and communities are shown in the output. I will talk about these later.

If you wish to see which routes in your routing table will be included by a particular regular expression, the command *show ip bgp regexp* followed by a regular expression shows all routes that match. For example, *show ip bgp regex ^\ (66000\)$* produces the following:

```
Router1# show ip bgp regex ^\(66000\)$
BGP table version is 8413446, local router ID is 192.168.129.133
Status codes: s suppressed, d damped, h history, * valid, > best, i - internal
Origin codes: i - IGP, e - EGP, ? - incomplete

   Network              Next Hop          Metric LocPrf Weight Path
*> 172.15.0.0/16        192.168.248.252                     0 (66000) i
*> 172.18.0.0/16        192.168.248.252                    10 (66000) i
*> 192.168.72.0/24      192.168.248.252                     0 (66000) i
*> 172.20.0.0/16        192.168.248.252                     0 (66000) i
```

In this example, we can see that one network, 172.18.0.0/16, has a weight different from the other networks. A particularly useful version of this command shows the routes are originated from a router:

```
Router1#show ip bgp regex ^$
BGP table version is 67829, local router ID is 172.15.11.3
Status codes: s suppressed, d damped, h history, * valid, > best, i - internal
Origin codes: i - IGP, e - EGP, ? - incomplete

    Network          Next Hop        Metric LocPrf Weight Path
*> 172.16.0.0        172.15.10.3       271          32768 i
*> 192.168.30.0      172.15.10.3       138          32768 i
*> 10.0.3.0/24       172.15.10.3       128          32768 i
```

You can see how routes have different values for different metrics. Locally originated routes have a default weight of 32768, while other routes have a zero weight. Other metrics, like "Metric," have different values for each route.

To test entire AS-path access lists, use the command *show ip bgp filter-list*. If you define an AS-path access list as follows:

```
as-path access-list 5 permit ^1_
as-path access-list 5 permit ^2$
```

capturing in a policy set all of the routes coming through AS 1 plus all the routes that originate from AS 2, the command *show ip bgp filter-list 5* produces the following output:

```
Router1# show ip bgp filter-list 5
BGP table version is 23029, local router ID is 192.168.18.100
Status codes: s suppressed, d damped, h history, * valid, > best, i - internal
Origin codes: i - IGP, e - EGP, ? - incomplete

    Network          Next Hop        Metric LocPrf Weight Path
*> 4.0.0.0/8        192.168.18.136                     0 1 2 i
*>                  192.168.18.138                     0 2 i
*> 172.23.0.0/16 192.168.18.136                        0 1 3 i
*                  192.168.18.137                      0 1 4 i
*> 172.24.0.0/16 192.168.18.138                        0 2 i
*> 192.168.10/24 192.168.18.136                        0 1 i
```

BGP community attribute

A very important attribute of routes in BGP is the *community* attribute, and as you might expect, there is a type of access list for building policy sets of them. Communities are four-byte numbers assigned to routes that flag routes for special processing by other routers. Routers can watch for communities on route advertisements and then take action on them. The uppermost bytes are an AS number, and the lower bytes are a number chosen by a network administrator.

Let's look at how community lists are constructed and how matching works. The community access list entry has the following format:

```
ip community-list {community list number} {permit|deny} string1 string2 .. string n
```

After the list number and permit/deny arguments, there are a series of communities. If any community of a route matches any of the communities on the entry, the route is added to a policy set. Here is an example:

```
ip community-list 100 permit 65000:1 65000:2 65000:3
ip community-list 100 permit 65001:1 65001:2 65001:3
```

Communities have two formats: an older format that is a long number (the Cisco default) and a newer format that divides the number into two numbers separated by a colon. Communities are 16-bit numbers and can range from 1 to 65535. The new format allows some structure to the community string in the form *a:b*. The first number (a) corresponds to the first (leftmost) 32 bits of the community string. The second number (b) corresponds to the second (rightmost) 16 bits of the string. ISPs often put their own AS as the first number to denote communities that relate to their infrastructure. To convert from the new format to the old format, use the following formula:

```
old format community string = a * 65536 + b
```

To convert to a new format from an old format string, convert the community string to a 32-bit binary number. The first number (a) is the decimal value of the leftmost 16 bits. The decimal equivalent of the rightmost 16 bits is the second number (b). For example, the new format community string 701:1 would convert to 701 × 65536 + 1 or 45940737. The new format of the old format community string 45940738 would be 701:2. In the older format, the previous example would be the following:

```
ip community-list 100 permit 4559840001 4559840002 4559840003
ip community-list 100 permit 4559905537 4559905538 4559905539
```

The configuration directive **ip bgp-community new-format** automatically converts the old format to the new format.

There are a few special predefined communities. The **Local-AS** community string instructs BGP not to send a route tagged with this string outside of the local AS. **No-export** prevents a route from being advertised to an external peer, while **No-advertise** tells BGP not to advertise the route from any peer. **Internet** communities means advertise the route to the Internet community.

Like AS-path access lists, the *show ip bgp* command can take community list entries or community lists as arguments to show only routes that match the community list entry or community list. The router command *show ip bgp community* followed by a community string shows all routes with that community:

```
Routerx# show ip bgp community 65000:1
BGP table version is 4953083, local router ID is 10.117.56.120
```

```
Status codes: s suppressed, d damped, h history, * valid, > best, i - internal
Origin codes: i - IGP, e - EGP, ? - incomplete

Network Next Hop Metric LocPrf Weight Path
*>i10.0.0.0 10.117.56.174 4294967294 100 0 (65001) i
*>i172.20.48.0/20 10.117.56.174 4294967294 100 0 (65001) i
*  i172.20.6.0/24 10.177.56.241 4294967294 100 0 (65002) i
*   172.21.7.0/24 10.177.56.241 4294967294 100 0 (65002) i
*  i172.21.94.0/23 10.177.56.241 4294967294 100 0(65002) i
*   172.24.125.0/24 10.177.56.241 4294967294 100 0 (65002) i
*  i172.25.252.0/23 10.177.56.174 4294967294 100 0 (65001) i
*  i172.26.92.0/24 10.177.56.241 4294967294 100 0 (65001) i
```

If you add the literal **exact**, only the routes with that community string are displayed. Similar to AS-path access lists, the command *show ip bgp community-list* followed by a community list name shows all routes that match that community list.

Generic route map format

To create generic policies for routing, we need two things: a way to identify routes to be affected by a policy and a way to set policies once those routes have been identified. Route maps are a series of entries that have exactly those two sets of elements. The name "route map" is entirely appropriate: routes are identified and mapped to a policy setting.

Each route map entry has the following format:

```
route-map route-map-name {permit|deny} {sequence number}
match clauses
policy settings
```

The *sequence number* determines the sequence in which route maps are evaluated. Entries with lower sequence numbers are evaluated before blocks with higher sequence numbers with the same route map name. *Match clauses* are policy set definitions, usually some kind of access list reference intended to match route characteristics. There can be multiple match clauses, and a route has to match all of the clauses in order to match the entry. **permit** and **deny** are the two possible keywords for route map entries. A **permit** says that a route with the match clause characteristics will have the policy settings applied to it. A **deny** says that a route that matches a match clause will no longer be evaluated by the route map, and further comparisons to other route map entries will stop. No route attributes are changed when a **deny** is encountered.

Here is an example of a route map:

```
route-map ROUTES-IN permit 10
match ip address 5 6
set local-preference 110
```

```
route-map ROUTES-IN deny 20
 match ip address 7

route-map ROUTES-IN permit 30
 match ip address 8
 set local-preference 90

access-list 5 permit 192.168.30.0
access-list 6 permit 192.168.31.0
access-list 7 permit 192.168.32.0
access-list 8 permit 192.168.33.0
```

The route map ROUTES-IN has three entries. Every route that is passed through
ROUTES-IN first goes through the entry with sequence number 10. If the destination network in the route matches access list 5 or access list 6, then the route's
local preference (I explain local preference later in the chapter) is set to 110. If
not, the route is checked if it matches the route-map entry with sequence 20. If it
matches access list 7, then no further matching is done because the entry is a deny
route map entry. The route is effectively ignored and not used or redistributed by
the route map. If the route matches access list 8, then it has its local preference set
to 90. If the route matches neither entry 10, 20, or 30, then the route's characteristics are left alone, and it is basically ignored.

In the previous example we matched against the network addresses to set route
characteristics. You don't necessarily need both a match clause and a policy setting, but you need at least one of them. The lack of a match clause implies that all
routes will match. The lack of policy setting means that no changes are made to
any matching routes. In later sections, I will describe how to match against other
parts of BGP routes, such as AS paths and communities.

Interior routing protocols and policy routing

A typical use of route maps involves redistributing routes. While you can use the
distribute-list router configuration and standard access lists to implement
policies, route maps can do things that you cannot do easily with access lists
alone. As an example, let's say we want to redistribute static routes to an EIGRP
routing process with the following policy:

Distribute all static routes to networks 172.16.20.0/24 172.16.25.0/24, 172.16.52.0/
24, 192.168.56.0/24, 192.168.57.0/24, and 192.168.59.0/24 to the routing process
EIGRP 100

In EIGRP 100, distribute only the certain static routes (172.16.20.0/24 172.16.25.0/
24, and 192.168.59.0/24) out of Fast Ethernet 1/0

We could implement this with:

```
ip access-list standard some-static-routes
 permit 172.16.20.0
 permit 172.16.25.0
 permit 172.16.52.0
 permit 192.168.56.0 0.0.1.0
 permit 192.168.59.0
ip access-list standard statics-for-Fast-1-0
 permit 172.16.20.0
 permit 172.16.25.0
 permit 192.168.59.0
router eigrp 100
 redistribute static
 distribute-list some-static-routes out static
 distribute-list statics-for-Fast-1-0 out FastEthernet 1/0
```

Note that every time we add static routes that would be distributed out of Fast-Ethernet 1/0, we have to update two access lists. We can get around this problem by using route maps:

```
ip access-list standard statics-not-for-Fast-1-0
 permit 172.16.52.0
 permit 192.168.56.0 0.0.1.0
ip access-list standard statics-for-Fast-1-0
 permit 172.16.20.0
 permit 172.16.25.0
 permit 192.168.59.0
route-map statics-in-map permit 10
 match ip address statics-not-for-Fast-1-0
route-map statics-in-map permit 20
 match ip address statics-for-Fast-1-0
router eigrp 100
 redistribute static route-map statics-in-map
 distribute-list statics-for-Fast-1-0 out FastEthernet 1/0
```

In this example, route maps make it easier to maintain the router configuration because they let us combine two separate access lists for one policy application.

Route maps also allow us to set different metrics for incoming routes. Let's say we add the following to our policy:

> Set the metric for static routes redistributed through interface fast Ethernet 1/0 to 1, while setting the metric for all other redistributed static routes to 3000

We can implement this new policy addition by changing **static-in-map** to the following map:

```
route-map statics-in-map permit 10
  match ip address statics-not-for-Fast-1-0
  set metric 3000
route-map statics-in-map permit 20
  match ip address statics-for-Fast-1-0
  set metric 1
```

The metric used in EIGRP is set depending on the static route.

Another use of route maps is routing based on the characteristics of incoming packets. Ordinarily, all of the packets coming into a router, regardless of their characteristics, are forwarded according to the route table. Policy routing allows us to route packets differently, depending on some characteristic of incoming packets that we may choose. Consider the router shown in Figure 6-1.

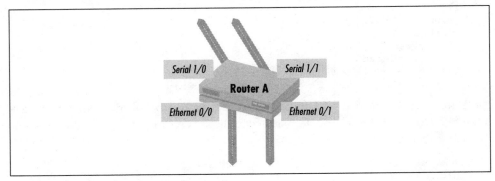

Figure 6-1. A router requiring policy routing

Let's say that we want to implement the following policy:

> All traffic coming in from Ethernet 0/0 should go out of Serial 1/0
>
> All traffic coming in from Ethernet 0/1 should go out of Serial 1/1

This policy cannot be implemented with any of the techniques covered so far. All of the routing done to this point has been based on filtering that's based on the destination address, not the origin. Cisco routers implement the following:

```
interface ethernet 0/0
 ip policy route FROM-ETHERNET-0-0
interface Ethernet0/1
 ip policy route FROM-ETHERET-0-0

route-map FROM-ETHERNET-0-0 permit 10
 match interface 0/0
 set next-hop Serial1/0
route-map FROM-ETHERNET-0-1 permit 10
 match interface Ethernet0/1
 set next-hop Serial1/1
```

In this example, we match the interface that traffic is coming in on using the match interface clause and set the next hop as the interface where we want traffic to go.

We can also use extended access lists as a way to build a policy set for policy routing. This allows us to implement much finer-grained control over how traffic flows. Let's say for the network in Figure 6-1, we have the following policy:

All SSL traffic (port 443) coming into the two Ethernet interfaces will go out of Serial 1/0

All other traffic will go out via Serial 1/1

We implement this policy with the following:

```
interface Ethernet0/0
 ip policy route FROM-ETHERNETS
interface ethernet 0/1
 ip policy route FROM-ETHERNETS

access-list 100 permit tcp any eq 443 any
access-list 100 permit tcp any any eq 443
access-list 101 permit ip any any

route-map FROM-ETHERNETS permit 10
 match ip address 100
 set next-hop Serial 1/0

route-map FROM-ETHERNETS permit 20
 match ip address 101
 set next-hop Serial 1/1
```

The route map FROM-ETHERNETS is applied to all traffic coming from the Ethernet segments. All SSL traffic (having port 443 as either source or destination) is given the next hop of Serial 1/0. All other traffic is sent out of Serial 1/1.

The command *show route-map* shows route maps along with how many packets have matched each clause. As an example, here is the output from a *show route-map* command used in policy routing:

```
Router1>show route-map FROM-ETHERNETS
route-map FROM-ETHERNETS, permit, sequence 10
  Match clauses:
    ip address (access-lists): 100
  Set clauses:
    next-hop Serial 1/0
  Policy routing matches: 823 packets, 426466 bytes
route-map FROM-ETHERNETS, permit, sequence 20
  Match clauses:
    ip address (access-lists): 101
  Set clauses:
    next-hop Serial 1/1
  Policy routing matches: 340 packets, 2123458 bytes
```

Only route maps used for this policy routing produce packet and byte counts. You can employ *show route-map* to show route maps used with routing protocols, but the packet counters do not increment.

BGP

This section shows how to use route maps and implement useful BGP routing policies. First, I use different kinds of match clauses to build policy sets. Then I relate different ways that route maps and other kinds of access lists can be used.

Match clauses in BGP

At the start of this chapter, I went over different kinds of access lists. In this section, I'll show how to use them to build policy sets that are part of match clauses in route maps.

Prefix lists are matched with the following format:

```
match ip address prefix-list {prefix-list name}
```

where **prefix-list name** is the name of the prefix list. Let's say we wanted to set prefixes of 172.28.0.0/16 that are less than or equal to /19 to have a local preference of 110 (we'll talk more about local preference later). We define a route map and prefix list with the following:

```
ip prefix-list prefixes-19-and-shorter seq 5 172.28.0.0/16 le 19

route-map VALID-INCOMING-ROUTES permit 10
  match ip address prefix-list prefixes-19-and-shorter
  set local-preference 110
```

and then apply this route map to a BGP neighbor. The prefix list **prefixes-19-and-shorter** defines a policy set, and in the route map, we take this policy set and apply a local preference of 110 to it.

Similarly, we can do the same with AS-path access lists:

```
as-path access-list 3 permit ^\(65001(_.*)*\).*$
as-path access-list 4 permit ^\(65002(_.*)*\).*$
access-list 3 permit any

route-map INCOMING-ROUTES permit 10
 match as-path 3
 set as-path prepend 65001

route-map INCOMING-ROUTES permit 20
 match as-path 4
 set as-path prepend 65002

route-map INCOMING-ROUTES permit 30
 match ip address 3

router bgp 65000
network 172.28.0.0
neighbor 192.168.30.1 route-map INCOMING-ROUTES in
neighbor 192.168.31.2 route-map INCOMING-ROUTES in
```

AS-path access list 3 builds a policy set of all routes originating from AS 65001. AS path access list 4 matches all routes coming directly from AS 65002. The route map `INCOMING-ROUTES` prepends an extra AS hop from all routes from neighboring AS 65001. It appends AS 65002 to all routes coming from AS 65002. All other routes are left alone. What is the result of this policy when we apply the route map to incoming routes? Routes from AS 65001 and AS 65002 have longer AS paths and are thus less preferred compared to routes from other autonomous systems. All other routes match the standard access list 3 in the last route map entry. Since there is no policy setting in this entry, routes with AS patterns that don't match the AS-path access lists are unaffected. Less traffic will go out through AS 65001 and AS 65002.

If you want to have a default behavior for routes (even if the default behavior is to do nothing), don't forget to put in a route map entry that matches everything. Otherwise, routes that don't match any route map entry are not included when you apply the route map.

To match a community string, use the route map command:

```
match community {community list number} [exact-match]
```

The *community list number* is the number of the community string access list. If a route has a community string that matches the community list (specified by the community list number), then the route map entry takes effect. If the optional keyword **exact-match** is present, the route's communities must exactly match the community list, not just have one community string that matches.

How do you use a community string? One option is to allow downstream autonomous systems to express route preferences. Take the route map:

```
route-map PREFERENCE-BY-COMMUNITY permit 10
 match community 1

set local preference 110
 route map PREFERENCE-BY-COMMUNITY permit 20
 match community 2
set local preference 100

route-map PREFERENCE-BY-COMMUNITY permit 30
 match community 3
 set local preference 90
ip community-list 1 permit 100
ip community-list 2 permit 200
ip community-list 3 permit 300
```

An autonomous system's network administrator who wishes to implement traffic preferences through local preference within an AS with the above route map can do so by setting communities. Local preference is a way of specifying how an AS will treat routes. All routes without an explicit local preference have a local preference of 100. Routes with higher local preferences are preferred over routes with lower local preferences. Some ISPs use this technique to allow multihomed customers to do preferential routing. The ISPs that provide this option apply a similar route map to routing updates from their customers.

Route maps as command qualifiers

Like standard access lists, route maps and AS path access lists can be qualifiers to route statements. Just as some routing protocol commands take an access list as an optional argument, some BGP4 directives take route maps or AS-path access lists as options. Let's look at some of these commands.

The BGP4 command *weight* can take the form:

```
neighbor [IP address] Weight [weight value]
```

weight is similar to administrative distance settings in that it can be used to determine the best path selection within a router. It is different in that the higher weight is preferred. An example use of *weight* is the following:

```
neighbor 192.168.50.3 weight 10
```

But we can specify which routes get that weight with a standard access list as a policy set:

```
access-list 1 permit 192.168.50.0
access-list 1 permit 172.28.0.0

router bgp 65004

 neighbor 192.168.50.1 distribute-list 1 weight 100
```

We can also filter based on an AS-path access list:

```
as-path access-list 1 permit ^65000$
router bgp 65004
 neighbor 192.168.50.1 filter-list 1 weight 100
```

The default path filter is an access list that permits all. By adding AS-path filters, we control the weight that we assign routes based on the routes' AS paths.

The *aggregate-address* command in BGP4 has several ways to use route maps to adjust what routes get aggregated. It has the following options that take a route map as a way of specifying the policy set that aggregation applies to:

- *suppress-map*

- *unsuppress-map*

- *advertise-map*

- *attribute-map*

Let's look at some of these options to see how route maps can be used as command arguments. The *suppress-map* option designates a route map that describes what addresses in an address block to advertise after aggregating. For example, let's aggregate all addresses in block 192.168.32.0 through 192.168.63.0 but continue to advertise address blocks 192.168.40.0 through 192.168.47.0. We would set up the following route map:

```
access-list 2 permit 192.168.40.0 0.0.7.0
route-map SUPPRESS-ADDRESSES permit 10
 match ip address 2
```

This route map is used in the following way:

```
router bgp 65000
 aggregate-address 192.168.32.0 0.0.31.0 suppress-map SUPPRESS-ADDRESSES
```

Unlike some other instances of route maps, this particular use of routes has no policy settings on each entry. In this case, it is used purely to build a policy set of routes that are not to be aggregated.

The *attribute-map* option lets us change the attributes of an aggregated route. For example, the following aggregate address command and route map:

```
route-map AGGREGATE-ATTRIBUTES permit 10
 set metric 10
 set community 701:1
router bgp 65000
 aggregate-address 192.168.32.0 0.0.31.0 attribute-map AGGREGATE-ATTRIBUTES
```

sets a route metric of 10 and adds a community attribute of 701:1 to the route aggregation. In this case, the route-map **AGGREGATE-ATTRIBUTES** has no match clause, meaning all routes match this entry.

"Flapping" networks—networks that appear and disappear—are a threat to routing stability, as large-scale route flapping can slow down routers. Networks that flap can be dampened, i.e., taken out of the routing table until a certain time period. Since this can be a severe penalty, there is a route map argument to the dampening command that allows a network administrator to declare what routes can be dampened. As an example, let's say that all routes tagged with the community string 700 are particularly troublesome routes and deserving of dampening. We would set up the following route map:

```
ip community-list permit 700
 route-map DAMPENED-ADDRESSES permit 10
 match ip community 700
```

and then use the following dampening statement:

```
router bgp 65000
 bgp dampening route-map DAMPENED-ADDRESSES
```

Implementing path preferences

A common application of route maps with BGP is the implementation of traffic preference policies. To implement route preferences in BGP, you first need to understand how BGP selects routes for placement in the routing table. BGP routes carry a set of attributes that are used to make routing decisions. Some of these attributes are changeable, functioning as administrative knobs that allow a network administrator to affect route selection while other attributes cannot be changed. Table 6-3 shows BGP route attributes in order of preference for deciding routes.

Table 6-3. BGP route attributes in order of preference

Attribute	Most preferred	Settable for individual route?	Default (if any)
Prefix length	Longer prefix length (more specific route)	Yes	
Connection to next hop	Do not consider if next hop is not reachable	No	
Synchronization	Do not consider if BGP path is not synchronized and synchronization is enabled	Yes (turn synchro-nization on or off)	Synchronization on
Weight	Higher	Yes	0
Local preference	Higher	Yes	100
Originated by router		Yes (by originat-ing with a **network** state-ment)	
AS path	Shorter	Yes	
Origin code (where route originated)	IGP < EGP < incomplete	No	Depends on origin of route
Multi-Exit Discriminator	Lower	Yes	
Prefer external (EBGP) over internal route (IBGP). Note that routes through confed-erations are consid-ered internal			
Prefer route that goes through closest IGP neighbor		Yes (by manipulat-ing IGP metrics)	

Table 6-3. BGP route attributes in order of preference (continued)

Attribute	Most preferred	Settable for individual route?	Default (if any)
If *maximum-paths* is enabled, install route if the best route and this route are external and from the same neighboring AS number			
If *maximum-paths* is not on, prefer the route with the lowest IP address value for Router ID	Lower	Yes	

When the BGP routing process sees multiple paths to a network, it looks for the most specific route, i.e., the route with the longest prefix. If a routing decision must be made for a destination IP address, the route with the more specific part of a network is used. For example, if BGP needs to decide how to route a packet to 192.168.32.5, and there are two routes that could match, one to 192.168.0.0/16 and another to 192.168.32.0/24, the route to 192.168.32.0/24 is used. If the next hop for a route is not available, the route is not considered. This may seem rather odd, but the next hop in a BGP route may not necessarily be the IP address of the router that sent the update, unlike IGP routing protocols such as RIP. BGP then looks at synchronization to decide whether to consider the route. If synchronization is turned on, and the route is learned via IBGP, the route is not considered if there is no IGP route for the network.

Next, BGP prefers the route with the highest weight. If weights are equal, the router installs the route with the highest local preference. If local preferences are the same, then the route that was originated by the router is used (originated with the network statement). Then, the route with the shortest AS path is chosen. If AS paths are the same, then the route with the lowest *origin code* is used. The origin code declares how the route originated. If a BGP routing process explicitly declares that a network is connected to it with a network statement, the origin is incomplete. If the path is learned via BGP from another AS, the origin code is EGP. If the route is learned via an IGP and redistributed into BGP (inadvisable but possible), the origin is IGP. BGP prefers explicitly declared networks over networks learned via BGP. Routes learned via an IGP are the least preferred.

If two or more routes have the same local preference, and AS paths are identical (not just the same length), then the route with the lowest Multi-Exit Discriminator is chosen. Next, external BGP routes are preferred over internal BGP. Note that routes from peers in a confederation are considered internal BGP routes. Next, the route preferred through the closest neighbor (via IGP metrics) is chosen. If multiple paths are enabled, any route that is external and comes from the same neighboring AS as the best route is installed. The last tiebreaker is the Originating Router ID. If everything is the same, the route with the lowest originator IP address is chosen. This may seem like an odd tiebreaker (what does the order of IP addresses have to do with route selection?), but it is the last-resort rule when a tiebreaker is needed.

It's worth noting network attributes that BGP does not consider. BGP has no notion of using current network conditions of bandwidth, delay, or congestion for making routing decisions. BGP may prefer a route that is more congested, has a smaller bandwidth, or has more latency. Network administrators can manipulate only the settable attributes listed previously to affect routing decisions.

To use these attributes effectively, you have to know to which direction these attributes apply, and the scope that changes to the attributes can propagate. Some of the BGP knobs that you can tune apply only to incoming route updates. Some apply to outgoing route updates, and others apply in both directions. Regarding scope, some changes apply only to the router where the attribute is applied (e.g., weight). Some attribute changes apply only within the local AS, and others apply everywhere. Table 6-4 describes BGP attributes that you can affect and the scope of where those changes take affect.

Table 6-4. Directionality and scope of adjustable BGP attributes

Attributes	Direction of influence	Scope
Weight	Inbound routing updates	Local router
Local preference	Inbound routing updates	Local AS
MED	Inbound and outbound routing updates	Adjacent AS (only within the same AS)
AS-path	Inbound and outbound routing updates	Everywhere
Communities	Inbound and outbound routing updates	Everywhere (although scope can be set)
Originator IP	Outbound routing updates	Everywhere (but often changed downstream)

All of these attributes of a route can be examined with variations of the *show ip bgp* command as shown previously.

The weight attribute

Note that weight is a Cisco proprietary feature of BGP, so you won't find it on other vendors' routers.

For a first example, lets revisit the scenario where an organization prefers to use a line that has a higher bandwidth for Internet access. A diagram of the situation is shown in Figure 6-2.

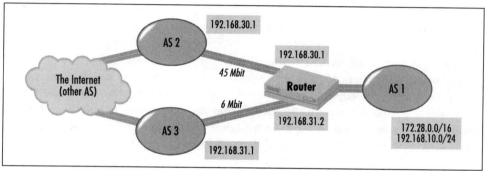

Figure 6-2. Preferring a higher bandwidth line using BGP

The line connecting the organization with AS 1 to AS 2 has a bandwidth 45 Mb. The line between AS 1 and AS 3 has a bandwidth of 6 Mb. Because of this difference, AS 1 wants to implement the following routing policy:

> Traffic to and from networks in AS 3 should go over the 6-Mb line unless the line is down. In that case, AS 3/ AS 1 traffic should use the 45-Mb line.

> All other traffic to and from the Internet should use the 45-Mb line unless the line is down. If the 45-Mb line is down, traffic should go through the 6-Mb line.

This policy lets most Internet traffic use the higher bandwidth link except for traffic between AS 1 and AS 3. This traffic uses the line directly between the two ASes. If a line is down, traffic uses the other line to get in and out of AS 1. AS 1 then gets what seems to be the best possible network performance while having failover if a link goes down.

There are many ways to implement this policy. Let's start by using the weight attribute for incoming route updates. Setting policy for incoming route updates directs traffic going out from AS 1:

```
! define AS path access lists and standard access lists to build policy sets
as-path access-list 5 permit ^3$
access-list 5 permit any
```

```
! build route map
route-map INCOMING-UPDATES-6Mbit-LINE permit 10
 match as-path 5
 set weight 30
route-map INCOMING-UPDATES-6Mbit-LINE permit 20
 match ip address 5
```

The route map `INCOMING-UPDATES-6Mbit-LINE` is used by BGP as follows:

```
router bgp 1
 network 172.28.0.0
 network 192.168.10.0
 !
 neighbor 192.168.30.1 remote-as 2
 neighbor 192.168.30.1 weight 20
 !
 neighbor 192.168.31.1 remote-as 3
 neighbor 192.168.31.1 route-map INCOMING-UPDATES-6Mbit-LINE in
```

In this example, I implement a route map entry that creates a policy set of all routes originating from AS 3. The AS-path access list 5 includes all these routes, which are given a weight of 30. All other routes from AS 3 do not get a weight (their default weight is 0). All the routes from AS 2 are given a weight of 20. As a result, all the routes from AS 2 have a higher weight except for those originating from AS 3. You can see the results of this policy using the *show ip bgp* command:

```
Router1# show ip bgp
BGP table version is 730292, local router ID is 192.168.31.2
Status codes: s suppressed, d damped, h history, * valid, > best, i - internal
Origin codes: i - IGP, e - EGP, ? - incomplete

    Network          Next Hop         Metric LocPrf Weight Path
*> 10.0.0.0/8       192.168.30.1                       20   2 5 i
*                   192.168.31.1                        0   3 5 i
*> 172.23.0.0/16 192.168.30.1                          20   2 i
*                   192.168.31.1                        0   3 2 i
*  172.24.0.0/16 192.168.30.1                          20   2 3 i
*>                  192.168.31.1                        30   3 i
*> 172.28.0.0/16 192.168.10.1            32768              i
*> 192.168.10/24 192.168.10.1            32768              i
```

Routes from AS 2 to networks like 10.0.0.0/8 and 172.23.0.0/16 that do not originate in AS 3 get a weight of 20. The same routes from AS 3 get a weight of 0. Thus traffic to 10.0.0.0/8 and 172.23.0.0/16 uses the 45-Mb link. Since network 172.24.0.0/16 originates in AS 3, the route for it from AS 3 gets a weight of 30, while the route from AS 2 gets a weight of 20. Thus traffic for network 172.24.0.0 would use the 6-Mb line.

AS-path prepending

We now have made outgoing traffic conform to our policy. What about incoming traffic? To influence inbound traffic we must make routes advertised out through

AS 2 look better than those through 3 but not bad enough to make traffic from 2 to 1 go via 3. Can we use weight here? Weight will not work because it only works on incoming routes and does not propagate past a single router. One way for AS 1 to influence incoming traffic is to add AS path hops to the less preferred route. The following route map implements this extra hop by adding a hop to the AS path:

```
! define route map
route-map TO-AS-3 permit 10
set as-path prepend 1
! router
router bgp 1
 network 172.28.0.0
 network 192.168.10.0
!
 neighbor 192.168.30.1 remote-as 2
 neighbor 192.168.30.1 weight 30
!
 neighbor 192.168.31.1 remote-as 3
 neighbor 192.168.31.1 route-map INCOMING-UPDATES-6Mbit-LINE in
 neighbor 192.168.31.1 route-map TO-AS-3 out
```

The AS paths that routers on the Internet see to AS 1 networks via AS 2 should be:

```
2 1
```

The path to AS 1 via AS 3 is:

```
3 1 1
```

From the Internet, the path through 2 is preferred, assuming that other autonomous systems apply no policies of their own. Thus the 45-Mb line is used for traffic coming in from the Internet to AS 1's networks, 172.28.0.0/16 and 192.168.10.0/24. Traffic from AS 3 uses the 6-Mb line since AS 3 sees the following path to 1 from the 6-Mb line:

```
1 1
```

The other path to AS 1's networks through AS 2 looks like this:

```
[other AS] 2 1
```

AS 3 should then send traffic to networks 172.28.0.0/24 and 192.168.10.0/24 via the direct 6-Mb line.

Let's say that the network topology we have been assuming is actually slightly different, such as in Figure 6-3. Instead of connecting to AS 3 and AS 2 through a single router, the paths to AS 2 and AS 3 go through a separate router.

Using weight to bias incoming routes doesn't work for setting preferences among incoming route updates. This is because the weight attribute does not propagate beyond the router where the weights are set. To deal with this situation, we have to find a BGP route attribute that can propagate to incoming routes and manipulate it

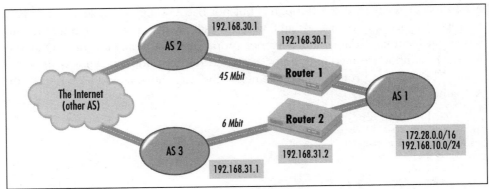

Figure 6-3. AS 1 connects to AS 2 and AS 3 through two routers (a variation of Figure 6-2)

appropriately. From Table 6-3, we can see that local preference affects incoming routes across an AS. We configure the following on Router 2:

```
! define AS path access lists and standard access lists to build policy sets
as-path access-list 5 permit ^3$
access-list 5 permit any
! build route map
route-map INCOMING-UPDATES-6Mbit-LINE permit 10
  match as-path 5
  set local-preference 100
route-map INCOMING-UPDATES-6Mbit-LINE permit 20
  match ip address 5
  set local-preference 80
```

Routes that live in AS 3 have a local preference of 100, but all other routes from AS 3 have a local preference of 80. Thus, traffic bound for AS 3 goes there directly through the 6-Mb line while all other traffic goes out the 45-Mb line. If the 45-Mb line goes down, traffic to the Internet will fail through the 6-Mb link.

AS path prepending can also be used in a similar way to manipulate traffic bound for the Internet. The following route map applied on Router 2 to the peering session with AS 3 can have the same effect:

```
! define AS path access lists and standard access lists to build policy sets
as-path access-list 5 permit ^3$
access-list 5 permit any
! build route map
route-map INCOMING-UPDATES-6Mbit-LINE permit 10
match as-path 5
route-map INCOMING-UPDATES-6Mbit-LINE permit 20
match ip address 5
set as-path prepend 3
```

This route map adds an extra AS hop to all routes coming in from AS 3 except for those routes originating in AS 3. Since AS-path changes propagate throughout an AS and even beyond it, this will work.

Communities

Communities can be another way to set traffic preferences. Some ISPs use community string settings in routes as a way to allow their customers to set routing. Let's say that the ISP running AS 3 has a policy that all routes received from its customers with community string 3:1 will have one AS hop of 3 prepended to the routes' AS path when the routes are advertised to the rest of the Internet. This would make traffic to the routes with the string stay within AS 3 (since they are only one hop away) but would make routes through AS 3 less preferred to the rest of the Internet. Customers of the ISP would not see the extra hop, only the ISP's peers and other autonomous systems getting routes from them. Let's also say that the ISP running AS 3 tags all of the routes originating from AS 3 and its directly connected customers with the community string 3:1000. This way, a multihomed customer of the 3 ISP, like AS 1, can know who is connected to 3, a few short hops away. With these community string settings, the following route maps applied to the AS 1 border routers could achieve the policy results we have been seeking:

```
! define AS path access lists and standard access lists to build policy sets
ip community-list 5 permit 3:1000
access-list 5 permit any
! build route map
route-map INCOMING-UPDATES-6Mbit-LINE permit 10
 match community 5
 set local-preference 100
route-map INCOMING-UPDATES-6Mbit-LINE permit 20
 match ip address 5
 set local-preference 80
! outgoing route map
route-map TO-AS-3 permit 10
 set community 3:1
```

AS 3 customers can connect directly to AS 1 using the 6-Mb line and not the longer path through AS 2.

There are a few things you need to know about using communities. If you are going to pass on communities, you need to use a BGP router command called *send-community*. Otherwise, your communities will not be passed on to neighboring ASes. Also, if you use the new community string format, you need to explicitly enable its use with the *ip bgp-community new-format* configuration command. In this example, we would use the BGP configuration command:

```
ip bgp-community new-format
router bgp 1
 network 172.28.0.0
 network 192.168.10.0
 neighbor 192.168.30.1 remote-as 2
!
 neighbor 192.168.31.1 remote-as 3
!
 neighbor 192.168.31.1 route-map INCOMING-UPDATES-6Mbit-LINE in
```

```
neighbor 192.168.31.1 route-map TO-AS-3 out
neighbor 192.168.31.1 send-community
```

Also, note that the *set community* command replaces whatever communities a route may have had previously. If you want to add a community string to those already in a route, use the keyword `additive` following the community string. Typically, a non-ISP organization does not need this setting, but if your organization has to transit another organization's traffic (and communities), this setting may be necessary.

Multi-Exit Discriminators

Another common scenario with multihomed organizations is having two or more lines to the Internet through the same ISP. The organization faces the same choices as in the previous set of examples: which lines to use for which networks. Having connections to the same ISP, however, allows for different choices in setting BGP metrics. A typical situation looks like the network in the Figure 6-4.

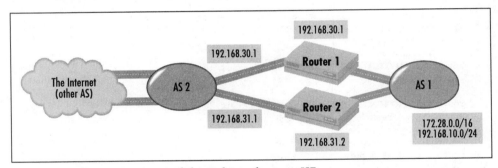

Figure 6-4. An organization multihomed into the same ISP

AS 1 connects to the Internet through AS 2 via two different lines. As an example policy, let's say the following:

Traffic for network 172.28.0.0/16 should use the lines between Router 1 and AS 2

Traffic for network 192.168.10.0/24 should use the line between Router 2 and AS 2

If one of these lines is down, then traffic should flow across the other line

There are a number of ways to implement this policy. We can use AS path preferences or, if available, communities. With AS path preferences, the route maps on the routers would be:

```
! Router 1 route map
access-list 1 permit 172.28.0.0
access-list 2 permit 192.168.10.0
!
route-map ROUTES-OUT permit 10
 match ip address 1
route-map ROUTES-OUT permit 20
 match ip address 2
```

```
    set as-path prepend 1
  !
 router bgp 1
  network 172.28.0.0
  network 192.168.10.0
  neighbor 192.168.30.1 remote-as 2
  neighbor 192.168.30.1 route-map ROUTES-OUT out
 !
 ! Router 2 route map
 access-list 1 permit 172.28.0.0
 access-list 2 permit 192.168.10.0
 !
 route-map ROUTES-OUT permit 10
 match ip address 2
 route-map ROUTES-OUT permit 20
 match ip address 1
 set as-path prepend 1
 !
 router bgp 1
  network 172.28.0.0
  network 192.168.10.0
  neighbor 192.168.30.1 remote-as 2
  neighbor 192.168.30.1 route-map ROUTES-OUT out
```

These route maps make the backup path to AS 2 less preferred with an additional AS hop. AS path prepending is not the only way to implement this policy. Since AS 1 connects to the Internet via the same AS for both links, it can use the *Multi-Exit Discriminator* (MED) metric to let AS 2 know which link is preferred for which network. The MED functions pretty much like its name; if there are multiple exits out of an AS to a network, it lets an AS discriminate between which exit is preferred. Like a routing metric, the lower MED is preferred. If we use MEDs to implement our policy, the route maps are as follows:

```
 ! Router 1 route map
 access-list 1 permit 172.28.0.0
 access-list 2 permit 192.168.10.0
 !
 route-map ROUTES-OUT permit 10
  match ip address 1
  set metric 10
 route-map ROUTES-OUT permit 20
  match ip address 2
  set metric 20
 !
 ! Router 2 route map
 access-list 1 permit 172.28.0.0
 access-list 2 permit 192.168.10.0
 !
 route-map ROUTES-OUT permit 10
  match ip address 2
  set metric 10
 route-map ROUTES-OUT permit 20
  match ip address 1
  set metric 20
```

In the two route maps, the preferred route through the link has a metric of 10, and the route that uses the link as backup has a metric of 20. The router at 192.168.30.1 sees the following in its BGP table:

```
Router1# show ip bgp regex ^1_
BGP table version is 7022, local router ID is 192.168.30.1
Status codes: s suppressed, d damped, h history, * valid, > best, i - internal

Origin codes: i - IGP, e - EGP, ? - incomplete

     Network           Next Hop         Metric LocPrf Weight Path
*>  172.28.0.0         192.198.30.2       10            0 1 i
i                      192.198.31.2       20            0 1 i
*   192.168.10.0       192.168.30.2       20            0 1 i
i>                     192.168.31.2       10            0 1 i
```

You can see that traffic to network 172.28.0.0/24 is preferred out through the line to Router 1 because of its lower metric. The router at 192.168.31.1 has the following in its table:

```
Router1# show ip bgp regex ^1_
BGP table version is 70222, local router ID is 192.168.31.1
Status codes: s suppressed, d damped, h history, * valid, > best, i - internal

Origin codes: i - IGP, e - EGP, ? - incomplete

     Network           Next Hop         Metric LocPrf Weight Path
*  172.28.0.0          192.198.30.2       10            0 1 i
i>                     192.198.31.2       20            0 1 i
*> 192.168.10.0        192.168.30.2       20            0 1 i
i                      192.168.31.2       10            0 1 i
```

If Router 1 and Router 2 learn the paths to networks 172.28.0.0/16 and 192.168.10.0/24 via an IGP, there is a way to use a route map to set the MED to the value of the IGP metric. Using an IGP metric as an MED sends traffic to the link closest to that network (as determined by the IGP metric value). The following implementation of our routing policy uses this technique, assuming that 172.28.0.0/16 is closer to Router 1 than Router 2 and 192.168.10.0/24 is closer to Router 2 than Router 1:

```
access-list 1 permit 172.28.0.0
access-list 1 permit 192.168.10.0
route-map ROUTES-OUT permit 10
 match ip address 1
 set metric internal
```

Using MEDs in this way simplifies the route map and allows the same route map to be used on both routers. This technique can be very useful when you have many connections to another AS and wish to have a simpler and standard route map for outbound route advertisements. If the internal topology of AS 1 changed and a network became closer (in terms of route metrics) to a particular gateway, the MED automatically reflects that and routing changes appropriately.

Peer groups

Each BGP neighbor typically requires at least one `neighbor` statement for a remote AS. When you add route map, path, and prefix filters, each neighbor may require three or more `neighbor` statements. To save time and make it easier to set policies on groups of neighbors, Cisco routers have an access list type of structure called *peer group*. You can define BGP neighbors as being members of a peer group, and then apply policy settings to that peer group (thus applying the settings to all of the neighbors). For example, let's say we wish to apply identical policies to BGP neighbors 172.28.3.5, 172.28.3.6, and 172.28.3.7, which are all in AS 65001. Instead of typing the same policy settings again and again for each neighbor, peer groups allow us do use the following:

```
router bgp 65000
  neighbor neighbors-group1 remote-as 65001
  neighbor neighbors-group1 route-map ROUTES-OUT-MAP out
  neighbor neighbors-group1 route-map ROUTES-IN-MAP in
  neighbor neighbors-group1 filter-list 1 in
  neighbor neighbors-group1 prefix-list nets-in in
  neighbor neighbors-group1 prefix-list nets-out out
  neighbor 172.28.3.5 peer-group neighbors-group1
  neighbor 172.28.3.6 peer-group neighbors-group1
  neighbor 172.28.3.7 peer-group neighbors-group1
```

This configuration saves 18 `neighbor` statements by applying policy to the peer group `neighbors-group1`. It also makes it easy to add definitions for a new neighbor with the same policy or change a policy setting for all of the neighbors in a peer group.

Note that you can use peer groups for just the settings that are identical. If in our previous example, all the neighbors are in different AS, we can still use peer groups to save statements with the following configuration:

```
router bgp 65000
  neighbor neighbors-group1 route-map ROUTES-OUT-MAP out
  neighbor neighbors-group1 route-map ROUTES-IN-MAP in
  neighbor neighbors-group1 filter-list 1 in
  neighbor neighbors-group1 prefix-list nets-in in
  neighbor neighbors-group1 prefix-list nets-out out
  neighbor 172.28.3.5 peer-group neighbors-group1
  neighbor 172.28.3.6 peer-group neighbors-group1
  neighbor 172.28.3.7 peer-group neighbors-group1
  neighbor 172.28.3.5 remote-as 65001
  neighbor 172.28.3.6 remote-as 65002
  neighbor 172.28.3.7 remote-as 65003
```

Each of the neighbors is in a different AS, but we still can use a peer group for all of the other settings, saving 15 `neighbor` statements.

Propagating route map changes

Once you have made changes in a route map, the changes do not take place until you force your BGP process (or your neighbor's BGP process) to recognize the changes. To do that, you need to use the *clear ip bgp* command. This command clears all of the BGP learned routes from the routing table, reads in all the routes from designated peers, and sends out any routes that need to be sent to those peers. When routes are read in or sent out, they are processed through any route map or AS-path access lists you may have modified. The command *clear ip bgp ** clears all the BGP sessions with all a router's BGP peers. You can reset the session with a specific peer by using an IP address instead an asterisk. For example, *clear ip bgp 192.168.72.3* clears the BGP session with peer 192.168.72.3.

Resetting BGP sessions can have a large impact on CPU utilization, especially if you are pulling in the full routing tables from the Internet or have many peers. To minimize this impact, I suggest that you clear BGP sessions one peer at a time. This will minimize the number of routes dropped during any one reset. To reduce impact even further, use the soft reconfiguration settings. You first need to configure each neighbor to use soft reconfiguration in the direction of the routing updates you want. For example, let's configure soft reconfiguration for both inbound and outbound routing updates and have a route map ROUTES-IN for inbound processing:

```
! route map in
route-map ROUTES-IN permit 10
 set local-preference 100
! route map out
access-list 1 permit any
route-map ROUTES-OUT permit 10
 match ip address 1
!
router bgp 1
 network 172.28.0.0
 network 192.168.10.0
 neighbor 192.168.30.1 remote-as 2
 neighbor 192.168.30.1 route-map ROUTES-IN in
 neighbor 192.168.30.1 route-map ROUTES-OUT out
 neighbor 192.168.30.1 soft-reconfiguration in
 neighbor 192.168.30.1 soft-reconfiguration out
```

Once this is set up, you can propagate policy changes with the *clear ip bgp soft* command. Note that route maps ROUTES-IN and ROUTES-OUT don't really do anything, since `local-preference` already has a default of 100. If we change ROUTES-IN, we can affect all incoming routes (and incoming routes only) by resetting the BGP session with *clear ip bgp 192.168.30.1 soft in*. Likewise, if we change ROUTES-OUT, we can affect only outgoing routes with *clear ip bgp 192.168.30.1 soft out*.

Debugging route maps and BGP

Debugging route maps is very similar to debugging access lists for routing policies since both deal with manipulating routes. For the most part, the same techniques I covered with routing access lists can be used to find problems with route maps. There are, however, some problems and commands unique to working with route maps, and I discuss these in this section.

First of all, you need to know the most convenient way to see the contents of route maps and AS-path access lists. While showing the running configuration shows you all your route maps, this may be time-consuming if you have a long configuration. The *show route-map* command prints out all your route maps. When followed by a route map name, a specific route map is displayed. Recall the route map I created called ROUTES-OUT:

```
route-map ROUTES-OUT permit 10
 match ip address 1
 set metric 10
route-map ROUTES-OUT permit 20
 match ip address 2
 set metric 20
```

The *show route-map* output of this route map looks like this:

```
Router1>show route-map ROUTES-OUT
route-map ROUTES-OUT, permit, sequence 10
  Match clauses:
    ip address (access-lists): 1
  Set clauses:
    Metric 10
  Policy routing matches: 0 packets, 0 bytes
route-map ROUTES-OUT, permit, sequence 20
  Match clauses:
    ip address (access-lists): 2
  Set clauses:
    Metric 20
  Policy routing matches: 0 packets, 0 bytes
```

The output divides each route map entry into match and set clauses. The `policy route matches` should be ignored when looking at route maps for BGP.

AS-path access lists are treated similarly to access lists. The *show ip as-path* command, followed by an optional access list number, displays AS-path access lists. The AS-path access list below:

```
as-path access-list 5 permit ^3$
```

appears as:

```
Router1>show ip as-path 5
AS path access list 5
    permit ^3$
```

One problem you may encounter is that despite extensive work on your route maps and associated access lists, the routing policy you have been trying to change may not be any different than when you started. The first reason to consider is that you may have forgotten to force your peers to recognize the change, either through a soft reconfiguration or a hard reset. A good way to check this is with the *show ip bgp* command. Output from this command shows a version ID for BGP:

```
Router1# show ip bgp
BGP table version is 23029, local router ID is 192.168.18.100
Status codes: s suppressed, d damped, h history, * valid, > best, i - internal
Origin codes: i - IGP, e - EGP, ? - incomplete
```

The BGP table version should increase after a change. Another way to check is with the *show ip bgp summary* command. This command will show you how long each BGP session for each of a router's peers has been up, and this information tells you the last time each session was reset or how long it has been down:

```
Router1# show ip bgp summary
BGP table version is 10302748, main routing table version 1030748
61505 network entries (182249/244040 paths) using 14333788 bytes of memory
25192 BGP path attribute entries using 2952896 bytes of memory
12170 BGP route-map cache entries using 194720 bytes of memory
0 BGP filter-list cache entries using 0 bytes of memory

Neighbor        V    AS MsgRcvd MsgSent   TblVer  InQ OutQ Up/Down  State
192.168.30.1    4     2 2713633  103161  1030743    0    0 2w2d
192.168.31.1    4     3  123449  103186  1030743    0    0 2w2d
```

In this example, you can see that this router connects to AS 2 and AS 3, and that each BGP connection has been running for more than two weeks. This is a better way to see if a reset has occurred.

The nature of the BGP route selection process creates a whole new set of ways to make a mistake. Often a route map change does not change actual policy because another route attribute was set that takes precedence over the changes you made. As an example, let's revisit the network in Figure 6-2. Let's say we want the 6-Mb line to be used only for backup. To affect the policy, we use the following:

```
! define AS path access lists and standard access lists to build policy sets
as-path access-list 5 permit^3$
access-list 5 permit any
!
! build route map
route-map INCOMING-UPDATES-6Mbit-LINE permit 10
 match ip address 5
 set as-path prepend 3 3
!
! define route map
route-map TO-AS-3 permit 10
 set as-path prepend 1 1
```

```
!
router bgp 1
 network 172.28.0.0
 network 192.168.10.0
 neighbor 192.168.30.1 remote-as 2
!
 neighbor 192.168.31.1 remote-as 3
 neighbor 192.168.31.1 route-map INCOMING-UPDATES-6Mbit-LINE in
 neighbor 192.168.31.1 route-map TO-AS-3 out
 neighbor 192.168.31.1 weight 15
```

AS-path prepending is used as a way to make the path through the 6-Mb line appear less preferred. Despite the route maps, however, traffic will still go out through 6-Mb line. Why? The path through the 192.168.31.1 has a higher weight than the other path through 192.168.30.1. Weight takes precedence over AS hops, and the BGP router configuration line that sets the weight needs to be deleted in order for the intended policy to work.

The directionality and scope of attribute changes is another potential problem. We may try to implement our previous policy using local preferences as shown:

```
! define AS path access lists and standard access lists to build policy sets
access-list 5 permit any
! build route map
route-map INCOMING-UPDATES-6Mbit-LINE permit 10
 match ip address 5
 set local-preference 80
! define route map
route-map TO-AS-3 permit 10
 set local-preference 80
!
router bgp 1
 network 172.28.0.0
 network 192.168.10.0
 neighbor 192.168.30.1 remote-as 2
    neighbor 192.168.31.1 remote-as 3
 neighbor 192.168.31.1 route-map INCOMING-UPDATES-6Mbit-LINE in
 neighbor 192.168.31.1 route-map TO-AS-3 out
```

While traffic does not go out of the 6-Mb line from AS 1, it still uses the 6-Mb line to AS 1. The route map TO-AS-3 does not work because local preference applies only to incoming routes. AS path prepending or communities (if supported by AS 3) are the only solutions for the route map TO-AS-3.

Another key attribute to look out for is prefix length. Remember that BGP uses the most specific route (longest prefix) to make a routing decision. Let's say that we had the following configuration for Router 1 for the network in Figure 6-4:

```
! Router 1 route map
access-list 1 permit 172.28.0.0
access-list 2 permit any
access-list 3 permit 172.28.35.0
```

```
!
route-map ROUTES-OUT permit 10
 match ip address 1
 set metric 10
route-map ROUTES-OUT permit 20
 match ip address 2
 set metric 20
!
route-map SUPPRESS-172-28 permit 10
 match ip addess 3
! bgp
router bgp 1
 network 172.28.10.0
 network 172.28.11.0
 network 172.28.23.0
 network 172.28.24.0
 network 172.28.25.0
 network 172.28.35.0
 network 12.28.36.0
 aggregate-address 172.28.0.0 255.255.0.0 suppress-map SUPPRESS-172-28
 network 192.168.10.0
 neighbor 192.168.30.1 remote-as 2
 neighbor 192.168.30.1 route-map ROUTES-OUT out
```

Recall that we want to route traffic for 172.28.0.0 through AS 2 and network 192.
168.10.0 through AS 3. We use only a few networks in network 172.28.0.0/16, but
we aggregate all of them together as a /16 network. The routing policy we intend
will not work, however, for traffic going to 172.28.35.0/24. Since we suppressed
aggregation for this part of 172.28.0.0/16, it is treated differently from the 172.28.0.
0/16 aggregate. Removing the **suppress-map** clause or adding the access list
entry:

```
access-list 1 permit 172.28.35.0
```

fixes the problem. You might wonder how such a **suppress-map** got left on. At
one point, a network administrator may have had a separate routing policy for that
route map and forgot to take it off at one point. Outdated configurations can be
another source of problems, especially if you have to change policies quickly and
often.

Many ISPs have a maximum length prefix length for a given IP address range that
they accept. ISPs that you purchase transit from are usually more generous in
terms of allowing a longer prefix length. If you are advertising networks to multiple ISPs outside of the traditional class B and class C spaces, I suggest that you
advertise routes to be a /19 or shorter. Otherwise you may find that some ISPs
reject routes with longer prefixes. This can result in unpredictable behavior, such
as some sites on the Internet being unreachable from particular networks while
others are reachable.

In this chapter:
- *A WAN case study*
- *A firewall case study*
- *An Internet routing case study*

7

Case Studies

In this chapter, I present three case studies that use access lists in common scenarios. These case studies show how different types of access lists can be used together in situations you may encounter. They also illustrate how the three key concerns we talked about—security, robustness, and business policy—are implemented in realistic situations. The first example deals with a single organization's intranet connected by a wide area network (WAN). I show how to use access lists to implement a secure and stable WAN. The second example goes over a common firewall configuration called the screened subnet architecture. Here, I use access lists to secure an organization's perimeter. The final case study covers how an organization connects to the Internet. This example shows how to use access lists to implement route preferences while still maintaining security.

A WAN case study

In this case study, we'll see how to use access lists in routers that make up a wide area network in the network shown in Figure 7-1. Like many large organizations, different departments control and manage different parts of this network. Site 1's network is run by a different organization from Site 2, neither of which run Site 3's network. Each of these three sites have separate address spaces, and each site runs a different routing protocol. The routers that connect the three sites, Routers A through F, are run by a separate organization, which uses yet another routing protocol. For our case study, I show the configurations of each of the WAN routers.

A few other facts are relevant to this example. Each WAN router connects to two different site networks. Routers A, C, and E use 2 in the last octet of each of these two networks. For example, Router A has interfaces 172.20.0.2 and 172.20.1.2.

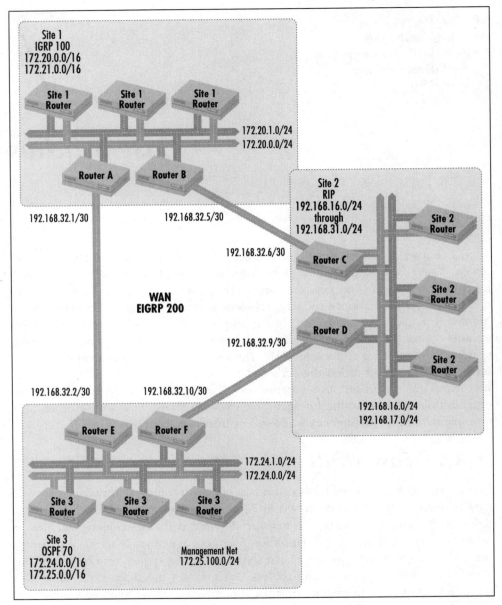

Figure 7-1. Network for WAN case study

Similarly, Routers B, D, and F have 3 in the last octet. As an example, Router B has interfaces 172.20.0.3 and 172.20.1.3. The WAN network administrators manage the WAN from hosts in network 172.25.100.0/24.

Security concerns

The WAN administrators do not allow local site network administrators to log in, so Telnet access needs to be limited to their administrative segment. We will also allow logins from the neighboring WAN router via the site network. This is useful for reaching WAN routers during cases when routing protocols are broken. In case the sites do manage to log on to a WAN router, we limit outgoing Telnet access to prevent the router from being used to stage attacks. To provide some visibility to the site network administrators, we allow read-only SNMP access to the sites, but read and write SNMP access is available only to the WAN administrative segment. Another security concern is that we do not want any spoofing of IP addresses. One site should not be able to mount attacks based on spoofing. A final concern is that we wish to harden our routers against attack by eliminating vulnerable services on them.

Robustness concerns

In a network environment like this, WAN administrators need to make sure that bad addressing information is not sent into the sites. In addition, WAN routers must not accept routes for inappropriate networks from their sites. Since the sites are stub networks, they only need to advertise their own network. Also, the WAN routers should be the only source of EIGRP 200 routing information from the local network.

Business concerns

In this organization's network, critical operations go on between Sites 2 and 3 and also between Sites 1 and 3. The link between Sites 2 and 3 is not used for failover if the link between Sites 1 and 2 goes down. If this link does go down, a business decision has been made that loss of connectivity between Sites 1 and 2 is less important than the application performance obtained by having bandwidth dedicated between 2 and 3. The organization's management has decided that the link between Sites 2 and 3 can be used, however, if the link between Sites 1 and 3 goes down, since that traffic is also deemed critical.

Site 1 router configurations

Here are the relevant parts of the configuration for Router A:

```
! limit points of vulnerability on router
no service tcp-small-servers
no service udp-small-servers
no service finger
!
ip subnet zero
```

```
! interfaces definitions
interface Ethernet0
 description  site 1 LAN interface
 ip address 172.20.0.2 255.255.255.0
 ip access-group 100 in
interface Ethernet1
 description  site 1 LAN interface
 ip address 172.20.1.2 255.255.255.0
 ip access-group 100 in
interface Serial 0
 description  serial interface to WAN
 ip address 192.168.32.1 255.255.255.252
 ip access-group 101 out
 ip access-group 102 in
! routing processes
router igrp 100
 network 172.20.0.0
 distribute-list 3 in Ethernet 0
 distribute-list 3 in Ethernet 1
 redistribute eigrp 200
!
router eigrp 200
 network 192.168.32.0 mask 255.255.255.248
 network 172.20.0.0
 redistribute igrp 100
 distance 90 192.168.32.2
 distance 90 172.20.0.3 0.0.1.0
 distance 255
! telnet access from management segment
access-list 1 permit 172.25.100.0 0.0.0.255
! telnet access from other WAN routers serial interfaces
access-list 1 permit 192.168.32.0 0.0.0.7
access-list 1 permit 192.168.32.8 0.0.0.3
! telnet access from other WAN routers Ethernet interfaces
access-list 1 permit 172.20.0.2 0.1.1.1
access-list 1 permt 172.24.0.2 0.1.1.1
! telnet access out on list 2 - limit to WAN routers
access-list 2 permit 172.20.0.2 0.1.1.1
access-list 2 permit 192.168.32.0 0.0.0.7
access-list 2 permit 192.168.32.8 0.0.0.3
! access-list for route distribution
access-list 3 permit 172.20.0.0 0.1.0.0
! SNMP access lists
! read write access for management segment
access-list 4 permit 172.25.100.0 0.0.0.255
! read only access for local site
access-list 5 permit 172.20.0.0 0.1.255.255
! limit incoming traffic to traffic from site
access-list 100 permit ip 172.20.0.0 0.1.255.255 any
! clobber traffic between site 1 and 2 on serial link
access-list 101 deny ip 172.20.0.0 0.1.255.255 192.168.16.0 0.0.15.255
access-list 101 permit ip any any
access-list 102 deny ip 192.168.16.0 0.0.15.255 172.20.0.0 0.1.255.255
access-list 102 permit ip any any
```

```
!
! SNMP access declarations
snmp community netman17225 rw 4
snmp community 172.20public ro 5
! line definitions
line vty 0 4
 access-class 1 in
 access-class 2 out
```

For security, we limit incoming Telnet sessions to the WAN routers and the management segment, 172.20.100.0/24 through access list 1. Outgoing Telnet is limited to the WAN routers with access list 2. If a WAN router login password is compromised, that router cannot be used to stage attacks into the sites. Services on the router are limited with the *no service* command. Access lists 4 and 5 limit SNMP access into the routers. To prevent spoofing attacks from one site to another, access list 100 limits packets only from Site 1 addresses to be distributed to the rest of organization.

For robustness, routes coming in from the site are filtered through access list 3, allowing on-the-site networks in. Also, we only listen to EIGRP 200 routing updates from the neighboring WAN routers. This policy is implemented with distance statements that set all routing updates from the WAN routers to distance 90 and set routing updates from all other routes to distance 255. To implement our business policy, we stop packets from Site 1 from going to Site 2 via Site 3. Note that this can be done in a number of places, but filtering the packets close to their source reduces the total amount of traffic on the WAN.

Router B has a similar configuration, differing only in the interface addresses:

```
! limit points of vulnerability on router
no service tcp-small-servers
no service udp-small-servers
no service finger
!
ip subnet zero
! interfaces definitions
interface Ethernet0
 description  site 1 LAN interface
 ip address 172.20.0.3 255.255.255.0
 ip access group 100 in
interface Ethernet1
 description  site 1 LAN interface
 ip address 172.20.1.3 255.255.255.0
 ip access-group 100 in
interface Serial 0
 ip address 192.168.32.5 255.255.255.252
 description  serial interface to WAN
! routing processes
router igrp 100
 network 172.20.0.0
 distribute-list 3 in Ethernet0
```

```
 distribute-list 3 in Ethernet1
 redistribute eigrp 200
!
router eigrp 200
 network 192.168.32.4 mask 255.255.255.252
 network 172.20.0.0
 redistribute igrp 100
 distance 90 192.168.32.6
 distance 90 172.20.0.2 0.0.1.0
 distance 255
! telnet access from management segment
access-list 1 permit 172.25.100.0 0.0.0.255
! telnet access from other WAN routers serial interfaces
access-list 1 permit 192.168.32.0 0.0.0.7
access-list 1 permit 192.168.32.8 0.0.0.3
! telnet access from other WAN routers Ethernet interfaces
access-list 1 permit 172.20.0.2 0.1.1.1
access-list 1 permt 172.24.0.2 0.1.1.1
! telnet access out on list 2 - limit to WAN routers
access-list 2 permit 172.20.0.2 0.1.1.1
access-list 2 permit 192.168.32.0 0.0.0.7
access-list 2 permit 192.168.32.8 0.0.0.3
! access-list for route distribution
access-list 3 permit 172.20.0.0 0.1.0.0
! SNMP access lists
! read write access for management segment
access-list 4 permit 172.25.100.0 0.0.0.255
! read only access for local site
access-list 5 permit 172.20.0.0 0.1.255.255
! limit incoming traffic to traffic from site
access-list 100 permit ip 172.20.0.0 0.1.255.255 any
!
! SNMP access declarations
snmp community netman17225 rw 4
snmp community 172.20public ro 5
! line definitions
line vty 0 4
 access-class 1 in
 access-class 2 out
```

Site 2 router configurations

Router C has a configuration similar to Routers A and B. It differs in the networks
filtered, interface numbers, and routing protocols used:

```
! limit points of vulnerability on router
no service tcp-small-servers
no service udp-small-servers
no service finger
!
ip subnet zero
! interfaces definitions
interface Ethernet0
 description  site 2 LAN interface
```

```
   ip address 192.168.16.3 255.255.255.0
   ip access-group 100 in
 interface Ethernet1
  description  site 2 LAN interface
  ip address 192.168.17.3 255.255.255.0
  ip access-group 100 in
 interface Serial 0
  description  serial interface to WAN
  ip address 192.168.32.6 255.255.255.252
 ! routing processes
router rip
 network 192.168.16.0
 network 192.168.17.0
 distribute-list 3 in Ethernet 0
 distribute-list 3 in Ethernet 1
 redistribute eigrp 200
 !
router eigrp 200
 network 192.168.16.0
 network 192.168.17.0
 network 192.168.32.4 mask 255.255.255.252
 distance 90 192.168.32.5
 distance 90 192.168.16.3 0.0.1.0
 distance 255
redistribute rip
! telnet access from management segment
access-list 1 permit 172.25.100.0 0.0.0.255
! telnet access from other WAN routers serial interfaces
access-list 1 permit 192.168.32.0 0.0.0.7
access-list 1 permit 192.168.32.8 0.0.0.3
! telnet access from other WAN routers Ethernet interfaces
access-list 1 permit 172.20.0.2 0.1.1.1
access-list 1 permt 172.24.0.2 0.1.1.1
! telnet access out on list 2 - limit to WAN routers
access-list 2 permit 192.168.16.0 0.0.1.1
access-list 2 permit 192.168.32.0 0.0.0.7
access-list 2 permit 192.168.32.8 0.0.0.3
! access-list for route distribution
access-list 3 permit 192.168.16.0 0.0.15.0
! SNMP access lists
! read write access for management segment
access-list 4 permit 172.25.100.0 0.0.0.255
! read only access for local site
access-list 5 permit 192.168.16.0 0.15.255.255
! limit incoming traffic to traffic from site
access-list 100 permit ip 192.168.16.0 0.15.255.255 any
!
! SNMP access declarations
snmp community netman17225 rw 4
snmp community 172.20public ro 5
! line definitions
line vty 0 4
 access-class 1 in
 access-class 2 out
```

Router D has some differences from Router C (other than just interface addresses) because we need to implement our routing policy that says that the link between Sites 2 and 3 will not be used for failover between Sites 1 and 2. There is no way to implement this policy using `distribute-list` statements, so we need to filter packets between Sites 2 and 3 to prevent traffic from Sites 1 and 2 from using the link. Although we filtered the packets leaving Site 1 bound for Site in Router A, we do the same in case we make a mistake in Router A:

```
! limit points of vulnerability on router
no service tcp-small-servers
no service udp-small-servers
no service finger
!
ip subnet zero
! interfaces definitions
interface Ethernet 0
 description  site 2 LAN interface
 ip address 192.168.16.3 255.255.255.0
 ip access-group 100 in
interface Ethernet 1
 description  site 2 LAN interface
 ip address 192.168.17.3 255.255.255.0
 ip access-group 100 in
interface Serial 0
 description  serial interface to WAN
 ip address 192.168.32.9 255.255.255.252
 ip access-group 101 in
 ip access-group 102 out
! routing processes
router rip
 network 192.168.16.0
 network 192.168.17.0
 distribute-list 3 in Ethernet 0
 distribute-list 3 in Ethernet 1
 redistribute eigrp 200
!
router eigrp 200
 network 192.168.16.0
 network 192.168.17.0
 network 192.168.32.8 mask 255.255.255.252
 redistribute rip
 distance 90 192.168.32.5
 distance 90 192.168.16.3 0.0.1.0
 distance 255
! telnet access from management segment
access-list 1 permit 172.25.100.0 0.0.0.255
! telnet access from other WAN routers serial interfaces
access-list 1 permit 192.168.32.0 0.0.0.7
access-list 1 permit 192.168.32.8 0.0.0.3
! telnet access from other WAN routers Ethernet interfaces
access-list 1 permit 172.20.0.2 0.1.1.1
access-list 1 permt 172.24.0.2 0.1.1.1
```

```
! telnet access out on list 2 - limit to WAN routers
access-list 2 permit 192.168.16.2 0.0.1.1
access-list 2 permit 192.168.32.0 0.0.0.7
access-list 2 permit 192.168.32.8 0.0.0.3
! access-list for route distribution
access-list 3 permit 192.168.16.0 0.0.15.0
! SNMP access lists
! read write access for management segment
access-list 4 permit 172.25.100.0 0.0.0.255
! read only access for local site
access-list 5 permit 192.168.16.0 0.15.255.255
access-list 6 deny 172.20.0.0 0.1.0.0
access-list 6 permit any
access-list
! limit incoming traffic to traffic from site
access-list 100 permit ip 192.168.16.0 0.15.255.255 any
! clobber traffic between site 1 and 2 on serial link
access-list 101 deny ip 172.20.0.0 0.1.255.255 192.168.16.0 0.0.15.255
access-list 101 permit ip any any
access-list 102 deny ip 192.168.16.0 0.0.15.255 172.20.0.0 0.1.255.255
access-list 102 permit ip any any
access
!
! SNMP access declarations
snmp community netman17225 rw 4
snmp community 172.20public ro 5
! line definitions
line vty 0 4
 access-class 1 in
 access-class 2 out
```

Site 3 router configurations

The configurations for Routers E and F are similar to the previous examples, except that they filter Site 1 and 2 packets in different directions and have different interface addresses and local routing protocols. Here's the configuration for Router E:

```
! limit points of vulnerability on router
no service tcp-small-servers
no service udp-small-servers
no service finger
!
ip subnet zero
! interfaces definitions
interface Ethernet 0
 description  site 3 LAN interface
 ip address 172.24.0.2 255.255.255.0
 ip access-group 100 in
interface Ethernet 1
 description  site 3 LAN interface
 ip address 172.24.1.2 255.255.255.0
```

```
 ip access-group 100 in
interface Serial 0
 description  serial interface to WAN
 ip address 192.168.32.2 255.255.255.252
 ip access-group 101 in
 ip access-group 102 out
! routing processes
router ospf 70
 network 172.24.1.0 mask 0.0.0.255 area 0
 network 172.25.0.0 mask 0.0.0.255 area 0
!
router eigrp 200
 network 172.24.0.0
 network 172.25.0.0
 network 192.168.32.0 mask 255.255.255.252
 distance 90 192.168.32.1
 distance 90 172.24.0.0 0.0.1.3
 distance 255
 redistribute ospf 70
! telnet access from management segment
access-list 1 permit 172.25.100.0 0.0.0.255
! telnet access from other WAN routers serial interfaces
access-list 1 permit 192.168.32.0 0.0.0.7
access-list 1 permit 192.168.32.8 0.0.0.3
! telnet access from other WAN routers Ethernet interfaces
access-list 1 permit 172.20.0.2 0.1.1.1
access-list 1 permt 172.24.0.2 0.1.1.1
! telnet access out on list 2 - limit to WAN routers
access-list 2 permit 172.24.0.2 0.1.1.1
access-list 2 permit 192.168.32.0 0.0.0.7
access-list 2 permit 192.168.32.8 0.0.0.3
! access-list for route distribution
access-list 3 permit 192.168.16.0 0.0.15.0
! SNMP access lists
! read write access for management segment
access-list 4 permit 172.25.100.0 0.0.0.255
! read only access for local site
access-list 5 permit 172.24.0.0 0.1.255.255
! limit incoming traffic to traffic from site
access-list 100 permit ip 172.24.0.0 0.1.255.255 any
! clobber traffic between site 1 and 2 on serial link
access-list 101 deny ip 172.20.0.0 0.1.255.255 192.168.16.0 0.0.15.255
access-list 101 permit ip any any
access-list 102 deny ip 192.168.16.0 0.0.15.255 172.20.0.0 0.1.255.255
access-list 102 permit ip any any
!
! SNMP access declarations
snmp community netman17225 rw 4
snmp community 172.20public ro 5
! line definitions
line vty 0 4
 access-class 1 in
 access-class 2 out
```

Finally, here is the configuration for Router F:

```
! limit points of vulnerability on router
no service tcp-small-servers
no service udp-small-servers
no service finger
!
ip subnet zero
! interfaces definitions
interface Ethernet0
 ip address 172.24.0.2 255.255.255.0
 ip access-group 100 in
interface Ethernet1
 ip address 172.24.1.2 255.255.255.0
 ip access-group 100 in
interface Serial 0
 ip address 192.168.32.2 255.255.255.252
 ip access-group 101 in
 ip access-group 102 out
! routing processes
router ospf 70
 network 172.24.1.0 mask 0.0.0.255 area 0
 network 172.25.0.0 mask 0.0.0.255 area 0
    redistribute eigrp 200
!
router eigrp 200
 network 172.24.0.0
 network 172.25.0.0
 network 192.168.32.0 mask 255.255.255.252
 redistribute ospf 70
 distance 90 192.168.32.9
 distance 90 172.24.0.0 0.0.1.2
 distance 255
! telnet access from management segment
access-list 1 permit 172.25.100.0 0.0.0.255
! telnet access from other WAN routers serial interfaces
access-list 1 permit 192.168.32.0 0.0.0.7
access-list 1 permit 192.168.32.8 0.0.0.3
! telnet access from other WAN routers Ethernet interfaces
access-list 1 permit 172.20.0.2 0.1.1.1
access-list 1 permt 172.24.0.2 0.1.1.1
! telnet access out on list 2 - limit to WAN routers
access-list 2 permit 172.24.0.2 0.1.1.1
access-list 2 permit 192.168.32.0 0.0.0.7
access-list 2 permit 192.168.32.8 0.0.0.3
! access-list for route distribution
access-list 3 permit 192.168.16.0 0.0.15.0
! SNMP access lists
! read write access for management segment
access-list 4 permit 172.25.100.0 0.0.0.255
! read only access for local site
access-list 5 permit 172.24.0.0 0.1.255.255
! limit incoming traffic to traffic from site
access-list 100 permit ip 172.24.0.0 0.1.255.255 any
```

```
! clobber traffic between site 1 and 2 on serial link
access-list 101 deny ip 172.20.0.0 0.1.255.255 192.168.16.0 0.0.15.255
access-list 101 permit ip any any
access-list 102 deny ip 192.168.16.0 0.0.15.255 172.20.0.0 0.1.255.255
access-list 102 permit ip any any
!
! SNMP access declarations
snmp community netman17225 rw 4
snmp community 172.20public ro 5
! line definitions
line vty 0 4
 access-class 1 in
 access-class 2 out
```

A firewall case study

The next case study covers a firewall implementation. Cisco routers packet filter traffic between bastion hosts and the Internet and between the bastion hosts and an organization's internal network. The main concern here is security. We want to make sure our bastion hosts are not exposed to wide ranges of problems and attacks, and also that if some of those hosts are compromised, they are not used as a launch point to attack the rest of the network. We also want to make sure that our own access to the router is reasonably secure. Other concerns are scalability and ease of management.

What are the key elements of this firewall complex? The firewall network has to support the following components:

- A general proxy supporting the socks protocol

- An SMTP mail relay

- A web caching proxy server listening on port 81

- A web server using standard HTTP

- A web server for secure transactions for serving SSL

- A remote access device for access into the internal network

All the routers and servers need to be administered, of course. To do this, we should consider the following rules:

- Network 172.28.32.0 has workstations for administration and for maintaining the proxy relay segments.

- Network 172.28.30.0/24 has workstations and servers for updating the web servers.

- The routers need to be administered with TACACS+ protocol for authentication, in addition to TFTP and Telnet. A compromise of a host in the firewall should not allow promiscuous snooping.

- Remote access uses an address pool of 172.28.64.0/24.

- Systems and routers use two NTP servers at 172.28.1.100 and 172.28.1.101.

- Routers use a TACACS+ server at 172.28.32.20.

- The organization connects to the Internet through a High Speed Serial Interface (HSSI) with IP address 192.168.33.2.

There are a few other things to consider:

- Design should be *scalable*: it should be easy to add servers without a major impact.

- In this environment, we control what systems go on segments: no hosts are put on a segment without our approval.

- Advertise only one network for ease of routing.

- There must be problem isolation: a problem with one segment shouldn't affect others.

Given these requirements and design considerations, the network shown in Figure 7-2 has been designed.

There are two routers and four DMZs in this design. DMZ stands for demilitarized zone, an area between an insecure area (the Internet) and a secured area (the internal area of the organization). The *screening router* filters (screens) packets going to the DMZs and provides a measure of protection to the hosts in the DMZs. The *choke router* restricts access (chokes) by DMZ hosts into the internal organization. Should a DMZ host be compromised, the choke router restricts its access to prevent further penetration. The first DMZ is dedicated to proxy services. The second DMZ is used for web services presented to the Internet. Servers accessible to the Internet are divided in this way for a number of reasons. Two different groups administer the web servers and the proxy systems. We don't want a compromise in one segment to allow attacks on other segments. While the ultimate extreme of this logic is to put each server on its own segment, this consumes a lot of address space and router interfaces, so we use a /26 for segments with hosts on them.

Another feature is a segment with no hosts on it, designed for maintaining the screening router. Telnet, TACACS+, and TFTP packets needed for router maintenance pass through the segment without being snooped on. Since we control the segment, we can ensure that no hosts will reside on it. This gives the design an added measure of security.

For the remote access segment, we use a small /30 network allowing in VPN connections. Users on the Internet connect to a tunnel server on this segment. The tunnel uses a pool address of 172.28.6.128/25, making incoming remote clients

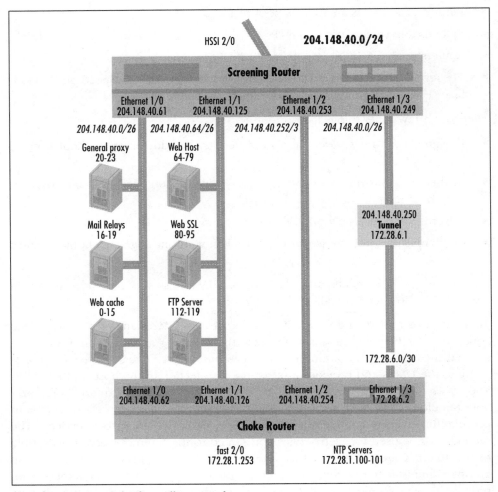

Figure 7-2. Network for firewall case study

look like they are from this address range. The same people administering the
proxy servers administer the remote access system. The VPN box requires Netbios
and other related ports for administration.

Screening router configuration

Given this network, I've constructed the following access list for the screening
router:

```
! limit points of vulnerability on router
no service tcp-small-servers
no service udp-small-servers
no service finger
```

```
!
ip classless
ip subnet zero
! NTP definitions
ntp update-calendar
ntp server 172.28.1.100
ntp server 172.28.1.101
ntp access-group query-only 12
! tacacs
aaa new-model
aaa authentication login default tacacs+ line
aaa authentication enable default tacacs+ enable
aaa authorization exec default tacacs+ none
aaa accounting exec default start-stop tacacs+
aaa accounting connection default start-stop tacacs+
aaa accounting system default start-stop tacacs+
! interfaces definitions
! proxy segment
interface etheret 1/0
 description interface to proxies
 ip address 204.148.40.61 255.255.255.192
 ip access-group 105 out
 ip access-group 106 in
 no ip directed-broadcast
! web server segment
interface Ethernet1/1
 description interface to web server segment
 ip address 204.148.40.125 255.255.255.192
 ip access-group 107 out
 ip access-group 108 in
 no ip directed-broadcast
! pass through segment
interface Ethennet1/2
 description pass through segment
 ip address 204.148.40.253 255.255.255.248
 ip access-group 103 out
 ip access-group 104 in
 no ip directed-broadcast
! tunnel
interface Ethernet1/3
 description tunnel segment
 ip address 204.148.40.249 255.255.255.252
 ip access-group 110 out
 ip access-group 109 in
 no ip directed-broadcast
interface hssi 2/0
 description HSSI interfce to Internet
 ip address 192.168.33.2 255.255.255.252
 ip access-group 102 out
 ip access-group 101 in
 no ip directed-broadcast
! routing processes
! vty access
access-list 10 permit 172.28.32.0 0.0.0.255
```

```
access-list 11 deny any
! NTP access
access-list 12 permit 172.28.1.100 0.0.0.1
! preventing spoofing - starting with private addresses
access-list 101 deny ip 172.16.0.0 0.15.255.255 any
access-list 101 deny ip 192.168.0.0 0.0.255.255 any
access-list 101 deny ip 10.0.0.0 0.255.255.255 any
! deny multicast
access-list 101 deny ip 224.0.0.0 0.255.255.255.255
! deny our own net from coming in
access-list 101 deny ip 204.148.40.0
! Let everything else in
access-list 101 permit ip any 204.148.40.0 0.0.0.25
! general outbound trafic - permit only our traffic  (no spoofing from us)
access-list 102 permit ip 204.148.40.0 .0.0.0.255 any
! rules for Pass thru DMZ
! no transit through this segment (outbound)
access-list 103 deny any any
! into pass through interface
! tacacs+
access-list 104 permit tcp 172.28.32.20 0.0.0.255 eq tacacs host 204.148.40.253 eq
tacacs
! telnet access
access-list 104 permit tcp 172.28.32.0 0.0.0.255 host 204.148.40.253 eq telnet
access-list 104 permit tcp host 204.148.40.252 host 204.148.40.253 eq telnet
! TFTP
access-list 104 permit tcp host 172.28.32.0 0.0.0.255 gt 1023 host 204.148.40.253
eq 69
! ping
access-list 104 permit icmp 172.28.32.0 0.0.0.255 host 204.148.40.253 echo
!
! to generic proxy segment
! established and echo first
access-list 105 permit any 204.148.40.0 0.0.0.63 established
access-list 105 permit icmp any 204.148.40.0 0.0.0.63 echo
access-list 105 permit icmp any 204.148.40.0 0.0.0.63 echo-reply
! to generic FTP proxy in
! deny access to socks port
access-list 105 deny any 204.148.40.0 0.0.0.63 eq 1080
! FTP data connection
access-list 105 permit tcp any eq 20 204.148.40.20 0.0.0.3 gt 1023
! DNS
access-list 105 permit udp any eq domain 204.148.40.0 0.0.0.63 eq domain
access-list 105 permit udp any eq domain 204.148.40.0 0.0.0.63 gt 1023
! mail relays
access-list 105 permit tcp any 204.148.40.16 0.0.0.3 eq smtp
! other icmp
access-list 105 permit icmp any 204.148.40.0 0.0.0.63 host-unreachable
!
! from generic proxy segment (inbound list)
! established
access-list 106 permit tcp 204.14.35.0 0.0.0.63 any established
! DNS
access-list 106 permit udp 204.148.40.0 0.0.0.63 any eq domain
```

```
access-list 106 permit tcp 204.148.40.0 0.0.0.63 any eq domain
! proxy access
access-list 106 permit tcp 204.148.40.20 0.0.0.3 any
! web proxy access
access-list 106 permit tcp 204.148.40.0 0.0.0.15 any
! mail
access-list 106 permit tcp 204.148.40.16 0.0.0.3 any eq smtp
! icmp
access-list 106 permit tcp 204.148.40.0 0.0.0.63 echo-reply
access-list 106 permit tcp 204.148.40.0 0.0.0.63 echo
!
! to web server segment
access-list 107 permit tcp any 204.148.40.64 0.0.0.63 established
access-list 107 permit icmp any 204.148.40.64 0.0.0.63 echo
access-list 107 permit tcp any 204.148.40.64 0.0.0.15 eq www
access-list 107 permit tcp any 204.148.40.80 0.0.0.15 eq 443
! FTP server
access-list 107 permit tcp any 204.148.40.112 0.0.0.7 range 20 21
access-list 107 permit tcp any eq 20 204.148.40.112 0.0.0.7 gt 1023
access-list 107 permit tcp any gt 1023 204.148.40.112 0.0.0.7 gt 1023
!
! from web server segment
access-list 108 permit 204.148.40.64 0.0.0.63 any established
! for FTP servers
access-list 108 permit 204.148.40.112 0.0.0.7 eq 20 any gt 1023
access-list 108 permit 204.148.40.64 0.0.0.63 any echo-reply
!
! to tunnel
access-list 109 permit gre any host 204.148.40.250
access-list 109 permit icmp any host 204.148.40.250 any
!
! from tunnel
access-list 110 permit gre host 204.148.40.250 any
access-list 110 permit icmp any host 204.148.40.250 any
! all routing via statics - no routing protocols run here
! route back into organizations' internal network
ip route 172.28.0.0 255.255.0.0 204.148.40.254
! default route to Internet
ip route 0.0.0.0 0.0.0.0 255.255.255.255 192.168.33.2
! snmp access
snmp community MyString ro 10
!
tacacs-server host 172.28.32.20
tacacs-server key MyKey123
! line access
line vty 0 4
 access-class 10 in
 access-class 11 out
```

To deal with possible spoofing of IP addresses, access lists 101 and 102 prevent spoofed packets from coming in from and going out to the Internet, respectively. In addition, the incoming and outgoing access lists prevent hosts on different subnets from sending out spoofed packets. Since there are incoming and outgoing access lists on each interface, the access list for each segment can be managed independently. Also, access to web service or proxy service is open to a range of IP addresses. This allows servers to be added without changes to access lists. On the proxy server segment, we block incoming attempts to the standard SOCKS proxy port. This is to prevent people on the Internet from using the proxy to attack other hosts or disguise their identities.

Notice that I have implemented some commands that reduce the number of access lists needed. The static route to 172.28.0.0/16 through the maintenance segment eliminates the need for routing protocols, which of course eliminates the need for routing access lists. The *no service tcp-small-servers*, *no service udp-small-servers*, and *no service finger* commands turn off router services. *no ip directed broadcast* eliminates the need for specific access list entries to filter broadcast attacks.

Choke router configuration

The choke router is configured as follows:

```
! limit points of vulnerability on router
no service tcp-small-servers
no service udp-small-servers
no service finger
!
ip classless
ip subnet zero
! NTP definitions
ntp update-calendar
ntp server 172.28.1.100
ntp server 172.28.1.101
ntp access-group query-only 12
! tacacs
aaa new-model
aaa authentication login default tacacs+ line
aaa authentication enable default tacacs+ enable
aaa authorization exec default tacacs+ none
aaa accounting exec default start-stop tacacs+
aaa accounting connection default start-stop tacacs+
aaa accounting system default start-stop tacacs+
! interfaces definitions
! proxy segment
interface Ethernet 1/0
  description interface to proxy segment
  ip address 204.148.40.62 255.255.255.192
  ip access-group 102 out
  ip access-group 103 in
  no ip directed-broadcast
! web server segment
interface Ethernet 1/1
  description interface to web server segment
  ip address 204.148.40.126 255.255.255.192
  ip access-group 104 out
```

```
  ip access-group 105 in
  no ip directed-broadcast
! pass through segment
interface Ethernet 1/2
  description pass through segment
  ip address 204.148.40.254 255.255.255.248
  ip access-group 106 out
  ip access-group 107 in
  no ip directed-broadcast
! tunnel
interface Ethernet 1/3
  description tunnel segment
  ip address 172.28.6.2 255.255.255.252
  ip access-group 108 out
  ip access-group 109 in
  no ip directed-broadcast
interface FastEthernet 2/0
  description interface to internal network
  ip address 172.28.1.253 255.255.255.0
  ip access-group 101 out
  ip access-group 100 in
  no ip directed-broadcast
! routing processes
! vty access
access-list 10 permit 172.28.32.0 0.0.0.255
access-list 11 deny any
! preventing spoofing from internal net
access-list 100 permit ip 172.28.0.0 0.0.255.255 any
! permit only traffic from DMZs
access-list 101 permit ip 204.148.40.0 0.0.0.255 172.28.0.0 0.0.255.255
access-list 101 permit ip 172.28.64.0 0.0.0.255 172.28.0.0 0.0.255.255
! Access to proxy segment
! start with established
access-list 102 permit tcp 172.28.0.0 0.0.255.255 204.148.40.0 0.0.0.63
established
! to proxy server port
access-list 102 permit tcp 172.28.0.0 0.0.255.255 204.148.40.0 0.0.0.15 eq 81
! mail
access-list 102 permit tcp 172.28.0.0 0.0.255.255 204.148.40.16 0.0.0.3 eq smtp
! generic socks proxy
access-list 102 permit tcp 172.28.0.0 0.0.255.255 192.168.3.20 0.0.0.3 eq 1080
access-list 102 permit icmp 172.28.0.0 0.0.255.255 204.148.40.0 0.0.0.63 echo
access-list 102 permit icmp 172.28.0.0 0.0.255.255 204.148.40.0 0.0.0.63 echo-
reply
! DNS
access-list 102 permit udp 172.28.0.0 0.0.255.255 eq domain 204.148.40.16 0.0.0.3
eq domain
access-list 102 permit udp 172.28.0.0 0.0.255.255 eq domain 204.148.40.16 0.0.0.3
gt 1023
! ssh access
access-list 102 permit tcp 172.28.0.0 0.0.255.255 204.148.40.20 0.0.0.3 eq 22
! from proxy segment
access-list 103 permit tcp 204.148.40.0 0.0.0.63 172.28.0.0 0.0.255.255
established
```

```
! mail in
access-list 103 permit tcp 204.148.40.16 0.0.0.3 172.28.0.0 0.0.255.255 eq smtp
! icmp
access-list 103 permit icmp 204.148.40.0 0.0.0.63 172.28.0.0 0.0.255.255 echo
access-list 103 permit icmp 204.148.40.0 0.0.0.63 172.28.0.0 0.0.255.255 echo-
reply
! DNS for SMTP boxes
access-list 103 permit udp 204.148.40.16 0.0.0.3 eq domain 172.28.0.0 0.0.255.255
eq domain
access-list 103 permit udp 204.148.40.16 0.0.0.3 gt 1023 172.28.0.0 0.0.255.255 eq
domain
! to web server segment
access-list 104 permit tcp 172.28.0.0 0.0.255.255 204.148.40.64 0.0.0.63
established
! access to web servers
access-list 104 permit tcp 172.28.0.0 0.0.255.255 204.148.40.64 0.0.0.63 eq www
access-list 104 permit tcp 172.28.0.0 0.0.255.255 204.148.40.64 0.0.0.63 eq 443
access-list 104 permit tcp 172.28.0.0 0.0.255.255 204.148.40.64 0.0.0.63 range
ftp-date ftp
! icmp
access-list 104 permit icmp 172.28.0.0 0.0.255.255 204.148.40.64 0.0.0.63 echo
! Netbios access
access-list 104 permit tcp 172.38.30.0 0.0.255.255 204.148.40.64 0.0.0.63 eq 139
access-list 104 permit udp 172.38.30.0 0.0.255.255 204.148.40.64 0.0.0.63 range
netbios-dgm netbios-ns
! from web segment
access-list 105 permit tcp 204.148.40.64 0.0.0.63 172.28.0.0 0.0.255.255
established
! FTP data connection
access-list 105 permit tcp 204.148.40.112 0.0.0.7 eq ftp-data 172.28.0.0 0.0.255.
255 gt 1023
! icmp
access-list 105 permit icmp 204.148.40.64 0.0.0.63 172.28.0.0 0.0.255.255 echo-
reply
! ntp
access-list 105 permit udp 204.148.40.64 0.0.0.63 eq ntp 172.28.1.100 0.0.0.1 eq
ntp
! pass thru segment access
! telnet and tacacs and tftp
access-list 106 permit tcp 172.28.32.0 0.0.0.255 host 204.148.40.253 eq telnet
access-list 106 permit tcp 172.28.32.20 0.0.0.255 eq tacacs host 204.148.40.253 eq
tacacs
access-list 106 permit udp 172.28.32.0 0.0.0.255 host 204.148.40.253 gt 1023
access-list 106 permit udp 172.28.32.0 0.0.0.255 eq 69 host 204.148.40.253 eq 69
! ntp
access-list 106 permit udp 172.28.1.100 0.0.0.1 eq ntp host 204.148.40.253 eq ntp
access-list 106 permit udp 172.28.1.100 0.0.0.1 gt 1023 host 204.148.40.253 eq ntp
! icmp
access-list 106 permit icmp 172.28.100.0 0.0.0.255 host 204.148.40.253 echo
! from pass through
! telnet back
access-list 107 permit tcp host 204.148.40.253 eq telnet 172.28.100.0 0.0.0.255 gt
1023
! tacacs
```

```
access-list 107 permit tcp host 204.148.40.253 eq tacacs 172.28.100.0 0.0.0.255 eq
tacacs
! tftp
access-list 107 permit udp host 204.148.40.253 eq 69 172.28.100.0 0.0.0.255 eq 69
access-list 107 permit udp host 204.148.40.253 gt 1023 172.28.100.0 0.0.0.255
! ntp
access-list 107 permit udp host 204.148.40.253 eq ntp 172.28.1.100 0.0.0.1 eq ntp
access-list 107 permit udp host 204.148.40.253 eq ntp 172.28.1.100 0.0.0.1 gt 1023
! icmp
access-list 107 permit icmp host 204.148.40.253 172.28.100.0 0.0.0.255 echo-reply
! to tunnel
access-list 108 permit ip 172.28.0.0 0.0.255.255 172.28.6.64 0.0.0.63
! NT services access for maintenance
access-list 108 permit tcp 172.28.30.0 0.0.0.255 host 172.28.6.5 eq 139
access-list 108 permit udp 172.28.30.0 0.0.0.255 host 172.28.6.5 range netbios-dgm
netbios-ns
! from tunnel
access-list 109 permit ip 172.28.6.64 0.0.0.63 172.28.0.0 0.0.255.255
access-list 109 permit tcp host 172.28.6.5 eq 139 172.28.30 0.0.0.255 gt 1023
access-list 109 permit tcp host 172.28.6.5 range netbios-dgm netbios-ns 172.28.30.
0 0.0.0.255 range netbios-dgm netbios-ns
! all routing via statics - no routing protocols run here
! route back into internal network
ip route 172.28.0.0.255.255.0.0 FastEthernet 2/0
! default route to Internet
ip route 0.0.0.0 0.0.0.0 255.255.255.255 192.168.33.2
! snmp access
snmp community MyString ro 10
!
tacacs-server host 172.28.32.20
tacacs-server key MyKey123
! line access
line vty 0 4
 access-class 10 in
 access-class 11 out
```

For segments like **maintenance** that have few TCP services, there's no need to put in an TCP **established** entry, since it doesn't save any lines and reduces total exposure.

An Internet routing case study

In this example, I show the use of access lists with Internet routing. Figure 7-3 shows a network diagram of an organization doing web hosting.

The organization has two sites, Site 1 and Site 2, each connected to two ISPs, A and B. ISP A has usage-based pricing while ISP B charges a flat rate. There are two sets of web servers, one on network 198.6.224.128/25 and another on 204.148.40.0/24. We want to get the best possible performance for the web hosts on 198.6.224.128/25. Traffic to and from 204.148.40.0/24 is a lower priority.

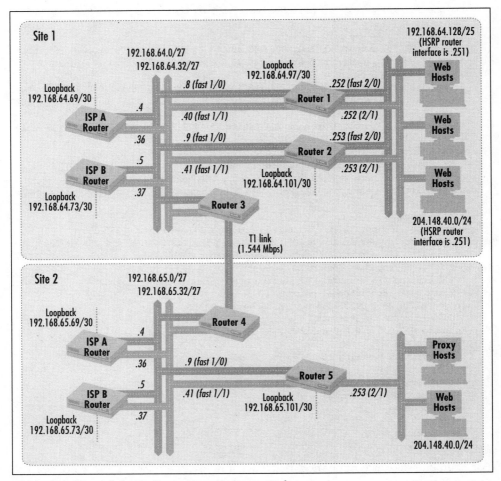

Figure 7-3. Network for an Internet routing case study

To ensure higher availability, two routers connect the web servers in Site 1 to the Internet. Using Cisco's Hot Standby Routing Protocol (HSRP), we have a path to and from the Internet even if one router is unavailable. We also have two different networks between the routers in front of the web servers and ISP routers. If one of the networks goes down, the other is still available to pass traffic to the Internet. Note also that both ISP routers are managed by their respective ISPs and not by the organization.

Site 2 contains some web servers as well as proxy servers for general use by that site. Of greatest interest is the fact that it is connected Site 1 and has connections to the same ISPs as Site 1.

Let's articulate the policies we wish to implement. In this example, I describe only the policies for Site 1.

Robustness concerns

The main robustness concerns center around making sure that improper routes are not accepted or distributed. Those concerns can be distilled into the following statements:

> Only networks 204.148.40.0/24 and 198.6.224.128/25 should be distributed out of the organization by Routers 1 and 2
>
> Local networks, the private IP networks, and multicast networks should not be accepted from the Internet

Security concerns

The main security concerns are to allow only what is necessary to the web servers and routers. This includes allowing only valid web traffic to the web servers and only appropriate routing traffic into the routers. These rules can be summarized as follows:

> BGP traffic allowed between loopbacks of the ISP routers and Routers 1 and 2
>
> EIGRP between all of the routers
>
> SNMP and Telnet access only from a management console (192.168.59.3/24) connected to fast Ethernet 3/0 (not shown on the diagram).
>
> Web and SSL access only to the web servers
>
> HSRP from the interfaces on the web servers segment
>
> Web servers should be able to ping the router interface on their segment
>
> The routers cannot be used or queried as time servers

These policies are implemented with packet-filtering lists and resource access lists.

Policy concerns

Good performance for the web servers on network 198.6.224.128/25 is a much higher priority than the performance of the web servers on segment 204.148.40.0/24. ISP B is on a pay-per-usage basis, so we wish to have the following policy to get good performance from the important web servers yet save money:

> Hosts in 198.6.224.128/25 will use both ISP A and B
>
> Hosts in 204.148.40.0 will use ISP A only

We also want to have traffic flow into the Internet gateway nearest the web servers. To do this, we implement the following policy:

If ISP A is unavailable in Site 1, then traffic for 198.6.224.128/25 should use ISP B in Site 1. Traffic should not come in via Site 2's ISP A connection

If ISP B is unavailable in Site 1, then traffic for 198.6.224.128/25 should use ISP A in Site 1. Traffic should not come in via Site 2's ISP B connection

If ISP A and B are unavailable in Site 1, then traffic should come in through Site 2's ISP connections

To help set routing policies, ISP B allows its customers to set communities to affect how a route is advertised. Table 7-1 describes each community and how it affects advertisements.

Table 7-1. ISP B's communities and their effects

Communities	Effect on route advertisement
ISPB:80	Local Preference is set to 80 (default is 100), so route is used as a last resort.
ISPB:120	Local Preference is set to 120 (default is 100), so route is preferred above all others.
ISPB:1	Prepend one of ISP B's AS numbers when route is advertised to ISP B's peers.
ISPB:2	Prepend two of ISP B's AS numbers when route is advertised to ISP B's peers.
ISPB:3	Prepend three of ISP B's AS numbers when route is advertised to ISP B's peers.

Note that ISP A has no such community settings. ISP A does, however, listen to MED settings on routes it hears from its customers.

Router configurations

In this section, I list the configurations for Routers 1 and 2. In the following example, named access lists are used. Here is the configuration for Router 1:

```
! limit points of vulnerability on router
no service tcp-small-servers
no service udp-small-servers
no service finger
!
ip classless
ip subnet zero
! interfaces definitions
! ISP Segment 1
interface FastEthernet1/0
 description ISP Segment 1
 ip address 192.168.64.8 255.255.255.224
 ip access-group ANTI-SPOOF-OUT out
 ip access-group ANTI-SPOOF-IN in
 no ip directed-broadcast
```

```
! ISP Segment 2
interface FastEthernet1/2
 description ISP Segment 1
 ip address 192.168.64.40 255.255.255.224
 ip access-group ANTI-SPOOF-OUT out
 ip access-group ANTI-SPOOF-IN in
 no ip directed-broadcast
! high priority web segment
interface FastEthernet2/0
 description high priority web segment
 ip address 198.6.224.252 255.255.255.128
 ip access-group TO-HIGH-PRIORITY-WEB-SEGMENT out
 ip access-group FROM-HIGH-PRIORITY-WEB-SEGMENT in

 no ip directed-broadcast
 standby 192 priority 200
 standby 192 preempt
 standby 192 ip 198.6.224.251
! lower priority web segment
interface FastEthernet2/1
 description low priority web segment
 ip address 204.148.40.252 255.255.255.0
 ip access-group TO-HIGH-PRIORITY-LOW-PRIORITY-WEB-SEGMENT out
 ip access-group FROM-LOW-PRIORITY-WEB-SEGMENT in
 ip policy route FROM-LOW-PRIORTY-WEB-SERVERS
 no ip directed-broadcast
 standby 172 priority 100
 standby 172 preempt
 standby 172 ip 204.148.40.251
! to management console
interface FastEthernet3/0
 description management segment
 ip address 192.168.59.252 255.255.255.0
 ip access-group TO-MANAGEMENT-SEGMENT out
 ip access-group FROM-MANAGEMENT-SEGMENT in
 no ip directed-broadcast
int Loopback0
 description loopback interface
 ip address 192.168.64.97 255.255.255.252
!
ip standard access-list DENY-ALL-OUT
 deny any
!
ip access-list standard DENY-ALL-ROUTES
 deny any
!
ip access-list standard HIGH-PRIORITY-WEB-SEGMENT
 permit 198.6.224.128
!
ip access-list standard HIGH-PRIORITY-WEB-SERVERS
 permit 198.6.224.128 0.0.0.127
!
ip access-list standard LOOPBACKS-IN
 permit 192.168.64.0 0.0.0.63
```

```
!
ip access-list standard LOW-PRIORITY-WEB-SEGMENT
 permit 204.148.40.0
!
ip access-list standard LOW-PRIORITY-WEB-SERVERS
 permit 204.148.40.0 0.0.0.255
!
ip access-list standard MANAGEMENT-SERVER
 permit 192.168.59.3 0.0.0.0
!
ip access-list standard PERMIT-ALL-ROUTES
 permit any
!
ip access-list standard VALID-ROUTES-IN
! deny private addresses
 deny 172.16.0.0 0.15.255.255
 deny 192.168.0.0 0.0.255.255 any
 deny 10.0.0.0 0.255.255.255.255 any
! deny multicast
 deny 224.0.0.0 0.255.255.255.255
! deny our own nets from coming in
 deny 198.6.224.128
 deny 204.148.40.0
 permit any
!
ip access-list standard VALID-ROUTES-OUT
 permit 192.168.64.0 0.0.0.255
 permit 198.6.224.128
 permit 204.148.40.0
!
! preventing spoofing in - starting with private addresses
ip access-list extended ANTI-SPOOF-IN
! Let in EIGRP
 permit eigrp 192.168.64.0 0.0.0.31 host 224.0.0.10
 permit eigrp 192.168.64.32 0.0.0.31 192.168.64.0 0.0.0.61
! Let in BGP
 permit tcp host 192.168.64.69 host 192.168.64.97 eq bgp
! Deny other private networks
 deny ip 172.16.0.0 0.15.255.255 any
 deny ip 192.168.0.0 0.0.255.255 any
 deny ip 10.0.0.0 0.255.255.255.255 any
! deny multicast
 deny ip 224.0.0.0 0.255.255.255.255
! deny our own nets from coming in
 deny ip 192.168.64.0 0.0.0.255 any
 deny ip 198.6.224.0 0.0.0.127 any
 deny ip 204.148.40.0 0.0.0.255 any
! Let everything else in
 permit ip any 204.148.40.0 0.0.0.255
 permit ip any 198.6.224.0 0.0.0.127
!
! general outbound trafic - permit only our traffic  (no spoofing from us)
ip access-list extended ANTI-SPOOF-OUT
 permit ip 198.6.224.128 0.0.0.255 any
 permit ip 204.148.40.0 0.0.0.255 any
```

```
!
! from web server segment
ip access-list extended FROM-HIGH-PRIORITY-WEB-SEGMENT
! allow in ip for ARP and HSRP
 permit ip 198.6.224.128 0.0.0.127 host 192.168.64.251
 permit ip 198.6.224.128 0.0.0.127 host 192.168.64.252
! web traffic
 permit tcp 198.6.224.128 0.0.0.1 27 eq www any gt 1023
 permit tcp 198.6.224.128 0.0.0.127 eq 443 any gt 1023
! permit ping of router interfaces
 permit icmp 198.6.224.128 0.0.0.127 host 198.6.224.251 echo
 permit icmp 198.6.224.128 0.0.0.127 198.6.224.252 0.0.0.1 echo
!
! from web server segment
ip access-list extended FROM-LOW-PRIORITY-WEB-SEGMENT
! allow in ip for ARP and HSRP
 permit ip 204.148.40.0 0.0.0.255 host 204.148.40.251
 permit ip 204.148.40.0 0.0.0.255 host 204.148.40.252
! web traffic
 permit tcp 204.148.40.0 0.0.0.255 eq www any gt 1023
 permit tcp 204.148.40.0 0.0.0.255 eq 443 any gt 1023
! ping from servers to local interface
 permit icmp 204.148.40.0 0.0.0.255 host 204.148.40.251 echo
 permit icmp 204.148.40.0 0.0.0.255 204.148.40.251.252 0.0.0.1 echo
!
ip access-list extended FROM-MANAGEMENT-SEGMENT
! telnet access
 permit tcp host 192.168.59.3 host 192.168.59.252 eq telnet
 permit tcp host 192.168.59.3 host 192.168.59.252 eq telnet
! TFTP
 permit tcp host 192.168.59.3 gt 1023 host 192.168.59.252 eq 69
! tacacs
 permit tcp host 192.168.59.3 eq tacacs host 192.168.59.252 eq tacacs
! ping
 permit icmp host 192.168.59.3 host 192.168.59.252 echo
!
ip access-list extended TO-HIGH-PRIORITY-WEB-SEGMENT
 permit tcp any 198.6.224.128 0.0.0.127 eq www
 permit tcp any 198.6.224.128 0.0.0.127 eq 443
! ping from servers
 permit icmp any 198.6.224.128 0.0.0.127 echo
!
ip access-list extended TO-LOW-PRIORITY-WEB-SEGMENT
 permit tcp any 204.148.40.0 0.0.0.255 eq www
 permit tcp any 204.148.40.0 0.0.0.255 eq 443
!
! to management segment
ip access-list extended TO-MANAGEMENT-SEGMENT
! no transit through this segment (outbound)
 deny any any
!
route-map FROM-LOW-PRIORITY-WEB-SERVERS permit 10
 match fast 2/0
 set ip next-hop 192.168.64.73
```

```
!
route-map INCOMING-ROUTES-FROM-SITE2 permit 10
 match ip PERMIT-ALL-ROUTES
 set local-preference 80
!
route-map ROUTES-OUT-TO-ISPA-SITE1 permit 10
 match ip HIGH-PRIORITY-WEB-SEGMENT
!
route-map ROUTES-OUT-TO-ISPA-SITE2 permit 10
 match ip HIGH-PRIORITY-WEB-SEGMENT
 set as-path prepend 1321 1321 1321
!
route-map ROUTES-OUT-TO-ISPB-SITE1 permit 10
 match ip HIGH-PRIORITY-WEB-SEGMENT
route-map ROUTES-OUT-TO-ISPB-SITE1 permit 20
 match ip LOW-PRIORITY-WEB-SEGMENT
!
route-map ROUTES-OUT-TO-ISPB-SITE2 permit 10
 match ip HIGH-PRIORITY-WEB-SEGMENT
 set community ISPB:80
route-map ROUTES-OUT-TO-ISPB-SITE2 permit 20
 match ip LOW-PRIORITY-WEB-SEGMEN2
 set community ISPB:80
!
! routing statements
router eigrp 800
 network 192.168.64.0 mask 255.255.255.224
 network 192.168.64.32 mask 255.255.255.224
 distribute-list DENY-ALL-ROUTES in fast 2/0
 distribute-list DENY-ALL-ROUTES in fast 2/1
 distribute-list LOOPBACKS-IN in fast 1/0
 distribute-list LOOPBACKS-IN in fast 1/1
 distribute-list VALID-ROUTES-OUT out
!
router bgp 1321
 no synchronization
 network 198.6.224.128 mask 255.255.255.128
 network 204.148.40.0
!
 neighbor external-peers ebgp-multihop 6
 neighbor external-peers update-source Loopback0
 neighbor external-peers next-hop-self
 neighbor external-peers distribute-list VALID-ROUTES-OUT out
 neighbor external-peers distribute-list VALID-ROUTES-IN in
 neighbor external-peers soft-reconfiguration in
 neighbor external-peers soft-reconfiguration out
 neighbor 192.168.64.69 peer-group external-peers
 neighbor 192.168.64.73 peer-group external-peers
 neighbor 192.168.65.69 peer-group external-peers
 neighbor 192.168.65.73 peer-group external-peers
!
 neighbor 192.168.64.69 remote-as 65000
 neighbor 192.168.64.69 route-map ROUTES-OUT-TO-ISPBA-SITE1 out
!
```

```
 neighbor 192.168.64.73 remote-as 65001
 neighbor 192.168.64.73 route-map ROUTES-OUT-TO-ISPB-SITE1 out
!
 neighbor 192.168.65.69 remote-as 65000
 neighbor 192.168.65.69 route-map ROUTES-OUT-TO-ISPBA-SITE2 out
 neighbor 192.168.65.69 route-map INCOMING-ROUTES-FROM-SITE2 in
!
 neighbor 192.168.65.73 remote-as 65001
 neighbor 192.168.65.73 route-map ROUTES-OUT-TO-ISPB-SITE2 out
 neighbor 192.168.65.73 route-map INCOMING-ROUTES-FROM-SITE2 in
! snmp access
snmp community MyString ro MANAGEMENT-SERVER
! line access
line vty 0 4
 access-class MANAGEMENT-SERVER in
 access-class DENY-ALL-OUT out
```

To deal with network robustness issues, we allow only our specific routes to be distributed out via EIGRP and BGP. Access list VALID-ROUTES-OUT restricts what is advertised via routing protocols. Only the loopback networks are accepted via EIGRP, which are restricted by the access list LOOPBACKS-IN. Our own networks, private addresses, and multicast networks are rejected by access list VALID-ROUTES-IN.

Several other access lists maintain security. The access list MANAGEMENT-SERVER restricts SNMP and Telnet access to the management console. The standard access list DENY-ALL-OUT prevents those with login access from attacking other sites on the web from the management console. Access list ANTI-SPOOF-IN prevents spoofed packets from entering the network, while ANTI-SPOOF-OUT prevents a compromised web server from becoming a source of spoofed packets. ANTI-SPOOF-IN has specific entries for allowing incoming EIGRP and BGP packets. There are incoming and outgoing access lists on the interfaces leading to the web servers. This allows the access lists for the high- and low-priority web servers to be managed independently—a change on one will not affect the others. The incoming access lists let in HSRP broadcasts. Only web traffic is permitted to the web servers. The no ip directed-broadcast command on the interfaces prevent the routers and servers from being used for broadcast-based attack, and TCP and UDP services are turned off with *no service* commands.

The traffic routing policy is implemented with route maps. Policy route map FROM-LOW-PRIORITY-WEB-SERVERS directs traffic from the low priority web servers to ISP B. The route map ROUTES-TO-ISPB-SITE2 sets the community string ISPB:80 on the routes from the low-priority web server network. This community makes the route to the low-priority servers less preferred through Site 2 and is used only if there is no path through ISP B in Site 1. It should be noted, however, that because of the policy route map on the low-priority web site segment, the next hop statement has to be manually changed to point to ISP B in Site

2 in order to completely fail over the low-priority segment. The route maps `ROUTES-TO-ISPA-SITE1` and `ROUTES-TO-ISPA-SITE2` do not include the low-priority network, so this network is never routed over ISP A in either site. To ensure that Site 2 is the last resort for the high-priority network, we prepend AS 1321 onto routes ISP A receives in Site 2 for the high-priority network. As a result, ISP B is used in Site 1 if ISP A goes down. For outgoing traffic, the route map `INCOMING-ROUTES-FROM-SITE2` makes all routes form ISP A and B in Site 2 a local preference of 80. This makes outgoing traffic go out Site 1 unless both ISPs there are down.

Note that we use `peer-group` in the BGP neighbor definitions to reduce the number of statements and simplify the configuration. Several commands, including two `distribute-list` statements for incoming and outgoing routes are repeated for each neighbor, and `peer-group` saves us from repeatedly entering them into the configuration.

The following configuration for Router 2 is added for completeness:

```
! limit points of vulnerability on router
no service tcp-small-servers
no service udp-small-servers
no service finger
!
ip classless
ip subnet zero
! interfaces definitions
! ISP Segment 1
interface FastEthernet1/0
 description ISP Segment 1
 ip address 192.168.64.9 255.255.255.224
 ip access-group ANTI-SPOOF-OUT out
 ip access-group ANTI-SPOOF-IN in
 no ip directed-broadcast
! ISP Segment 2
interface FastEthernet1/2
 description ISP Segment 1
 ip address 192.168.64.41 255.255.255.224
 ip access-group ANTI-SPOOF-OUT out
 ip access-group ANTI-SPOOF-IN in
 no ip directed-broadcast
! high priority web segment
interface FastEthernet2/0
 description high priority web segment
 ip address 198.6.224.253 255.255.255.128
 ip access-group TO-HIGH-PRIORITY-WEB-SEGMENT out
 ip access-group FROM-HIGH-PRIORITY-WEB-SEGMENT in

 no ip directed-broadcast
 standby 192 priority 200
 standby 192 preempt
 standby 192 ip 198.6.224.251
```

```
! lower priority web segment
interface FastEthernet2/1
 description low priority web segment
 ip address 204.148.40.253 255.255.255.0
 ip access-group TO-HIGH-PRIORITY-LOW-PRIORITY-WEB-SEGMENT out
 ip access-group FROM-LOW-PRIORITY-WEB-SEGMENT in
 ip policy route FROM-LOW-PRIORTY-WEB-SERVERS
 no ip directed-broadcast
 standby 172 priority 100
 standby 172 preempt
 standby 172 ip 204.148.40.251
! to management console
interface FastEthernet3/0
 description management segment
 ip address 192.168.59.253 255.255.255.0
 ip access-group TO-MANAGEMENT-SEGMENT out
 ip access-group FROM-MANAGEMENT-SEGMENT in
 no ip directed-broadcast
int Loopback0
 description loopback interface
 ip address 192.168.64.101 255.255.255.252
!
ip standard access-list DENY-ALL-OUT
 deny any
!
ip access-list standard DENY-ALL-ROUTES
 deny any
!
ip access-list standard HIGH-PRIORITY-WEB-SEGMENT
 permit 198.6.224.128
!
ip access-list standard HIGH-PRIORITY-WEB-SERVERS
 permit 198.6.224.128 0.0.0.127
!
ip access-list standard LOOPBACKS-IN
 permit 192.168.64.0 0.0.0.63
!
ip access-list standard LOW-PRIORITY-WEB-SEGMENT
 permit 204.148.40.0
!
ip access-list standard LOW-PRIORITY-WEB-SERVERS
 permit 204.148.40.0 0.0.0.255
!
ip access-list standard MANAGEMENT-SERVER
 permit 192.168.59.3 0.0.0.0
!
ip access-list standard PERMIT-ALL-ROUTES
 permit any
!
ip access-list standard VALID-ROUTES-IN
! deny private addresses
 deny 172.16.0.0 0.15.255.255
 deny 192.168.0.0 0.0.255.255 any
 deny 10.0.0.0 0.255.255.255.255 any
```

```
! deny multicast
 deny 224.0.0.0 0.255.255.255.255
! deny our own nets from coming in
 deny 198.6.224.128
 deny 204.148.40.0
 permit any
!
ip access-list standard VALID-ROUTES-OUT
 permit 192.168.64.0 0.0.0.255
 permit 198.6.224.128
 permit 204.148.40.0
!
! preventing spoofing in - starting with private addresses
ip access-list extended ANTI-SPOOF-IN
! Let in EIGRP
 permit eigrp 192.168.64.0 0.0.0.31 host 224.0.0.10
 permit eigrp 192.168.64.32 0.0.0.31 192.168.64.0 0.0.0.61
! Let in BGP
 permit tcp host 192.168.64.69 host 192.168.64.97 eq bgp
! Deny other private networks
 deny ip 172.16.0.0 0.15.255.255 any
 deny ip 192.168.0.0 0.0.255.255 any
 deny ip 10.0.0.0 0.255.255.255 any
! deny multicast
 deny ip 224.0.0.0 0.255.255.255.255
! deny our own nets from coming in
 deny ip 192.168.64.0 0.0.0.255 any
 deny ip 198.6.224.0 0.0.0.127 any
 deny ip 204.148.40.0 0.0.0.255 any
! Let everything else in
 permit ip any 204.148.40.0 0.0.0.255
 permit ip any 198.6.224.0 0.0.0.127
!
! general outbound trafic - permit only our traffic   (no spoofing from us)
ip access-list extended ANTI-SPOOF-OUT
 permit ip 198.6.224.128 0.0.0.255 any
 permit ip 204.148.40.0 0.0.0.255 any
!
! from web server segment
ip access-list extended FROM-HIGH-PRIORITY-WEB-SEGMENT
! allow in ip for ARP and HSRP
 permit ip 198.6.224.128 0.0.0.127 host 192.168.64.251
 permit ip 198.6.224.128 0.0.0.127 host 192.168.64.252
! web traffic
 permit tcp 198.6.224.128 0.0.0.1 27 eq www any gt 1023
 permit tcp 198.6.224.128 0.0.0.127 eq 443 any gt 1023
! permit ping of router interfaces
 permit icmp 198.6.224.128 0.0.0.127 host 198.6.224.251 echo
 permit icmp 198.6.224.128 0.0.0.127 198.6.224.252 0.0.0.1 echo
!
! from web server segment
ip access-list extended FROM-LOW-PRIORITY-WEB-SEGMENT
! allow in ip for ARP and HSRP
 permit ip 204.148.40.0 0.0.0.255 host 204.148.40.251
```

```
 permit ip 204.148.40.0 0.0.0.255 host 204.148.40.252
! web traffic
 permit tcp 204.148.40.0 0.0.0.255 eq www any gt 1023
 permit tcp 204.148.40.0 0.0.0.255 eq 443 any gt 1023
! ping from servers to local interface
 permit icmp 204.148.40.0 0.0.0.255 host 192.168.64.251 echo
! ping from servers to local interface
 permit icmp 204.148.40.0 0.0.0.255 host 204.148.40.251 echo
 permit icmp 204.148.40.0 0.0.0.255 204.148.40.251.252 0.0.0.1 echo
!
ip access-list extended FROM-MANAGEMENT-SEGMENT
! telnet access
 permit tcp host 192.168.59.3 host 192.168.59.252 eq telnet
 permit tcp host 192.168.59.3 host 192.168.59.252 eq telnet
! TFTP
 permit tcp host 192.168.59.3 gt 1023 host 192.168.59.252 eq 69
! tacacs
 permit tcp host 192.168.59.3 eq tacacs host 192.168.59.252 eq tacacs
! ping
 permit icmp host 192.168.59.3 host 192.168.59.252 echo
!
ip access-list extended TO-HIGH-PRIORITY-WEB-SEGMENT
 permit tcp any 198.6.224.128 0.0.0.127 eq www
 permit tcp any 198.6.224.128 0.0.0.127 eq 443
! ping from servers
 permit icmp any 198.6.224.128 0.0.0.127 echo
!
ip access-list extended TO-LOW-PRIORITY-WEB-SEGMENT
 permit tcp any 204.148.40.0 0.0.0.255 eq www
 permit tcp any 204.148.40.0 0.0.0.255 eq 443
!
! to management segment
ip access-list extended TO-MANAGEMENT-SEGMENT
! no transit through this segment (outbound)
 deny any any
!
route-map FROM-LOW-PRIORITY-WEB-SERVERS permit 10
 match fast 2/0
 set ip next-hop 192.168.64.73
!
route-map INCOMING-ROUTES-FROM-SITE2 permit 10
 match ip PERMIT-ALL-ROUTES
 set local-preference 80
!
route-map ROUTES-OUT-TO-ISPA-SITE1 permit 10
 match ip HIGH-PRIORITY-WEB-SEGMENT
!
route-map ROUTES-OUT-TO-ISPA-SITE2 permit 10
 match ip HIGH-PRIORITY-WEB-SEGMENT
 set as-path prepend 1321 1321 1321
!
route-map ROUTES-OUT-TO-ISPB-SITE1 permit 10
 match ip HIGH-PRIORITY-WEB-SEGMENT
route-map ROUTES-OUT-TO-ISPB-SITE1 permit 20
 match ip LOW-PRIORITY-WEB-SEGMENT
```

```
!
route-map ROUTES-OUT-TO-ISPB-SITE2 permit 10
 match ip HIGH-PRIORITY-WEB-SEGMENT
 set community ISPB:80
route-map ROUTES-OUT-TO-ISPB-SITE2 permit 20
 match ip LOW-PRIORITY-WEB-SEGMEN2
 set community ISPB:80
!
! routing statements
router eigrp 800
 network 192.168.64.0 mask 255.255.255.224
 network 192.168.64.32 mask 255.255.255.224
 distribute-list DENY-ALL-ROUTES in fast 2/0
 distribute-list DENY-ALL-ROUTES in fast 2/1
 distribute-list LOOPBACKS-IN in fast 1/0
 distribute-list LOOPBACKS-IN in fast 1/1
 distribute-list VALID-ROUTES-OUT out
!
router bgp 1321
 no synchronization
 network 198.6.224.128 mask 255.255.255.128
 network 204.148.40.0
!
 neighbor external-peers ebgp-multihop 6
 neighbor external-peers update-source Loopback0
 neighbor external-peers next-hop-self
 neighbor external-peers distribute-list VALID-ROUTES-OUT out
 neighbor external-peers distribute-list VALID-ROUTES-IN in
 neighbor external-peers soft-reconfiguration in
 neighbor external-peers soft-reconfiguration out
 neighbor 192.168.64.69 peer-group external-peers
 neighbor 192.168.64.73 peer-group external-peers
 neighbor 192.168.65.69 peer-group external-peers
 neighbor 192.168.65.73 peer-group external-peers
!
 neighbor 192.168.64.69 remote-as 65000
 neighbor 192.168.64.69 route-map ROUTES-OUT-TO-ISPBA-SITE1 out
!
 neighbor 192.168.64.73 remote-as 65001
 neighbor 192.168.64.73 route-map ROUTES-OUT-TO-ISPB-SITE1 out
!
 neighbor 192.168.65.69 remote-as 65000
 neighbor 192.168.65.69 route-map ROUTES-OUT-TO-ISPBA-SITE2 out
 neighbor 192.168.65.69 route-map INCOMING-ROUTES-FROM-SITE2 in
!
 neighbor 192.168.65.73 remote-as 65001
 neighbor 192.168.65.73 route-map ROUTES-OUT-TO-ISPB-SITE2 out
 neighbor 192.168.65.73 route-map INCOMING-ROUTES-FROM-SITE2 in
! snmp access
snmp community MyString ro MANAGEMENT-SERVER
! line access
line vty 0 4
 access-class MANAGEMENT-SERVER in
 access-class DENY-ALL-OUT out
```

A

Extended Access List Protocols and Qualifiers

Table A-1. IP protocols

Protocol name	IP protocol number
AH	51
EIGRP	88
ESP	50
GRE	47
ICMP	1
IGMP	2
IGRP	9
IP	0–255
IPINIP	94
NOS	4
OSPF	89
TCP	6
UDP	17

Table A-2. Qualifiers for ICMP

Type or code	
administratively-prohibited	host-precedence-unreachable
alternate-address	host-redirect host-tos-redirect
conversion-error	host-tos-unreachable
dod-host-prohibited	host-unknown
dod-net-prohibited	host-unreachable
echo	information-reply
echo-reply	information-request
general-parameter-problem	mask-reply
host-isolated	mask-request

Table A-2. Qualifiers for ICMP (continued)

Type or code	
mobile-redirect	reassembly-timeout
net-redirect	redirect
net-tos-redirect	router-advertisement
net-tos-unreachable	router-solicitation
net-unreachable	source-quench
network-unknown	source-route-failed
no-room-for-option	time-exceeded
option-missing	timestamp-reply
packet-too-big	timestamp-request
parameter-problem	traceroute
port-unreachable	ttl-exceeded
precedence-unreachable	unreachable
protocol-unreachable	

Table A-3. TCP and UDP qualifers

IP Protocol	Qualifer	Port number (if any)
UDP	biff	512
UDP	bootpc	68
UDP	bootps	67
UDP	discard	9
UDP	domain	53
UDP	dnsix	90
UDP	echo	7
UDP	mobile-ip	434
UDP	nameserver	42
UDP	netbios-dgm	137
UDP	netbios-ns	138
UDP	ntp	123
UDP	rip	520
UDP	snmp	161
UDP	snmptrap	162
UDP	sunrpc	111
UDP	syslog	514
UDP	tacacs-ds	49
UDP	talk	517
UDP	tftp	69
UDP	time	37
UDP	who	513
UDP	xdmcp	177
TCP	bgp	179

Table A-3. TCP and UDP qualifers (continued)

IP Protocol	Qualifer	Port number (if any)
TCP	chargen	19
TCP	daytime	13
TCP	discard	9
TCP	domain	53
TCP	echo	7
TCP	finger	79
TCP	ftp	21
TCP	ftp-data	20
TCP	gopher	70
TCP	hostname	101
TCP	irc	194
TCP	klogin	543
TCP	kshell	544
TCP	lpd	515
TCP	nntp	119
TCP	pop2	109
TCP	pop3	110
TCP	smtp	25
TCP	sunrpc	111
TCP	syslog	514
TCP	tacacs-ds	65
TCP	talk	517
TCP	telnet	23
TCP	time	37
TCP	uucp	540
TCP	whois	43
TCP	www	80

Table A-4. Common application ports and directionality

Service	Protocol	Source port (on client unless specified)	Destination port (on server unless specified)
FTP (control connection)	TCP	> 1023	21
FTP (data connection)	TCP	20 (from server)	> 1023 (to client)
FTP PASV data connection	TCP	> 1023	20

Table A-4. Common application ports and directionality (continued)

Service	Protocol	Source port (on client unless specified)	Destination port (on server unless specified)
FTP PASV data connection as implemented by many browsers	TCP	> 1023	> 1023
Secure Shell (SSH)	TCP	> 1023	22
Telnet	TCP	> 1023	23
SMTP	TCP	> 1023	25
TACACS	UDP	49	49
DNS	UDP	53 > 1023	53
DNS (for zone transfers and for large queries in presence of large packet loss)	TCP	> 1023	53
TFTP	UDP	> 1023	69
POP3	TCP	> 1023	110
IDENT (often used by mailers)	TCP	> 1023	113
NNTP (News)	TCP	> 1023	119
NTP (Network Time Protocol)	UDP	123	123
Netbios services	UDP	137, 138 > 1023	137, 138
Netbios file sharing	TCP	> 1023	139
SNMP	UDP	> 1023	161
SSL	TCP	> 1023	443
REXEC	TCP	> 1023	512
RLOGIN	TCP	< 1024	513
RSH	TCP	< 1024	514
SOCKS	TCP	> 1023	1080
Squid Proxy	TCP	> 1023	3128
Syslog	UDP	> 1023	514

B

Binary and Mask Tables

Table B-1. 8-bit binary/decimal conversion chart from 0 to 255

Decimal	Binary	Decimal	Binary	Decimal	Binary	Decimal	Binary
0	00000000	64	01000000	128	10000000	192	11000000
1	00000001	65	01000001	129	10000001	193	11000001
2	00000010	66	01000010	130	10000010	194	11000010
3	00000011	67	01000011	131	10000011	195	11000011
4	00000100	68	01000100	132	10000100	196	11000100
5	00000101	69	01000101	133	10000101	197	11000101
6	00000110	70	01000110	134	10000110	198	11000110
7	00000111	71	01000111	135	10000111	199	11000111
8	00001000	72	01001000	136	10001000	200	11001000
9	00001001	73	01001001	137	10001001	201	11001001
10	00001010	74	01001010	138	10001010	202	11001010
11	00001011	75	01001011	139	10001011	203	11001011
12	00001100	76	01001100	140	10001100	204	11001100
13	00001101	77	01001101	141	10001101	205	11001101
14	00001110	78	01001110	142	10001110	206	11001110
15	00001111	79	01001111	143	10001111	207	11001111
16	00010000	80	01010000	144	10010000	208	11010000
17	00010001	81	01010001	145	10010001	209	11010001
18	00010010	82	01010010	146	10010010	210	11010010
19	00010011	83	01010011	147	10010011	211	11010011
20	00010100	84	01010100	148	10010100	212	11010100
21	00010101	85	01010101	149	10010101	213	11010101
22	00010110	86	01010110	150	10010110	214	11010110

Table B-1. 8-bit binary/decimal conversion chart from 0 to 255 (continued)

Decimal	Binary	Decimal	Binary	Decimal	Binary	Decimal	Binary
23	00010111	87	01010111	151	10010111	215	11010111
24	00011000	88	01011000	152	10011000	216	11011000
25	00011001	89	01011001	153	10011001	217	11011001
26	00011010	90	01011010	154	10011010	218	11011010
27	00011011	91	01011011	155	10011011	219	11011011
28	00011100	92	01011100	156	10011100	220	11011100
29	00011101	93	01011101	157	10011101	221	11011101
30	00011110	94	01011110	158	10011110	222	11011110
31	00011111	95	01011111	159	10011111	223	11011111
32	00100000	96	01100000	160	10100000	224	11100000
33	00100001	97	01100001	161	10100001	225	11100001
34	00100010	98	01100010	162	10100010	226	11100010
35	00100011	99	01100011	163	10100011	227	11100011
36	00100100	100	01100100	164	10100100	228	11100100
37	00100101	101	01100101	165	10100101	229	11100101
38	00100110	102	01100110	166	10100110	230	11100110
39	00100111	103	01100111	167	10100111	231	11100111
40	00101000	104	01101000	168	10101000	232	11101000
41	00101001	105	01101001	169	10101001	233	11101001
42	00101010	106	01101010	170	10101010	234	11101010
43	00101011	107	01101011	171	10101011	235	11101011
44	00101100	108	01101100	172	10101100	236	11101100
45	00101101	109	01101101	173	10101101	237	11101101
46	00101110	110	01101110	174	10101110	238	11101110
47	00101111	111	01101111	175	10101111	239	11101111
48	00110000	112	01110000	176	10110000	240	11110000
49	00110001	113	01110001	177	10110001	241	11110001
50	00110010	114	01110010	178	10110010	242	11110010
51	00110011	115	01110011	179	10110011	243	11110011
52	00110100	116	01110100	180	10110100	244	11110100
53	00110101	117	01110101	181	10110101	245	11110101
54	00110110	118	01110110	182	10110110	246	11110110
55	00110111	119	01110111	183	10110111	247	11110111
56	00111000	120	01111000	184	10111000	248	11111000
57	00111001	121	01111001	185	10111001	249	11111001
58	00111010	122	01111010	186	10111010	250	11111010

Table B-1. 8-bit binary/decimal conversion chart from 0 to 255 (continued)

Decimal	Binary	Decimal	Binary	Decimal	Binary	Decimal	Binary
59	00111011	123	01111011	187	10111011	251	11111011
60	00111100	124	01111100	188	10111100	252	11111100
61	00111101	125	01111101	189	10111101	253	11111101
62	00111110	126	01111110	190	10111110	254	11111110
63	00111111	127	01111111	191	10111111	255	11111111

Table B-2. Subnet masks and wildcard mask per prefix lengths

Prefix length	Subnet mask in dotted quad notation	Access list mask that matches all hosts	Valid networks with this prefix length
/8	255.0.0.0	0.255.255.255	{1-126,128-223}.0.0.0
/9	255.128.0.0	0.127.255.255	{1-126,128-223}.{0,128}.0.0
/10	255.192.0.0	0.63.255.255	{1-126,128-223}.{0,64,128,192}.0.0
/11	255.224.0.0	0.31.255.255	{1-126,128-223}.{0,32,64,96,128,160,192,224}.0.0
/12	255.240.0.0	0.15.255.255	{1-126,128-223}.{0,16,32,48,64,80,96,102}.0.0 {1-126,128-223}.{128,144,160,176,192,208,224,240}.0.0
/13	255.248.0.0	0.7.255.255	{1-126,128-223}.{0,8,16,24,32,40,48,56}.0.0 {1-126,128-223}.{64,72,80,88,96,104,112,120}.0.0 {1-126,128-223}.{128,136,144,152,160,168,176,184}.0.0 {1-126,128-223}.{192,200,208,216,224,232,240,248}.0.0
/14	255.252.0.0	0.3.255.255	{1-126,128-223}.{0,4,8...248,252}.0.0
/15	255.254.0.0	0.1.255.255	{1-126,128-223}.{0,2,4...252,254}.0.0
/16	255.255.0.0	0.0.255.255	{1-126,128-223}.{0-255}.0.0
/17	255.255.128.0	0.0.127.255	{1-126,128-223}.{0-255}.{0,128}.0
/18	255.255.192.0	0.0.63.255	{1-126,128-223}.{0-255}{0,64,128,192}.0
/19	255.255.224.0	0.0.31.255	{1-126,128-223}.{0-255}{0,32,64,96}.0 {1-126,128-223}.{0-255}{128,160,192,224}.0
/20	255.255.240.0	0.0.15.255	{1-126,128-223}.{0-255}.{0,16,32,48 }.0 {1-126,128-223}.{0-255}.{64,80,96,102}.0 {1-126,128-223}.{0-255}.{128,144,160,176}.0 {1-126,128-223}.{0-255}.{192,208,224,240}.0

Table B-2. Subnet masks and wildcard mask per prefix lengths (continued)

Prefix length	Subnet mask in dotted quad notation	Access list mask that matches all hosts	Valid networks with this prefix length
/21	255.255.248.0	0.0.7.255	{1-126,128-223}.{0-255}.{0,8,16,24}.0 {1-126,128-223}.{0-255}.{32,40,48,56}.0 {1-126,128-223}.{0-255}.{64,72,80,88 }.0 {1-126,128-223}.{0-255}.{96,104,112,120}.0 {1-126,128-223}.{0-255}.{128,136,144,152}.0 {1-126,128-223}.{0-255}.{160,168,176,184}.0 {1-126,128-223}.{0-255}.{192,200,208,216}.0 {1-126,128-223}.{0-255}.{224,232,240,248}.0
/22	255.255.252.0	0.0.3.255	{1-126,128-223}.{0-255}.{0,4,8…248,252}.0
/23	255.255.254.0	0.0.1.255	{1-126,128-223}.{0-255}.{0,2,4…252,254}.0
/24	255.255.255.0	0.0.0.255	{1-126,128-223}.{0-255}.{0-255}.0
/25	255.255.128.0	0.0.0.127	{1-126,128-223}.{0-255}.{0-255}.{0,128}
/26	255.255.192.0	0.0.0.63	{1-126,128-223}.{0-255}.{0-255}.{0,64,128,192}
/27	255.255.224.0	0.0.0.31	{1-126,128-223}.{0-255}.{0-255}.{0,32,64,96} {1-126,128-223}.{0-255}.{0-255}.{128,160,192,224}
/28	255.255.240.0	0.0.0.15	{1-126,128-223}.{0-255}.{0-255}.{0,16,32,48 } {1-126,128-223}.{0-255}.{0-255}.{64,80,96,102} {1-126,128-223}.{0-255}.{0-255}.{128,144,160,176} {1-126,128-223}.{0-255}.{0-255}.{192,208,224,240}
/29	255.255.248.0	0.0.0.7	{1-126,128-223}.{0-255}.{0-255}.{0,8,16,24} {1-126,128-223}.{0-255}.{0-255}.{32,40,48,56} {1-126,128-223}.{0-255}.{0-255}.{64,72,80,88 } {1-126,128-223}.{0-255}.{0-255}.{96,104,112,120} {1-126,128-223}.{0-255}.{0-255}.{128,136,144,152} {1-126,128-223}.{0-255}.{0-255}.{160,168,176,184} {1-126,128-223}.{0-255}.{0-255}.{192,200} {1-126,128-223}.{0-255}.{0-255}.{208,216} {1-126,128-223}.{0-255}.{0-255}.{224,232} {1-126,128-223}.{0-255}.{0-255}.{240,248}
/30	255.255.252.0	0.0.0.3	{1-126,128-223}.{0-255}.{0-255}.{0,4,8…248,252}
/31	255.255.254.0	0.0.0.1	{1-126,128-223}.{0-255}.{0-255}.{0,2,4…252,254}
/32	255.255.255.255	0.0.0.0	{1-126,128-223}.{0-255}.{0-255}.{0-254}

C

Common
Application Ports

Table C-1. *Common application source and destination ports*

Service	Protocol	Source port (on client unless specified)	Destination port (on server unless specified)
DNS	UDP	53 > 1023	53
DNS (for zone transfers and for large queries in presence of large packet loss)	TCP	> 1023	53
FTP (control connection)	TCP	> 1023	21
FTP (data connection)	TCP	20 (from server)	> 1023 (to client)
FTP PASV data connection	TCP	> 1023	20
FTP PASV data connection as implemented by many browsers	TCP	> 1023	> 1023
IDENT (often used by mailers)	TCP	> 1023	113
Netbios name service	UDP	137 > 1023	137
Netbios datagram service	UDP	138 > 1023	138
Netbios file sharing	TCP	> 1023	139
NNTP (News)	TCP	> 1023	119

Table C-1. Common application source and destination ports (continued)

Service	Protocol	Source port (on client unless specified)	Destination port (on server unless specified)
NTP (Network Time Protocol)	UDP	123	123
POP3	TCP	> 1023	110
REXEC	TCP	> 1023	512
RLOGIN	TCP	< 1024	513
RSH	TCP	< 1024	514
SMTP	TCP	> 1023	25
SNMP	UDP	> 1023	161
SOCKS	TCP	> 1023	1080
Squid Proxy	TCP	> 1023	3128
SSH (Secure Shell)	TCP	> 1023	22
SSL	TCP	> 1023	443
Syslog	UDP	> 1023	514
TACACS	UDP	49	49
Telnet	TCP	> 1023	23
TFTP	UDP	> 1023	69

Index

We'd like to hear your suggestions for improving our indexes. Send email to *index@oreilly.com*.

About the Author

Jeff Sedayao is a network engineer with Intel Online Services, the web and application hosting division of Intel Corporation. From 1987 through 1999, he architected and maintained Intel's Internet connectivity, starting with a simple 2400-bps email link through CSNET and ending up with multiple sites connecting to the Internet with multiple ISPs at multi-megabit speeds. He has always been fascinated with policy and policy implementation, ranging from using Cisco IOS access lists for routing and firewall policies to sendmail configurations and address space design. As part of Intel Online Services, his main interests include network usage and performance issues, DNS and email implementation, and addressing and routing policy.

Colophon

Our look is the result of reader comments, our own experimentation, and feedback from distribution channels. Distinctive covers complement our distinctive approach to technical topics, breathing personality and life into potentially dry subjects.

The animal on the cover of *Cisco IOS Access Lists* is a burro. "Burro" is, more or less, just another word for donkey, but it is also used specifically to mean a type of small feral donkey found in the southwestern United States and in Mexico.

Donkeys (*Equus asinus*) are descended from the African wild ass. They stand three to five feet tall at the shoulder, have a short mane, tufted tail, and big ears, and live for about 25 years. They were domesticated over 5,000 years ago, and they are still often used as pack animals, due to their surefootedness on rough terrain. Donkeys can be mated with horses, but the offspring of these matings are usually sterile. A female donkey (called a jennet or jinny) mated with a male horse produces an animal called a hinny. The offspring of a male donkey (jackass) and a female horse is a mule.

The feral burros of the southwestern U.S. and Mexico are the descendants of escaped and freed pack animals. Some believe the large feral burro population is driving desert bighorn sheep into extinction, by competing with them—successfully, it would seem—for scarce desert resources.

Emily Quill was the production editor, Matt Hutchinson was the copyeditor, and Mary Anne Weeks Mayo was the proofreader for *Cisco IOS Access Lists*. Colleen Gorman and Catherine Morris performed quality control reviews, and Edith Shapiro provided production assistance. Lucie Haskins wrote the index.

Ellie Volckhausen designed the cover of this book, based on a series design by Edie Freedman. The cover image is a 19th-century engraving from *Old-Fashioned Animal Cuts*. Emma Colby produced the cover layout with QuarkXPress 4.1 using Adobe's ITC Garamond font.

Melanie Wang designed the interior layout based on a series design by Nancy Priest. Anne-Marie Vaduva converted the files from Microsoft Word to FrameMaker 5.5.6 using tools created by Mike Sierra. The text and heading fonts are ITC Garamond Light and Garamond Book; the code font is Constant Willison. The illustrations that appear in the book were produced by Robert Romano and Jessamyn Read using Macromedia FreeHand 9 and Adobe Photoshop 6. This colophon was written by Leanne Soylemez.

Whenever possible, our books use a durable and flexible lay-flat binding. If the page count exceeds this binding's limit, perfect binding is used.